NATHANIEL HAWTHORNE

Transcendental Symbolist

MARJORIE J. ELDER

OHIO UNIVERSIT

1969

Preface

THIS STUDY was undertaken because the rather thorough studies of Emerson's aesthetics and the fewer studies of Hawthorne's views of art seemed to offer an area of relationship worthy of investigation. Further, such investigation was prompted by the many recent and extensive criticisms of Hawthorne which show no regard for literary history, ignore Hawthorne's own purposes, and impose upon his works preconceived critical theories which often fail to interpret him satisfactorily.

Hawthorne scholars await with delight the completion of the definitive edition, *The Centenary Edition of the Works of Nathaniel Hawthorne,* now being published by Ohio State University Press, under the editorial direction of William Charvat (1905–1966), Roy Harvey Pearce, Claude M. Simpson, Matthew J. Bruccoli, Fredson Bowers, and L. Neal Smith. At this writing four volumes are available: *The Scarlet Letter* (I, 1962), *The House of the Seven Gables* (II, 1965), *The Blithedale Romance* and *Fanshawe* (III, 1964), and *The Marble Faun* (IV, 1968). Since the numerous tales and sketches are not available at this date in the Centenary Edition, I have thought it well to refer consistently to the Riverside Edition. Though the major line of argument is not affected by this decision, I regret not being able to make use throughout of the best available text.

v

In addition to my indebtedness to the Emerson and Hawthorne scholars whose books and articles I have found useful, I should like to express appreciation to Walter Blair and Merlin Bowen for their helpful criticisms, to Norman Holmes Pearson and Nolan Smith for their kindness in answering queries on Hawthorne's letters, to Napier Wilt for his suggestions when I began research in American literature, to Mary C. Dodd for her inspirational teaching of Hawthorne at the undergraduate level, to Inland Steel-Ryerson Foundation, Inc., for the fellowship grant which made the completion of the work possible, and to my mother for her inspiring interest in my Hawthorne studies.

I wish also to express my appreciation to Ohio State University Press for their permission to quote from Randall Stewart's edition of *The American Notebooks by Nathaniel Hawthorne* (Yale University Press, 1932; copyrighted by Ohio State University Press, 1960); and to The Modern Language Association of America for their permission to quote from *The English Notebooks by Nathaniel Hawthorne*, edited by Randall Stewart (New York: Modern Language Association of America; London: Oxford University Press, 1941).

M.J.E.

Marion, Indiana
December, 1968

Contents

NATHANIEL HAWTHORNE

*Transcendental
Symbolist*

Hawthorne and the Transcendentalists

NATHANIEL HAWTHORNE never pronounced himself an unqualified "Transcendentalist," but he did think of himself as an Artist living at a time when Transcendentalists, "under one name or another," had "their share in all the current literature of the world."[1] And among his close friends and associates were numbered such persons as Sophia and Elizabeth Peabody, Margaret Fuller, Amos Bronson Alcott, Ralph Waldo Emerson, and Henry David Thoreau—all thoroughgoing "disciples of the Newness."[2]

When the philosophic concepts of various Transcendentalists led them into conflict with widely accepted theological views, Hawthorne remained unconcerned with Transcendentalism as a "religion." Yet as Artist he was always concerned, as the most casual reader knows, with man's relation to God.

When Transcendentalism turned to extreme reforms such as vegetarianism or the refusal to wear cotton cloth because slaves produced it, Hawthorne was not numbered with the extremists. Even when the influence of this moral philosophy shaped major reforms such as the abolition of slavery and the emancipation of women, Hawthorne remained more occupied, artistically, with reform in the human heart, such reform as should influence man's relation to society.

The concern here, then, is with Hawthorne as Artist; the question is not whether he was a Transcendentalist but whether he was a Transcendental symbolist. Hence it is the Transcendental aesthetic and Hawthorne's relation to that philosophy that is explored. That exploration begins with Hawthorne's associations with the Transcendentalists, to discover the many opportunities he had of conversing with and reading from his Transcendentalist friends. Then the Transcendental aesthetic must be understood as defined by these friends, showing the permeating influence both by reference to the aesthetics of non-Transcendentalists and to Hawthorne's acknowledgement of the influence upon himself. With such a background, Hawthorne's aesthetic theories will be investigated through all primary sources, and his practice of Art may be understood by his own terms. Herein lies the justification for the epithet "Transcendental Symbolist."

The philosophy known as Transcendentalism was distinctly a New England product. Inspired by German idealism, taking the name "transcendental" and the central thought from Immanuel Kant, Unitarian ministers found here an enlivening influence for their somewhat cold and intellectual objections to Puritanism. However, since most American Transcendentalists felt the German thought as an indirect influence through the philosophy of Coleridge, the preachments of Carlyle, and the poetry of Wordsworth, it was sensed more as a spirit of the times than as a metaphysical scheme. And since the religious philosophy had its roots in the New England Christian tradition, many of the Transcendental concepts were an extension or a spiritualizing of Christian tenets— with, one might say, both "orthodox" and "unorthodox" conclusions. With infusions of Orientalism, Platonism, and French Fourierism, the profoundly idealistic American Transcendentalism became a movement that was spiritual and practical rather than purely metaphysical. But at its core was the belief in a "transcendental" knowledge for all men.

The clergyman William Ellery Channing (1780–1842) had marked a development in Unitarian thought toward Transcendentalism in "Unitarian Christianity Most Favorable to Piety," published in 1826. Not until the 1830's, however, did the philosophy really flourish. In fact, the publication in 1836 of Emerson's *Nature*, the first relatively complete statement of Transcendental philosophy, might be said to mark the beginning of the golden years. That same year introduced Bronson Alcott's *Conversations on the Gospels* and saw the beginning of The Transcendental Club, which would continue its meetings for more than a decade, with Emerson, Alcott, Margaret Fuller, Elizabeth Peabody, George Ripley and others of the group in attendance.

Emerson's "The American Scholar" was delivered in 1837 at Harvard as was his "Divinity School Address" of 1838. Margaret Fuller's conversations, developing out of her associations with Elizabeth Peabody and with Bronson Alcott in the Temple School, began in 1839 and continued to be widely discussed. By 1841 the Brook Farm social community under George Ripley was a fact. *The Dial*, the organ of the movement, which grew out of the meetings of The Transcendental Club, appeared between July, 1840, and April, 1844.[3]

The picture of Nathaniel Hawthorne as a man unaware of this world in which he lived, maintaining his genius in solitude, has been largely corrected by recent scholars. Randall Stewart carefully details Hawthorne's travels and associations during even the so-called "solitary years" between 1825 and 1837. He also indicates Hawthorne's wide and varied reading during this period and mentions his editing the *American Magazine of Useful and Entertaining Knowledge* from March through August, 1836.[4] Marion L. Kesselring has shown that Hawthorne was often reading recently published works, and he indicates no less than five of Coleridge's works in Hawthorne's library borrowings between 1833 and 1836 and more than one withdrawal of Wordsworth's poetry (1837 Philadelphia edition) in 1837 and 1838.[5] Hawthorne certainly was not ignorant of any ideas so pervasive as those of New England Transcendentalists in the 1830's—particularly since he numbered leading Transcendentalists among his closest friends.

Interestingly enough, it was Hawthorne's first volume of collected tales that both "opened an intercourse with the world"[6] and drew him into close association with the Transcendentalists.

For it was the publication of *Twice-Told Tales*, in 1837, that brought the unknown writer to the attention of Transcendentalist Elizabeth Peabody. Though the Peabody home was but a short distance from the Hawthorne home in Salem, the families had been mere neighbors until Elizabeth invited the newly discovered author and his sisters to call. Her sister Sophia, a semi-invalid, was not present at Hawthorne's earliest visits, but the friendship with Elizabeth led to Hawthorne's meeting Sophia in the autumn of 1838 and the beginning of a friendship which by the end of the year had grown into love. During the courtship of three and a half years, its length extended by the financial inability of the young author to maintain a household, Hawthorne corresponded with Sophia from the Boston Custom House, where he was a measurer in 1839–40, and from Brook Farm, where he spent some months in 1841. By July of 1842, when Hawthorne married and took his bride to "The Old Manse" in Concord, he had not only become acquainted with the Transcendental doctrines of the Peabody sisters; he had also become personally acquainted with leading Transcendentalists with whom he was to be associated during the years in Concord.

Both Sophia and Elizabeth were ardent Transcendentalists, closely associated with leaders of the movement. As early as 1833, Elizabeth started a series of conferences in which Transcendental ideas were discussed. With Elizabeth's assistance as teacher and recorder, Bronson Alcott opened the Temple School in Boston in 1834. Alcott's school, a Transcendentalist's attempt to free young minds and develop the innate imagination and virtue of children, stressed conversations in which the teacher turned the pupils' minds in upon themselves for the discovery of truth. From these conversations, Elizabeth compiled *The Record of a School* (1835), which was followed by Alcott's *Conversations on the Gospels* (1836–37). When public reaction against the latter work forced the school to close after struggling along with only a few pupils until 1839, Elizabeth Peabody returned to her parents' home in Salem. Since Sophia had occasionally assisted in recording the

Alcott pupils' conversations, Hawthorne probably discussed Alcott's venture with both of the Peabody sisters.

Margaret Fuller, a leading Transcendentalist, had some connection with the Temple School as recorder. But more characteristic of her contribution to the flow of Transcendental thought were her "Conversations," begun in 1839 under Elizabeth Peabody's auspices and to some extent based on the earlier series of conferences. Margaret's Conversations, taking the form of "classes" under her direction, continued until 1844. Both Sophia and Elizabeth, as well as Alcott and Emerson, participated in certain 1841 meetings reported by Caroline H. Dall.[7] Besides more formal conferences there were informal conversations which took place in the Peabody bookstore, which Elizabeth opened in Boston in 1839. Here Transcendentalists got together to discuss questions of the day and to review new books. Here Brook Farm, a community of Transcendentalists, was considered for many months before it became an actuality. Hawthorne, slaving at the Custom House, may have spent little time there. Nevertheless, he did visit the bookshop, and to aid Miss Peabody in her publishing ventures, in 1840, he had her issue his *Grandfather's Chair*.

But Hawthorne was not particularly eager to meet a literary lioness such as Margaret Fuller without Sophia present. In 1839 he wrote that though he had been invited to dine at Mr. Bancroft's with Margaret, "Providence had given me some business to do; for which I was very thankful."[8] Nor, as he wrote to Sophia in 1841, was he highly sympathetic with Margaret's Conversations. Nevertheless, it is likely that he was present at some of the talks which Margaret Fuller conducted at Brook Farm. He wrote in his notebooks of Frank Dana's picnic party, that Margaret and Emerson "came forth into the little glade where we were assembled. Here followed much talk."[9] Early in his Brook Farm experience, he described for Sophia Miss Fuller's "Transcendental heifer," "not an amiable cow," but with "a very intelligent face," and "of a reflective cast of character."[10] And the friendship between Margaret and Sophia was close enough that Sophia wrote Margaret of her engagement to Hawthorne, receiving a reply in which Miss Fuller highly complimented both parties.

Because of his frequently publicized attempts at reforms, Alcott seems to have been thought of as the leader of New England Transcendentalists in the early 1830's, though Emerson, particularly after the Divinity School Address in 1838, came to be regarded as their spokesman. Alcott and Emerson met in 1835, and their association increased through The Transcendental Club. Since the club, founded in 1836 and continuing until about 1850, had no formal organization, no list of members, and no officers, these meetings, too, became something like informal "conversations." Among "regular members" Emerson, Alcott, Fuller, Elizabeth Peabody, and Thoreau are all named; though Hawthorne was probably not a member, despite Lindsay Swift's association of his name with the club,[11] it is quite possible that he was occasionally in the company after he moved to Concord.

Hawthorne's more immediate communication with Emerson began through the agency of the Peabody household. It was Elizabeth who, in 1838, showed Emerson one of Hawthorne's early writings, "Footprints on the Seashore." Though Emerson "complained that there was no inside to it," that "Alcott and he together would make a man,"[12] Elizabeth reported in 1839 that Emerson "seemed all congenial about" Hawthorne, though he had not yet read his writings.[13] This congeniality no doubt grew in part from Emerson's knowledge of the engagement of Hawthorne to his admirer Sophia Peabody. For it was clear that Sophia was an ardent admirer of Emerson. On May 14, 1838, she told her sister Elizabeth of "an exquisite visit from Waldo,"[14] and commented in highly Transcendental terms:

> It seems to me sometimes as if every material object and every earthly event were only signs of something higher signified; and at such times all particulars are merged into one grand unit. Then I feel as if I could read a minute portion of the universe. How everything hurries into its place the moment we are high

enough to catch the central light! . . . I suppose Mr. Emerson holds himself in that lofty region all the time. . . . I think Mr. Emerson is the greatest man that ever lived.[15]

The concepts of immanence and of the mystic perception of their significance are basic Transcendental beliefs. Hawthorne was somewhat less enthusiastic about Emerson, as one might expect. He politely refused a ticket proffered by Sophia for one of the Concord sage's lectures:

> Dearest, I have never had the good luck to profit much, or indeed any, by attending lectures; so that I think the ticket had better be bestowed on somebody who can listen to Mr. Emerson more worthily. My evenings are very precious to me.[16]

A few days later, though, he showed some interest by apologetically wishing that he had asked whether she wanted him to attend. In June of the following year, he was still recognizing her associations with the "Emersonians" but did not accept Mr. Emerson's invitation to Concord and wished Sophia to express his regrets properly and let Emerson know what a "business-machine" he was.[17]

The friendship of Sophia Peabody and Emerson insured the easy availability to Hawthorne of Emerson's first two important publications, for Sophia was given presentation copies of both *Nature* (1836) and *Essays, First Series* (1841). Hawthorne himself received *Essays, Second Series* (1844). Specific evidence that Hawthorne read *Nature* is his quotation from it in the *American Notebooks*,[18] and Julian Hawthorne assures us that his father read with enjoyment both Emerson's essays and his poetry.[19]

Hawthorne had another opportunity to become familiar with Transcendental ideas when he took up his residence at George Ripley's Brook Farm community on April 12, 1841, where he remained for six or seven months; there he had meetings not only with Emerson and Margaret Fuller, occasional visitors, but with a group of minor Transcendentalists. Emerson records in his *Journal*, in 1843: "Hawthorne boasts that he lived at Brook Farm during its heroic age: then all were intimate and each knew the other's work: priest and cook conversed at night of the day's work."[20] Though Hawthorne held two shares of stock at $500 a share, was elected a Director of Finance and made a Trustee of the Brook Farm estate, it is unlikely that he was ever much in sympathy with the enterprise as an embodiment of Transcendental tenets. Still one may be sure that, as a habitually observant writer, he listened to a number of conversations on Transcendental ideals and beliefs.

Hawthorne probably left Brook Farm some time in November, 1841, and early in the following year, to Emerson's delight, became interested in making his home in Concord. While Hawthorne and Sophia were in Concord on May 7, to see about renting the Manse, they called on Emerson. Emerson's pleasure in Concord's becoming a literary center is seen in his telling some four different correspondents of Hawthorne's interest in the Manse and the prospective move of Hawthorne and his bride to that home.[21] When Hawthorne met Emerson in the Athenaeum in late May, Emerson referred to "their" (the Hawthornes') garden at "The Old Manse" and reported it coming along well.[22] On July 9, 1842, Hawthorne and Sophia Peabody were married, and their brief wedding journey ended at "The Old Manse" in Concord. There they were to spend three years.

When the Hawthornes moved to Concord, Thoreau as well as Emerson already lived in the community. When Alcott came home from England in October, 1842, he visited Concord, and in 1844, the Alcotts moved to "The Hillside." Margaret Fuller was a frequent guest at the Emersons' or at her sister's and did not forget to call upon her friends the Hawthornes. Emerson, Thoreau, Alcott, Fuller—Hawthorne was part of a Transcendental literary community.

Conversations, formal and informal, planned and unplanned, seem to characterize one phase of the Transcendentalist movement. Whether he sought conversations or avoided them as he often did, Hawthorne of Concord was certain to find himself conversing occasionally with Transcendentalist neighbors and friends.

In his notebooks Hawthorne speaks of several visits with Emerson. There were, for instance, a walk to Walden Pond and a trip to the Shaker village. Though the conversation was not always of "Transcendental matters," sometimes it seems to have taken that turn. In April of 1843, Hawthorne records "as good a talk as I ever remember experiencing" with Emerson and says that they had discussed Margaret Fuller and her significance, Ellery Channing and his poetry, Thoreau and the problems of having him as a resident of Emerson's home. They talked about Brook Farm "and the singular moral aspects which it presents," and the desirability of having its history written.[23]

Hawthorne was present, too, when Emerson entertained Alcott upon his return from England with his English socialist friends Lane and Wright.[24] He once dined at Emerson's in company with Mr. Hedge,[25] and at least once before leaving Concord he evidently attended the Monday evening club. George William Curtis describes the silence and solemnity of the first awkward meeting of that gathering of philosophers, with Orphic Alcott invading the silence with a "saying," while Hawthorne, "a statue of night and silence, sat, a little removed, under a portrait of Dante, gazing imperturbably upon the group."[26]

Hawthorne mentions one particular conversation with Margaret Fuller when he met her by chance as he was returning from Emerson's through the woods. They talked about

> . . . Autumn—and about the pleasures of getting lost in the woods . . . and about the experiences of early childhood, whose influence remains upon the character after the recollection of them has passed away—and about the sight of mountains from a distance, and the view from their summits—and about other matters of high and low philosophy.[27]

Two of these topics—the recollections from early childhood and the shifting views of mountains—are clearly "Transcendental" in nature.

Thoreau's visits to "The Old Manse" began within a few weeks after the Hawthornes moved there[28] and continued until Thoreau left Concord for a brief time to tutor in Staten Island, New York.

Hawthorne, who respected Thoreau as a "keen and delicate observer of nature,"[29] was impressed by his knowledge of nature's
secrets and recorded specific facts that Thoreau had told him.
Passages in Hawthorne's notebooks about the purchase of the boat
Musketaquid (which had made the trip recorded in *A Week on the
Concord*) show that Thoreau's mystical ability to "will" the boat as
almost a part of himself appealed to Hawthorne. Something of
Thoreau's philosophical influence is surely evident when Hawthorne writes in this connection, "Oh that I could run wild!—that
is, that I could put myself into a true relation with nature, and be
on friendly terms with all congenial elements."[30] When Thoreau
called just before his departure for Staten Island, he and Hawthorne talked of the spiritual advantages of changing place and
about *The Dial* and Mr. Alcott. Hawthorne wished that Thoreau
might remain in Concord, "he being one of the few persons, I
think, with whom to hold intercourse is like hearing the wind
among the boughs of a forest-tree; and with all this wild freedom,
there is a high and classic cultivation in him too."[31] Hawthorne's
words of commendation echo Transcendental doctrines developed
by Thoreau.

The Transcendental periodical, *The Dial*, founded before
Hawthorne moved to Concord, carried articles not only by Emerson, Fuller, Alcott, and Thoreau, but by a substantial number of
minor Transcendentalists. In notebooks of "The Old Manse"
period, Hawthorne mentions *The Dial* and specifically calls attention to three articles, one by Margaret Fuller, one by Thoreau,
and one on Bronson Alcott's works. Both Miss Fuller's and Thoreau's articles were unsigned, but Hawthorne indicated in his
comments that he knew who had written them.[32]

Hawthorne reports that he found little help in the article on
Alcott, saying, "It is not very satisfactory, and has not taught me
much," but it is interesting to find him studying Charles Lane's
rather lengthy criticism of Alcott.[33] Hawthorne's own evaluation
of Alcott had appeared a few months earlier in "The Hall of
Fantasy," where he pictured Emerson "surrounded by an admiring
crowd of writers and readers of the Dial, and all manner of Tran-

scendentalists and disciples of the Newness." Perhaps even recalling that evening at Emerson's when Alcott and his English friends had unfolded their social ideas, Hawthorne writes, "Here, also was Mr. Alcott, with two or three friends, whom his spirit had assimilated to itself and drawn to his New England home, though an ocean rolled between." He continues:

> There was no man in the enchanted hall, whose mere presence, the language of whose look and manner, wrought such an impression as that of this great mystic innovator. So calm and gentle was he, so holy in aspect, so quiet in the utterance of what his soul brooded upon, that one might readily conceive his Orphic Sayings to well upward from a fountain in his breast, which communicated with the infinite abyss of Thought.

And Hawthorne, as narrator, remarks that "doubtless there is the spirit of a system in him, but not the body of it."[34] Such a commentary makes it clear that he had given careful consideration to Alcott's views before he looked to see what a critic had to say about him.

The article of Margaret Fuller's to which Hawthorne refers is "Canova." Here Miss Fuller evaluates the artist Canova in Transcendental terms—with emphasis on his lack of real genius and an appreciation for his ability to talk about art. Hawthorne found this article "good."[35]

Though he said that Thoreau is "more exclusive than is desirable, like all other Transcendentalists, so far as I am acquainted with them," Hawthorne appreciated Thoreau's article, "Natural History of Massachusetts," as a bit of Transcendental philosophy:

> Methinks this article gives a very fair image of his mind and character—so true, minute, and literal in observation, yet giving the spirit as well as the letter of what he sees, even as a lake reflects its wooded banks, showing every leaf, yet giving the wild beauty of the whole scene.[36]

As will be noticed in the study of Hawthorne, his approval of Thoreau's blending of the actual with the ideal, in a reflection which pictures each detail as a part of the whole, is not only Transcendental in spirit: it corresponds with Hawthorne's own aesthetic intentions and practices.

Thus through the years of Hawthorne's courtship and associations with the Peabody family, through the immediate contacts with Transcendentalists at Brook Farm, through increasing associations with Emerson, Thoreau, Fuller, and Alcott during his residence at "The Old Manse" in Concord, through an active interest in the Transcendental writings of Emerson, Thoreau, Alcott, and Fuller, Hawthorne had unusually good opportunities to encounter Transcendental beliefs. Hawthorne did not consider himself a Transcendentalist and, in fact, more than once voiced objections to Transcendentalism as a philosophy.[37] But not only did he also speak specific appreciations, he was acute enough to realize something of the extent of the Transcendental influence upon himself and others. Before this matter is discussed, however, the Transcendental aesthetic must be defined.

Transcendental Aesthetic Theories

EMERSON'S AESTHETIC THEORY

A DISCUSSION of Transcendental aesthetic theories may well begin with the Emersonian aesthetic, which was more completely formulated than the artistic beliefs of Alcott, Fuller, or Thoreau, and partly for that reason was more influential upon other writers. Emerson's aesthetic theory, partly stated in such essays as "The Poet," "Beauty," and "Plato; or The Philosopher," is never completely detailed in a single essay. It must therefore be studied throughout his work. And because of its close relationship with Emerson's metaphysical views, it must be considered in conjunction with them.

The theory comprises three areas: Emerson's view of Truth, his idea of the nature of the Artist, and his concept of the Work of Art. His view of Truth will be discovered in his assertion of the Real (the Perfect) shadowed in the Actual (the imperfect)—in Nature and Man. His Artist will be seen as Representative Man, enabled by faith, intuition, the pursuit of Beauty, and Nature's dynamic language, to become the Seer and Sayer. The Work of Art is an expression of Unity (Truth, Beauty) by variety (the symbol) made possible by the action of Imagination on the Actual. The Artist paints by means of light (symbolic both of the seeing eye and the light of Imagination enabling the saying). The Artist's purpose, governing all the details of his Work of Art, is to express

Truth. By the light of Imagination upon the Actual, he paints Nature at the thought level in correspondence with Man, the central figure; he paints Man revealing outwardly even more of his inner character than he reveals in Actuality. Finally, he orders all things in a succession of events governed causally by the character who acts at both the partial and universal levels in the conflict with sin.

The Concept of Truth: The Over-Soul

Emerson's aesthetic theory is so intricately interrelated with his metaphysical beliefs that any clear consideration of his ideas on art begins with an understanding of the Over-Soul in its relations to Nature and Man. This "Unity," this "eternal *One*," is called by many names: it is "that great nature in which we rest," "that common heart," "that overpowering reality," "the wise silence," "the universal beauty," the "deep power," "the whole," "the Highest Law."[1] In the assertion of the existence of the Over-Soul and the interpretation of its relation to this world lie Emerson's metaphysical beliefs.

The Over-Soul is the Unity or the Whole which unifies the particulars seen in Nature and Man. The unity accomplished by the Over-Soul is observable in certain general relationships between the All and the "parts." First, the Soul is *over* nature and man in the sense of Universal Law; Emerson asserts in "Spiritual Laws" that "there is a soul at the centre of nature and over the will of every man, so that none of us can wrong the universe."[2] Again, the Soul is present *in* all Nature, an "inferior incarnation of God,"[3] and in all persons, in every period of life. Thirdly, the Soul acts *through* all particulars as the "principle which is the basis of things, which all speech aims to say, and all action to evolve."[4] This relationship is causal, whether the Over-Soul be thought of as First Cause, continuing essence, or final Unity. This All, then, is over all, in all, through all.

Or, the Over-Soul may be spoken of as "Truth, whose centre is everywhere and its circumference nowhere, whose existence we cannot disimagine; the soundness and health of things."[5] This

Truth is one with both Goodness and Beauty, and the Identity may be referred to with equal accuracy as "eternal beauty" or "moral sentiment." Emerson's explanation is, "Truth, and goodness, and beauty, are but different faces of the same All,"[6] and "Truth and Beauty always face each other and each tends to become the other."[7] All changing appearances rest on this living "reality," this eternal Truth.

Yet the substitution of such words as "Unity" and "Truth" for the Over-Soul do not define the concept. The Over-Soul in its essence remains not only undescribed but indescribable; "above the thought is the higher truth."[8]

> In many forms we try
> To utter God's infinity,
> But the boundless hath no form,
> And the Universal Friend
> Doth as far transcend
> An angel as a worm.
>
> The great idea baffles wit,
> Language falters under it,
> It leaves the learned in the lurch;
> Nor art, nor power, nor toil can find
> The measure of the eternal Mind,
> Nor hymn, nor prayer, nor church.[9]

Though the Over-Soul is beyond the reach of man's mind, Emerson saw the visible creation as its manifestation in material forms. He insisted that every individual fact "is the end or last issue of spirit."[10] Thus the Universe becomes "the externalization of the soul,"[11] and "every natural fact is a symbol of some spiritual fact."[12]

Because of this relationship, man may infer the eternal from the evanescent show. Emerson quotes Plato as crying, "Yet things are knowable!" and says, "They are knowable because being from one, things correspond. There is a scale; and the correspondence of heaven to earth, of matter to mind, of the part to the whole, is our guide."[13] This correspondence reveals itself in an ascending scale of culture, "from the first agreeable sensation which a sparkling gem or a scarlet stain affords the eye, up through fair outlines and details of the landscape, features of the human face and form, signs and tokens of thought and character in manners, up to the ineffable mysteries of the intellect."[14] Since the correspondence is of the part to the whole, every individual thing "teaches the unity of cause, the variety of appearance."[15] And always that which constitutes beauty in the pitiful individuality of objects is this very cosmical quality, this "power to suggest relation to the whole world."[16] Thus, "the splendor of meaning . . . plays over the visible world,"[17] and "heaven and earth" reflect "the infinite Beauty" "in all lovely forms."[18]

The meaning of each object is assured because of the presence in each and all of many aspects of the central Identity. "The true doctrine of omnipresence is that God reappears with all his parts in every moss and cobweb."[19] This means more than merely saying that some thought is behind each object; it means that the whole sense, all Nature's laws, "may be read in the smallest fact."[20] This being true, the highest minds explore "the double . . . quadruple . . . centuple or much more manifold meaning, of every sensuous fact."[21] For "in nature, each individual symbol plays innumerable parts, as each particle of matter circulates in turn through every system. The central identity enables any one symbol to express successively all the qualities and shades of real being."[22]

Not only is infinite Beauty shadowed in Nature, but it is reflected in Man's mind and soul. "Man is conscious of a universal soul within or behind his individual life. . . . This universal soul he calls Reason." This Reason is the same essence that is called Spirit, considered in relation to Nature.[23] Using a favorite symbol, Emerson describes Man's inner light thus: "From within or from behind, a light shines through us upon things and makes us aware that we are nothing, but the light is all."[24]

Hence Man is *of* that Unity, with "that gleam of light which flashes across his mind from within,"[25] with God having entered "doors to the mind, never left open by the individual."[26] Emerson lamented that men did not know how divine is man, that they had not seen his inner light,[27] for he saw "this open channel to the highest life" as "the first and last reality,"[28] and believed "the ground of hope" to be "in the infinity of the world; which infinity reappears in every particle, the powers of all society in every individual, and of all mind in every mind."[29]

But it is not easy to read the shadows of infinite Beauty either in Nature or Man, for the beautiful reality lies beneath the surfaces of things. The common eye may be satisfied with the surfaces though "the wise eye knows that it is the surface, and, if beautiful, only the result of interior harmonies, which, to him who knows them, compose the image of higher beauty."[30]

While Emerson does not emphasize the evil in Nature, he admits that there are "hints of ferocity in the interiors of nature," that "Providence has a wild, rough, incalculable road to its end, and it is of no use to try to whitewash its huge, mixed instrumentalities, or to dress up that terrific benefactor in a clean shirt and white neckcloth of a student of divinity."[31] Elsewhere he says that "war, plague, cholera, famine, indicate a certain ferocity in nature, which, as it had its inlet by human crime, must have its outlet by human suffering."[32] But since Emerson sees evil as negative, he affirms the Good as positive, insisting

> But in the darkest, meanest things
> There alway, alway something sings.
> . . . .
> But in the mud and scum of things
> There alway, alway something sings.[33]

Emerson is aware that the Reality, the Beauty, the Over-Soul, permeates Man as the Perfect in the imperfect.[34] He talks of humanity's mar, saying of the forms, "Unfortunately every one of them bears the marks as of some injury; is marred and superficially defective."[35] He argues from the greatest and wisest man—"none of them seen by himself, and his performance compared with his promise or idea, will justify the cost of that enormous apparatus of means by which this spotted and defective person was at last procured."[36] And he argues from the most hopeless among humanity—"one born in blight."[37]

Emerson's affirmative philosophy accepts the "testimony of negative facts, as every shadow points to the sun."[38] He feels that Beauty is never entirely absent, that "every face, every figure, suggests its own right and sound estate."[39] The great Unity is beyond the evil, the good beyond the meanness; sorrow is in the appearances, but felicity beyond.[40] The reason for the lack of unity in the world lies in man's being disunited with himself; thus "The problem of restoring to the world original and eternal beauty is solved by the redemption of the soul."[41]

The Artist

Since man stands on a point between spirit and matter and is "native of both elements," he has some idea "that one re-presents the other; that the world is the mirror of the soul; and that it is his office to show this beautiful relation, to utter the oracles of the mind in appropriate images from nature."[42] But while it is true that "in the deep heart of man a poet dwells,"[43] and that the imagination is not inactive in any man, yet for most men inspiration is occasional. But in the Poet, the imagination is intoxicating;[44] the powers of seeing and saying are balanced; he handles what others dream of, and he is representative of man by virtue of "being the largest power to receive and to impart."[45] And what does the poetic imagination of the Sayer, the Namer, effect for men?

> A poet comes who lifts the veil; gives them glimpses of the laws of the universe; shows them the circumstance as illusion; shows that nature is only a language to express the laws, which are grand and beautiful;—and lets them, by his songs, into some of the realities.[46]

The highest ground for the Transcendental Poet is the worship of the Unity, self-surrender to the moral sentiment.[47] Without this tremendous belief in Truth, the Poet will not reach the heights which he should reach. Emerson finds Homer, Chaucer, Spenser, Shakespeare, and Milton "poets by the free course which they allow to the informing soul, which through their eyes beholds again and blesses the things which it hath made."[48] But the poets' belief is not alone in the great Unity; they also "know that this correspondence of things to thoughts is far deeper than they can penetrate,—defying adequate expression; that it is elemental, or in the core of things."[49] In other words, they also believe that the manifold works of Nature express the soul, all sensual objects corresponding to thought. Closely related to that belief is a third faith—faith in the revelation in the Poet's own mind. In citing two things that a novelist must do, Emerson declares that "first, the aspirations of the mind are to be revered, that is, Faith."[50] The faith of the Poet, then, is in the Beauty, Truth, Goodness—the Unity—shadowed in Nature's objects and in his own mind; and by that faith he speaks. "All sins," Emerson declared in a letter to his friend John Sterling, "literary and aesthetic and scientific, as well as moral, grow out of unbelief at last." And he added, "I certainly did not mean, when I took up this paper, to write an essay on Faith, and yet I am always willing to declare how indigent I think our poetry and all literature is become for want of that."[51] Transcendentalism certainly supplied the deficiency by being an "excess of Faith."[52]

So far does the Poet need to trust the revelation of his mind that he writes by revelation or intuition until he himself seems not to write but to be written through. Again and again Emerson suggests the idea of the submission, surrender, resignation, passivity of the Poet. In a dozen different figures of speech he expounds the doctrine of inspiration. At the heart of the doctrine is the belief that "the universal soul is the alone creator of the useful and the beautiful."[53] Therefore, the Poet's only will in inspiration is the surrender of his will to the Universal Power. By such submission the Poet uses an imagination which "exists by sharing the ethereal currents,"[54] so that the first time a poem is heard it sounds rather "as if copied out of some invisible tablet in the Eternal mind than as if arbitrarily composed by the poet."[55]

Sometimes the Poet testifies to a driving power within him, or he speaks of miraculous revelation that leaves him stupid with wonder. This enlarged power called Inspiration, of which the Poet is made aware, is "a power to carry on and complete the metamorphosis of natural into spiritual facts," and "every real step is by what a poet called 'lyrical glances,' by lyrical facility, and never by main strength and ignorance."[56]

Emerson's Poet, as a result, does not feel himself to have been the true author of his work:

> Ah, not to me these dreams belong!
> A better voice peals through my song.[57]

"He knows that he did not make his thought,—no, his thought made him, and made the sun and the stars."[58] Hence, "the ardors of piety agree at last with the coldest skepticism,—that nothing is of us or our works,—that all is of God. . . . All writing comes by the grace of God, and all doing and having."[59] In "The Problem" Emerson so interprets Michael Angelo in a phrase that has been adopted into the language, "He builded better than he knew":

> The hand that rounded Peter's dome
> And groined the aisles of Christian Rome
> Wrought in a sad sincerity;
> Himself from God he could not free;
> He builded better than he knew;—
> The conscious stone to beauty grew.[60]

Despite Emerson's assertions of the poetic inspiration and the spontaneity of revelation through the Poet, he admits that a writer is something like a skater, going partly where he will and partly where his skates take him.[61] This seems to suggest that there might be some possible area of active effort on the writer's part. At least "he pursues a beauty, half seen, which flies before him."[62] The pursuit of Beauty (or effortful contemplation of Identity) becomes a contemplation of its revelation in Nature, the manifold. However, there is a sense in which Nature does not like to be observed: "The beauty that shimmers in the yellow afternoons of October, who ever could clutch it? Go forth to find it, and it is gone; 't is only a mirage as you look from the windows of diligence." If the mere outward beauty is hunted too eagerly, the observer will be mocked by its unreality:

> But this beauty of Nature which is seen and felt as beauty, is the least part. The shows of day, the dewy morning, the rainbow, mountains, orchards in blossom, stars, moonlight, shadows in still water, and the like, if too eagerly hunted, become shows merely, and mock us with their unreality.[63]

Hence, the man of Beauty, in his observation of Nature, explores rather "the double meaning, or . . . the quadruple or the centuple or much more manifold meaning, of every sensuous fact."[64] He is "enamored of thoughts and laws." "Guided by them, he is ascending from an interest in visible things to an interest in that which they signify, and from the part of a spectator to the part of a maker."[65] Emerson quotes Plato that "long familiarity with the objects of intellect" is one of the prerequisites for perception.[66] And when Emerson himself says in "Intellect," "Then, in a moment, and unannounced, the truth appears," he adds, "but the oracle comes because we had previously laid siege to the shrine."[67]

Then with the Truth lying like a burden on his mind, "the burden of truth to be declared,—more or less understood; . . . it constitutes his business and calling in the world to see those facts through, and to make them known."[68] Emerson insists that "The thought of genius is spontaneous," but he does admit that "the power of picture or expression, in the most enriched and flowing nature, implies a mixture of will, a certain control over the spontaneous states, without which no production is possible."[69] Here there is active effort involved in the artist's exercise of will in distributing and expressing the inspired ideas.

Nature offers all her creatures to the Poet "as a picture-language."[70] "Whatever he beholds or experiences, comes to him as a model and sits for its picture."[71] And since "all good is eternally reproductive," "the beauty of nature re-forms itself in the mind . . . for new creation."[72] Since "all the endless variety of things make an identical impression,"[73] when Nature offers to the Poet the fascinating variety of symbols, each is so much a part of the perfect Whole, that it "is a microcosm, and faithfully renders the likeness of the world."[74]

Always the poetic vision is an increased sensibility of the imagination, to pierce through the outward fact to its meaning,[75] to see the "eternal spiritual beauty" through superficial beauty,[76] to perceive "the independence of the thought on the symbol, the stability of the thought, the accidency and fugacity of the symbol."[77]

> Whilst common-sense looks at things or visible Nature as real and final facts, poetry, or the imagination which dictates it, is a second sight, looking through these, and using them as types or words for thoughts which they signify.[78]

So by the help of Nature's picture-language and the intoxicating imagination to see through the symbols to the meaning, the Poet lets the light of his imagination fall upon an object that his thought may be seen.[79] He uses the analogies Nature shows everywhere of the visible to the invisible world, by converting land, sea, air, animals—all into symbols of thought. The outward creation becomes his alphabet. Treating Nature as apparent and thought as the only reality,[80] he makes things beautiful by re-attaching things to nature and to the Whole.[81] Having listened to conversation and beheld all objects in Nature, he gives back, "not them, but a new and transcendent whole,"[82] like Nature, ultimating his thought in a thing.[83] For poetry as a talent "is a magnetic tenaciousness of an image, and by the treatment demonstrating that this figment of thought is as palpable and objective to the poet as is the ground on which he stands, or the walls of houses about him."[84] But the imagination flows rather than freezes; when the

Poet has read the meaning of the form, he will not rest, but "makes the same objects exponents of his new thought." He will not nail a symbol to one sense, "for all symbols are fluxional."[85]

The Work of Art

Previous studies of Emerson's aesthetic theory have emphasized his indebtedness to Plato's twice-bisected line with its ascending scale for the operations of the soul, where the mind ranges from diversity at the base—seen in Nature's manifold effects—to Identity at the top—the cause of Nature's effects. First hinted by W. T. Harris, in 1882, this "Platonic structure" was more carefully analyzed and used to interpret specific works of Emerson by Walter Blair and Clarence Faust, in 1944, and has since become a basis for such interpretations as those of Vivian Hopkins and Sherman Paul.[86] Emerson believed "a key to the method and completeness of Plato is his twice bisected line,"[87] a line dividing the visible and intelligible worlds, the former into images and objects, the latter into opinions and truths, thus providing an ascending scale for the four operations of the soul—conjecture, faith, understanding, and reason. The mind is urged to range up this scale, to ask for one cause of many effects; again, the mind is forced to move down the scale, turning to variety, where Nature is the manifold. In every natural object are a real and an ideal power; poetry, by seeking to show unity through variety ("that is, always by an object or symbol,"[88]) unites these impossibilities of the real and the ideal. It can be readily seen that a work of art expressing Unity by Variety is, by that very accomplishment, a "miniature of Nature."[89] Yet Emerson believed that the work of art is a "new and transcendent whole,"[90] by which belief he implies that the representation is more beautiful than Nature. This is true because the work of art ascends on the scale of being; where in Nature's objects are seen only the shadows of the higher beauties of the soul, in Art the soul or mind itself is expressed—in a symbol. Thus the symbol will partake of two things, Nature and the Artist's Imagination; that is, actual objects acted upon by the thought. In Emerson's *Journals* one notation on pictures is applicable here:

Art. Two things in picture:

(1) Representation of Nature, which a photograph gives better than any pencil, . . . and which is a miracle of delight to every eye.

(2) An ideal representation, which, by selection and much omission, and by adding something not in Nature, but profoundly related to the subject, and so suggesting the heart of the thing, gives a higher delight, and shows an artist, a creator.[91]

That Emerson saw this combination of the Actual and the Ideal as the Artist's work in writing as certainly as in painting is made clear by his analysis of Couture's rules of drawing as applicable to writing. In his lecture "The Preacher," appeared these suggestions.

Couture's rules of drawing are swiftly translatable into rules of writing. "Draw directly or actually a perpendicular and a horizontal line through the centre of the object." . . . The perpendicular line would be their relation to truth; the horizontal, their relation to the world around them.[92]

In another metaphor Emerson says, "The poet, like the electric rod, must reach from a point nearer to the sky than all surrounding objects down to the earth, and down to the dark wet soil, or neither is of use."[93] It takes the Artist's Imagination working upon things to turn "every dull fact into pictures and poetry, by making it an emblem of thought."[94] For actualities, things by themselves, may be pretty or elegant but are not beautiful until the Imagination lifts them out of individuality and they take on cosmical quality; that is, until they express the Unity by a symbol. As Emerson says,

My boots and chair and candlestick are fairies in disguise, meteors and constellations. . . . Chaff and dust begin to sparkle and are clothed about with immortality. And there is a joy in perceiving the representative or symbolic character of a fact, which no bare fact or event can ever give.[95]

So if the Imagination touches any actual individuality to lift it from the area of bare fact to the area of symbol, the work of art will have expressed Unity by variety. But the work itself partakes of *both* the Actuality and the Imagination.

"Light is the first of painters"

The symbolizing of the Actual *through the Imagination* is effected in part by what Emerson called, in speaking of Couture's drawing rules, "suggestive description." Emerson quotes a second rule from the same source and interprets it thus:

> Couture proceeds,—"Half close the eyes and look at the object long: find where is the strongest light, and the degrees of light, and thus see only the masses, without the details. Then do the like to see where is the strongest shadow, and the less strong. Draw these with vigor. Keep three quarters of your eye on Nature, and only one quarter on your work." Now apply these rules to your writing. "Half close the eyes and look at the object long and find the strongest light." That is—Don't think of your chamber, or boarding-house, or the daily routine of life or instruction, but search your memory for the happiest passages, the best thought, the best intercourse, some crowning result that has characterized the curriculum or the society, the height of hope, the fruitfullest truth—then you have the strongest light, and minor lights, and will see masses and not details.[96]

In Emerson's analysis of Beauty in *Nature*, he says, "light is the first of painters." Part of the delight we take in Nature's forms is owing to the eye, "the best of artists." He explains the composing power of the eye:

> By the mutual action of its structure and of the laws of light, perspective is produced, which integrates every mass of objects, of what character soever, into a well colored and shaded globe, so that where the particular objects are mean and unaffecting, the landscape which they compose is round and symmetrical.[97]

And he goes on to say that "as the eye is the best composer, so light is the first of painters. There is no object so foul that intense light will not make it beautiful."[98] Here Emerson suggests a unifying

of particulars into symmetrical composition and the use of light
for bringing out principal and subordinate ideas. The reflected
Beauty will be heightened, as it is when reflected in Nature:

> Every one may see, as he rides on the highway through an unin-
> teresting landscape, how a little water instantly relieves the
> monotony: no matter what objects are near it,—a gray rock, a
> grass-patch, an alder-bush, or a stake,—they become beautiful
> by being reflected.[99]

It is no wonder that Emerson saw the mirror as one of the symbols
of the age.[100]

If the ideal representation selects, omits, adds, to the things
found in Nature (as Emerson said in "Two things in picture," cited
above), if the eye is the best composer and light the first of painters,
there is a close connection between the mirror of Nature[101] and the
work of the Artist. But the biggest question is, how, in the work of
art, are the selections, omissions, additions to be decided upon.
Here Emerson clearly sees "veracity first of all, and forever. *Rien
de beau que le vrai.*"[102] The form does not make the thought, but
the thought makes the form. This is true throughout Emersonian
metaphysics, and he maintains the truth here. Even though intu-
itively the form and thought "are equal in the order of time, . . .
in the order of genesis the thought is prior to the form."

> Not metres, but a metre-making argument . . . makes a poem,—
> a thought so passionate and alive that like the spirit of a plant
> or an animal it has an architecture of its own, and adorns nature
> with a new thing.[103]

Emerson believes that Art should be as sincere as God and Nature.
Ingenuity, skilful contrivance, finish are not enough. "We should
see in it the great belief of the artist, which caused him to make it
so as he did, and not otherwise. . . . And this design must shine
through the whole performance."[104] There is no choice to the
Artist. His selections, additions, omissions from Nature must all be
brought into relationship with his sincere idea, his message; and
that message if it reaches the highest beauty will have pervading it
"the moral tone," the Truth. "Man, never so often deceived," says

Emerson, "still watches for the arrival of a brother who can hold him steady to a truth until he has made it his own."[105]

But in the Artist's selection from Nature's mirror he seeks to concentrate the world's radiance on one point in such a way as to suggest by the single object the universal or the whole, for things are only beautiful in the whole. His result will be an "expression of nature, in miniature."[106] In his work he will express the Unity by variety, just as Nature does. And as in Nature "all the endless variety of things make an identical impression,"[107] so in thought the same Unity is pervasive. "Every universal truth which we express in words, implies or supposes every other truth. . . . Every such truth is the absolute Ens seen from one side. But it has innumerable sides."[108]

The Artist's purpose governs all the details. Emerson criticizes a miscellaneous beauty, where the Artist makes additions here and there, "instead of unfolding the unit of his thought. Beautiful details we must have, or no artist; but they must be means and never other. The eye must not lose sight for a moment of the purpose."[109] But "as soon as a man masters a principle and sees his facts in relation to it, fields, waters, skies, offer to clothe his thoughts in images."[110]

As truth is the Whole, made of many particulars, so the Truth of the work of art is unified through particulars, chosen because related to the main principle.

"The frame" for "the central figure"

The central figure in Nature is Man. In Reality Man and Nature are in unison, the beauty of Nature corresponding to the beauty of noble thoughts and actions. Emerson says, in the "living picture," "when a noble act is done,—perchance in a scene of great natural beauty; . . . are not . . . heroes entitled to add the beauty of the scene to the beauty of the deed?"[111] Nature fits as a frame the picture of Man, because Nature is "metaphor of the human mind."[112] The very changes in Nature will speak thought:

> Every hour and change corresponds to and authorizes a different state of mind, from breathless noon to grimmest midnight. Na-

ture is a setting that fits equally well a comic or a mourning piece.[113]

Since Man is thus related to Nature, the Poet is not only authorized but obliged to make transfers in Nature in order to betray the "rhymes and echoes that pole makes with pole,"[114] to discover to the reader this true relationship. To do this he must make the scene fit the deed, by selections, omissions, additions—that is, simply by such transfers in Nature as are necessary to symbolize the correspondence of objects and thought. Then the Poet will discover that "good tableaux do not need declamation. Nature tells every secret once."[115] In the choice and arrangement of details from Nature—details which agree with the Poet's picture of Man—he finds his best arguments. Emerson says,

> If you agree with me, . . . I may yet be wrong; but if the elm-tree thinks the same thing, if running water, if burning coal, if crystals, if alkalies, in their several fashions say what I say, it must be true.[116]

In giving not a real landscape—the Poet cannot give "air, light, motion, life, dampness, heat, and actual infinite space"—but "the suggestion of a better, fairer creation than we know; he should crowd a greater number of beautiful effects into his picture than co-exist in any real landscape."[117] When Emerson says "beautiful effects," he means details with meaning, for he admits that he "cannot greatly honor minuteness in details, so long as there is no hint to explain the relation between things and thoughts."[118] But the addition of "beautiful effects" with meaning will draw the mind toward the beautiful Unity.

"Characters . . . more true to the laws of thought"

Since every spirit builds its house, "all form is an effect of character,"[119] "human character evermore publishes itself,"[120] and "every act of the man inscribes itself . . . in his own manners and face."[121] This provides two levels on the scale of being: first, the actual man, his character publishing itself in his appearance, talk, and action; second, the ideal man, that is, his mind. Emerson admires an author's knowing and treating his characters as real,[122] but if the author combines with the actuality the higher level of the ideal, they will be "made more true to the laws of thought." Shakespeare's characters "are so sharply drawn as if always he was painting from real life, and yet all are idealized or made more true to the laws of thought than heroes in actual life are ever found."[123] This being true, it follows that the Artist should add surface details as evidences of inner spirit, each detail of appearance to shadow a truth in the character's mind. His selections, additions, and omissions exercised on the actual character will make the character "more true to the laws of thought," while every particular about the character shadows forth its specific truth. And the variety of specific truths will draw the mind toward the Unity of which all are parts.

Emerson says it is "the perception of real affinities between events (that is to say, of *ideal* affinities, for those only are real), [which] enables the poet . . . to make free with the most imposing forms and phenomena of the world, and to assert the predominance of the soul."[124] This means that the poet redisposes the objects of Nature and "makes them revolve around the axis of his primary thought."[125] From a succession of objects it is possible to see both "the immensity of the world" and that the "excellence of all things is one."[126]

But "what seems the *succession* of thought is only the distribution of wholes into causal series,"[127] Emerson says. What, then, makes the causal series? What but the relation of act to actor. Emerson objects when "the novelist plucks this event here and that fortune there, and ties them rashly to his figures, to tickle the fancy of his readers with a cloying success or scare them with shocks of tragedy."[128] "Nature," on the contrary, "has a magic by which she fits the man to his fortunes, by making them the fruit of his character."[129] What the Poet must remember is that "a man's action is only a picture-book of his creed. . . . Your condition, your employment, is the fable of *you*."[130] Since character, then, is emitted in the events that "exude from and accompany" a man, "events expand with the character."[131] Thus the causal relation of events is established.

This causal relation of events operates, however, at two levels. Every man is both a universalist, working out the universal problem, and a partialist, justified in his individuality.[132] At the universal level, "every crime is punished, every virtue rewarded, every wrong redressed, in silence and certainty"; "retribution is the universal necessity."[133] At the individual or partial level, all this is still true, but at the same time, "No law can be sacred to me but that of my nature"; "the only right is what is after my constitution; the only wrong what is against it."[134] The Universal Mind means Unity, but Nature is the manifold; and in Nature, each character is accountable to that Mind within him, which may, in the partial sense, be thought of as requiring fidelity to his own nature.

Emerson believed that speculation tended to Unity, action to diversity,[135] and that those two levels gave different views:

> Self-accusation, remorse, and the didactic morals of self-denial and strife with sin, are in the view we are constrained by our constitution to take of the fact seen from the platform of action; but seen from the platform of intellection there is nothing for us but praise and wonder.[136]

From this it can be argued that the Poet's characters in action may well work out the Beautiful Unity at the level where the view shows much of the conflict with sin.

In the work of art, then, the Poet "turns the world to glass, and shows us all things in their right series and procession."[137] He shows us not Nature merely, for the power of his creative imagination transcends the sensible objects, making them thoughts, so that he speaks with Nature's language, a variety of details—of scenes, characters, events—each symbolic of specific truth, each related to his primary thought, and each and all revelatory of The Identity—The Truth—The Eternal, Spiritual Beauty.

THE AESTHETIC OF OTHER TRANSCENDENTALISTS

Following this examination in some detail of the Emersonian aesthetic, the investigation may now turn to phases of that aesthetic shared by such Transcendentalists as Amos Bronson Alcott, Margaret Fuller, and Henry David Thoreau. Each distinctly individual, these three Transcendentalists gave varied expression to similar theories. Alcott's Transcendental theories took the shape of "Orphic Sayings" and impractical reforms; Miss Fuller's of conversations, art criticism, and vindication of women's rights; Thoreau's of an identification of art and life.

Amos Bronson Alcott

As Hawthorne said, Bronson Alcott seemed to have the spirit of a system if not the body of it.[138] And, if one wishes to give a kind of organization to his vague disorganized sayings, it is possible simply to trace through the "Orphic Sayings" which appeared in *The Dial* point by point agreements with the Emersonian aesthetic. Since the sayings have only a superficial pattern, simply being numbered, given general titles, and occasionally grouped by related topics, perhaps a kind of table of pertinent comments will suggest something of the Alcott substance and manner. For the reader's convenience, however, the over-all order used in the discussion of Emerson will be adopted.

"Orphic Sayings" of Alcott
Selected from *The Dial*, I[139]

The Over-Soul

Life eludes all scientific analysis. Each organ and function is modified in substance and varied in effect, by the subtile energy which pulsates throughout the whole economy of things, spiritual and corporeal. The each is instinct with the all; the all unfolds and reappears in each. Spirit is all in all. God, man, nature, are a divine synthesis, whose parts it is impiety to sunder (p. 93).

Every soul feels at times her own possibility of becoming a God; she cannot rest in the human, she aspires after the Godlike. This instinctive tendency is an authentic augury of its own fulfilment (p. 87).

Shadowed in Things of Earth

Divinely seen, natural facts are symbols of spiritual laws (p. 86).

The soul makes a double statement of all her facts; to conscience and sense; reason mediates between the two. Yet though double to sense, she remains single and one in herself; one in conscience, many in understanding; one in life, diverse in function and number (p. 88).

In the Midst of Evil

All unrest is but the struggle of the soul to reassure herself of her inborn immortality; to recover her lost intuition of the same, by reason of her descent amidst the lusts and worship of the idols of flesh and sense (p. 87).

The Position of the Artist

Out of the invisible God, he comes to abide awhile amongst men; yet neither men nor time shall remain as at his advent. He is a creative element, and revises men, times, life itself. A new world pre-exists in his ideal. He overlives, outlives, eternizes the ages, and reports to all men the will of the divinity whom he serves (pp. 90–91).

The Artist's Faith and Intuition

The prophet, by disciplines of meditation and valor, faithful to the spirit of the heart, his eye purified of the motes of tradition, his life of the vestiges of usage, ascends to the heights of immediate intuition: he rends the veil of sense; he bridges the distance between faith and sight, and beholds spiritual verities without scripture or mediator (p. 91).

The Pursuit of Beauty

All departures from perfect beauty are degradations of the divine image. . . . Beauty is fluent; art of the highest order represents her always in flux, giving fluency and motion to bodies solid and immovable to sense. The line of beauty symbolizes motion (p. 97).

Nature's Language

It is life, not scripture; character, not biography, that renovates mankind. The letter of life vitiates its spirit. Virtue and genius refuse to be written (p. 355).

The Work of Art

The prophet and bard are original men, and their lives and works being creations of divine art, are inimitable (p. 355).

The Light

The prophet, whose eye is coincident with the celestial ray, receives this into his breast, and intensifying there, it kindles on his brow a serene and perpetual day (p. 357).

The Truth

Facts, reported, are always false. Only sanctity and genius are eyewitnesses of the same; and their intuition, yet not their scriptures, are alone authentic. Not only all scripture, but all thought is fabulous. Life is the only pure fact, and this cannot be written to sense; it must be lived, and thus expurgate all scriptures (p. 357).

Nature as Scene

Yet nature is not separate from me; she is mine alike with my body; and in moments of true life, I feel my identity with her; I breathe, pulsate, feel, think, will, through her members, and know of no duality of being. It is in such moods of soul that prophetic visions are beheld, and evangeles published for the joy and hope of mankind (p. 94).

Character as Central

Character is the only legitimate institution; the only regal influence. Its power is infinite (p. 91).

Always is the soul portraying herself; the statue of our character is hewn from her affections and thoughts (p. 352).

Plot

Their problem is ever to pierce the coarse and superficial rind of diversity, and discover the unity in whose core is the heart and seed of all things (p. 92).

The quotations show that, though Emerson explored and stated many details more completely, in general and in particular Alcott's aesthetic theories are very similar to those of Emerson. In Alcott's view, art and life tend to flow together more than in the Emersonian analysis, and the Artist does not stand out from other men quite as clearly. Further, Alcott's emphasis on intuition, together with his tendency to ignore the world of the senses (though he sees "the actual and ideal" as "twins of one mother, Reality"[140]) makes his theory more vague and less tangible than Emerson's.

Margaret Fuller

In a sketch Margaret Fuller left of the Transcendentalists, she talks of those who adhere "to the faith of the soul with that unusual earnestness which the world calls 'mad.'" Among those considered "mad" she counts not only "the young poet who valued insight of nature's beauty, and the power of chanting to his fellowmen a heavenly music" but also the "friends, and lovers, who see, through all the films of human nature, in those you love, a divine energy, worthy of creatures who have their being in very God." And Margaret considered herself to belong to these "children of light."[141]

In "The One in All" she identifies the pervading Unity:

> One presence fills and floods the whole serene;
> Nothing can be, nothing has ever been,
> Except the one truth that creates the scene.[142]

"A single thought transfuses every form"[143] she asserts. In conversations on the fine arts, she speaks about "poesy as the ground of all the fine arts, and also of the true art of life; it being not merely truth, not merely good, but the beauty which integrates both." Then she interprets the individual surrounded by prose, thought of as "the manifestation of the temporary, in opposition to the eternal, always trenching on it, and circumscribing and darkening." She speaks of "the acceptance of this limitation" and believes "we should inwardly cling to the truth that poesy" is "the natural life of the soul," while admitting "that prose" is "the necessary human condition."[144]

For Margaret, the Poet, the maker, is divine. She believes Nature to be "the literature and art of the divine mind" and "human literature and art the criticism on that."[145] "Poesy" is "the expression of the sublime and beautiful"; "the human mind, apprehending the harmony of the universe, and making new combinations by its laws." She feels that Poetry should "sing to the ear, paint to the eye, and exhibit the symmetry of architecture. If perfect, it will satisfy the intellectual and moral faculties no less than the heart and the senses."[146]

Thus Margaret Fuller held the Emersonian view of the all-pervading Truth manifested as poetry in the midst of life's prose and the view of the divinely inspired Artist copying Nature in a work of beauty structured to speak on both ideal and actual levels.

Henry David Thoreau

In Thoreau, recognized disciple of Emerson, the Transcendental theories of art find individual and quite extensive expression. His *Week on the Concord and Merrimack Rivers*, taken as a whole, is such an expression. Conscious of the spiritual meanings reflected in the river, the central figure—man and Poet—moves through time, breathing his songs with the same breath by which he lives—a breath from the gods. Between spirit (the river) and matter (all Nature and books) winds the boat of his thought. Gifted with senses for high seeing, his vision along and beside the river makes him understand the laws of Nature, which *are* morality. His life *is* the meaning.

Thoreau gave explicit statement to facets of the Transcendental aesthetic which show beliefs similar to Emerson's. In the *Week*, he speaks of seeing, smelling, hearing, tasting, feeling, the "everlasting Something to which we are allied," our maker, abode, destiny, "our very Selves; the one historic truth, . . . the actual glory of the universe."[147] He sees a Nature behind the ordinary, "a beauty in the form or coloring of the clouds which addresses itself" to the imagination, that can be accounted for scientifically to the understanding but not to the imagination; it is the symbolicalness that speaks to the imagination.[148]

"The Man of Genius," for Thoreau, "is an originator, an inspired or demonic man, who produces a perfect work in obedience to laws yet unexplored." However, the Artist is near the Genius because he "detects and applies the law from observation of the works of Genius, whether of man or nature." Though there has never been a man of pure Genius, neither has there ever been a man completely destitute of genius.[149] Thus Poetry becomes a miracle of inspiration and "the peculiarity of a work of genius" is the "absence of the speaker from his speech."[150] The Artist's belief and effort are much like any man's faith and effort. A man's faith is not to be confused with his creed; it is the faith that counts,[151] and faith "is not a remembered assurance, but a use and enjoyment of knowledge." When a man is in actual contact with Truth he does not have to believe but is "related to her in the most direct and intimate way."[152] Then he attempts to "live a *thread* of life," "in the midst of this labyrinth," with "the laws of earth . . . for the feet" and "the laws of heaven . . . for the head," the latter being merely "the former sublimed and expanded." By observing the laws for both the inferior and the superior man, he "neither stoops nor goes on tiptoe, but lives a balanced life, acceptable to nature and to God."[153] This is the life between spirit and matter.

In Thoreau's aesthetic, the Poet speaks by using Nature's language. In fact, since Poetry is a natural fruit, "it is as if nature spoke." "Nature furnishes him not only with words, but with stereotyped lines and sentences."[154] The very images and pictures of a poet like Ossian seem to occupy "much space in the land-scape."[155] Chaucer is good because, like Nature, he does not put the flowers and nuts in a heap.[156] Even the rhythms of language come from Nature; Walter Raleigh is a good stylist because he uses a natural emphasis, "like a man's tread," with "a breathing space between the sentences."[157]

So the Work of Art becomes a *life*, wherein is discoverable the "restored original" of which Nature is the reflection.[158] Wherever he wanders, "the universe is built round" Man, and Man is "central still."[159] And the composition is as if the life had grown outward when expressed.[160]

Thus, in his individual way Thoreau, too, expressed the Transcendental aesthetic. With greater emphasis on the actual facts of Nature, he tended toward natural philosophy, particularly in his later works, but his insistence on the fusion of art and life is an extending of the Transcendental aesthetic.[161]

THE TRANSCENDENTAL AESTHETIC OF NON-TRANSCENDENTALISTS

The Transcendental aesthetic theories were not by any means confined to the Transcendentalists but had echoes in writers as far from Transcendentalism as the Brahmins Longfellow, Lowell, and Holmes and that rather hearty objector to the Transcendental philosophy, Herman Melville.

The Brahmins

Though all the Brahmins evidence Transcendental influence,[162] Longfellow will prove the most significant here because of his lifelong friendship with Hawthorne. Graduating in the same college class at Bowdoin in 1825, the two men became more closely associated after Longfellow's very favorable review of *Twice-Told Tales*.[163]

Longfellow created two artist-type characters: Flemming, the hero of *Hyperion* (1839), who is given the poetic imagination; and Mr. Churchill, the romance writer who fails to produce a work in

Kavanaugh (1849). Some understanding of Flemming's beliefs and of Longfellow's analysis of Mr. Churchill's ability and the sources of his failure will suggest Longfellow's theories.

Kavanaugh begins with a paragraph that has Transcendental overtones, with words that are said to express the vague thought floating through Mr. Churchill's brain:

> Great men stand like solitary towers in the city of God, and secret passages running deep beneath external nature give their thoughts intercourse with higher intelligences, which strengthens and consoles them, and of which the labourers on the surface do not even dream![164]

Flemming confesses a love for "that tranquility of soul, in which we feel the blessing of existence, and which in itself is a prayer and a thanksgiving," and decides that when Nature seems unsympathetic with man, the fault is in our own imperfections, not hers.[165] Yet Longfellow does not follow out the Transcendental relation between man and nature. When he writes,

> Oh, let not the soul that suffers dare to look Nature in the face, where she sits majestically aloft in the solitude of the mountains! for her face is hard and stern, and turns not in compassion upon her weak and erring child, . . .[166]

he is not expressing a correspondence between Man and Nature which demands obedience to inner or outer law, but simply using Nature to point his moral.

In Longfellow's view of inspiration, however, in one respect he comes nearer the Transcendentalists. He says: "The highest exercise of imagination is not to devise what has no existence, but rather to perceive what really exists, though unseen by the outward eye,—not creation, but insight."[167] He defines Flemming's thoughts as "twin-born; the thought itself, and its figurative semblance in the outer world." He adds, "Thus, through the quiet, still waters of his soul each image floated double, 'swan and shadow.' "[168] Michael Angelo, with his "faith in the Ideal,"[169] is an artist who sees a statue in every block of marble, sees it as distinctly as if it stood before him and has only to hew away the stone to reveal it to other eyes.[170] The Poet has a kind of double gift. All men have the vague images that float in the soul, but the "Active Intellect," "the power to put these shapes and images in Art, to embody the indefinite," is the Poet's peculiar gift. "He knows not even whence nor how this is."[171] Longfellow insists that the active effort of the Artist is partly a matter of will; Mr. Churchill's failure is a lack of will; he needed to take hold of materials near at hand and use them to create his Romance.

Mr. Churchill's definition of literature indicates a kind of Transcendental moral purpose and shows also that Longfellow saw the Artist as using Nature largely for decorative purposes: the Poet says,

> Literature is rather an image of the spiritual world, than of the physical, is it not?—of the internal, rather than the external. Mountains, lakes, and rivers are, after all, only its scenery and decorations, not its substance and essence.[172]

But Flemming, in one of his flights, comes closer to the Transcendental view: "Art is the revelation of man; and not merely that, but likewise the revelation of Nature, speaking through man. Art pre-exists in Nature, and Nature is reproduced in Art."[173] Longfellow felt that spiritual meanings would be lacking unless Art was built on experience, that only a play of fancies would result and figures would lack inner life unless the Artist looked near at hand to build on common life.[174] He states artistic success symbolically in "Moonlight":

> Illusion! Underneath there lies
>   The common life of every day;
> Only the spirit glorifies
>   With its own tints the sober gray.[175]

Such Transcendental hints in Longfellow, friend of Hawthorne and admirer of Emerson—though not of Transcendentalism as a philosophy—have considerable weight in showing the far-reaching influences of the Transcendental aesthetic.

Herman Melville

Melville's objections to Emersonian Transcendentalism may probably be centered in three faults that he found in the philosophy: it tended to pride, it lacked "heart," and it was too idealistic, lacking physical zest. Each of these objections is related to his artistic theories. The pride he disliked was the pride that insinuated a too complete knowledge of Truth.[176] The lack of heart he lamented hindered the Artist from being all an Artist should be.[177] The idealism of the theory resulted from a remoteness from actuality which prevented a deep sense and clear picturing of the "blackness" in the world.[178]

But despite these objections, a number of echoes of Emersonian Transcendentalism are discoverable in Melville. Remembering that Melville's ideas on art developed with his practice and were never fully stated, never fully completed, the thoughtful reader still finds hints at a great central Truth, intimations of an inspired Artist, and suggestions that the world of mind or the Work of Art combined elements of nature and novelty, elements which have some correspondence to what Hawthorne called Actuality and Imagination.

When Melville writes in *Mardi* (1849), "I and all mine revolve round the great central Truth, sun-like, fixed and luminous forever in the foundationless firmament,"[179] or even in *Moby Dick* (1851), of the meaningless, all-meaning whale; when he asserts God's omnipresence as "our divine equality"[180] or lets Ahab wonder "What things real are there, but imponderable thoughts?"[181] these are surely hints toward that Truth which Melville believed it was the Artist's work to pursue. And when Babbalanja intimates to Media "things infinite in the finite; and dualities in unities,"[182] or Ahab cries, "O Nature, and O soul of man! how far beyond all utterance are your linked analogies! not the smallest atom stirs or lives on matter, but has its cunning duplicate in mind,"[183] or "All visible objects . . . are but as pasteboard masks. . . . strike through the mask!"[184] these too are echoes of a vision of meanings shadowed in things of earth. As Melville develops a device to reflect Truth in the doubloon nailed to the mast of the *Pequod*, which will mirror an image of the world to each character who looks, he insists: "And some certain significance lurks in all things, else all things are little worth, and the round world itself but an empty cipher. . . ."[185]

In Melville's view of the Poet, he insisted that a writer must have both brain and heart. And he saw the Artist as a Truth-seeker, whose name really only stands "for the mystical, ever-eluding Spirit of all Beauty, which ubiquitously possesses men of genius."[186] Moved "by some mystic impulse," he explores "the world of mind."[187] With "the essence of all ideas . . . infused,"[188] the "iron-mailed hand clenches" that of the Artist "in a vice, and prints down every letter" in spite of him.[189]

What use does the Artist make of Nature? To some extent Nature becomes a light or inspiration to the Mardian artist Lombardo, who never wrote "by rushlight." "His lamp swung in heaven.— He rose from his East, with the sun; he wrote when all nature was alive."[190] And when Lombardo's work is criticized for lacking cohesion, being "all episode," Babbalanja defends it by comparing it with the actual world of Mardi:

> And so is Mardi itself:—nothing but episodes; valleys and hills; rivers, digressing from plains; vines, roving all over; boulders and diamonds; flowers and thistles; forests and thickets; and, here and there, fens and moors. And so, the world in the Koztanza.[191]

At least this implies that the work compares with Nature in such a way that the symbols become both organic and fluxional.

For Melville the Work of Art is a world made up of two elements difficult to name clearly, but the one has to do with the actual world and the other with the action of the Imagination. Though he uses varied terms, Melville suggests these two elements again and again. In writing of what he means to do in *Mardi*, he comments that Polynesia furnishes "a great deal of rich poetical material," and continues by saying that to bring it out suitably requires a "play of freedom & invention."[192] He defines the work by saying that "it opens like a true narrative" and adds that "the romance & poetry of the thing thence grow continually, till it becomes a story wild enough ... & with a meaning too."[193] In *The Confidence Man* (1857), Melville calls the Work of Art "another world, and yet one to which we feel the tie,"[194] and counts himself among those who expect literature to be more real than life itself. In Babbalanja's analysis the two elements are called "matter and mind," united, he says, in the work he so much admired, the Koztanza.[195] As Melville says again, people want novelty in a Work of Art, but "they want nature, too; but nature unfettered, exhilarated, in effect transformed."[196]

If Truth-seeking is the Artist's work, then the meaning of the Work of Art, perhaps one should say "the part and parcel allegoricalness of the whole,"[197] becomes of major importance. Melville saw the meanings as growing with the work, as fluxional or fluid— quite as the Transcendentalists saw them. But he placed a greater emphasis on the impossibility of arriving at final, complete answers, enhancing the ambiguity of meaning in the work. The ambiguous method follows the Artist's belief:

> Upon the whole, it might rather be thought, that he, who, in view of its inconsistencies, says of human nature the same that, in view of its contrasts, is said of the divine nature, that it is past finding out, thereby evinces a better appreciation of it than he who, by always representing it in a clear light, leaves it to be inferred that he clearly knows all about it.[198]

Melville did not see Man and Nature in a purely Transcendental fashion. As Merlin Bowen has demonstrated, Melville pitted the "self" against the "universe," showing in this basic antagonism the hostility or indifference of the universe.[199] This is surely different from a basic agreement between the soul of Man and the Spirit of Nature.

When it comes to characters, Melville says that a novelist usually picks up any character "in town," that in nearly all "there is discernible something prevailingly local, or of the age." He insists that even a really original character has this in common with other invented personages—"it cannot be born in the author's imagination."[200] Yet the imaginative element is there, too. The "rare worthies" in Lombardo's Koztanza he met first "in his reveries; they were walking about in him, sour and moody: and for a long time were shy of his advances; but still importuned, they at last grew ashamed of their reserve; stepped forward; and gave him their hands."[201]

These, then, are Transcendental reflections in Melville's aesthetic theories: in his views of Truth seen in things of earth; of the inspired Poet, driven to write, copying Nature to some extent; of the Work as a combination of the Actual and the Imagined (or, to use his words, "material" and "poetry"); of meanings growing out of the work; of characters taken from actual life and developed in thought.[202] Opposed as he was to Emersonian Transcendentalism as a philosophy, Melville's symbolic method of striking through the mask was thoroughly Transcendental.

CONCLUSION

Writers on Transcendentalism seem to have found it difficult to overstate the influence of Emerson and his fellow-Transcendentalists. Goddard writes:

> To the benefits which have flowed from the teaching and example of the transcendentalists we fortunately have ample witness. The influence of Emerson on such men as Arnold and Tyndall, men so unlike Emerson in many ways and in many ways so unlike each other, is typical of the inspiration which this movement spread abroad.[203]

And Frothingham makes even greater claims:

> Transcendentalism was an episode in the intellectual life of New England; an enthusiasm, a wave of sentiment, a breath of mind. . . . Its influence on thought and life was immediate and powerful. Religion felt it, literature, laws, institutions. The various reforms owed everything to it. New England character received from it an impetus that never will be spent.[204]

In the present study, however, we have concerned ourselves with the pervasiveness of the Transcendental aesthetic. It is clear that the Transcendental aesthetic theories, carefully formulated and published by Emerson (in both lecture and book form), were far-reaching in their influence on his American contemporaries. When men as distant from the Transcendentalists as Longfellow and Melville evidence this influence, it would be unlikely that Hawthorne, rather closely associated with the Transcendentalists, and with Longfellow and Melville too, should be untouched by the Transcendental aesthetic. This is particularly true because it was just at the time when Hawthorne was forming his own theories about art that he came into close association with the Transcendentalists, who were then, one might say, at their height. A look at the dates of Hawthorne's early works dealing with art is significant. His associations with the Transcendentalists began, it will be remembered, several years before he moved to Concord; his expression of his own ideas of the Artist began to appear the year after he moved to Concord. Hawthorne published "The Hall of Fantasy," in the *Pioneer* in February, 1843; "The Artist of the Beautiful" in the *Democratic Review* in June, 1844; "Rappaccini's Daughter" with a preface on art in the *Democratic Review* in December, 1844; "The Old Manse," in the collection *Mosses from an Old Manse* in 1846.

Hawthorne, himself, sensed the influence of Emersonian Transcendentalism. In three of the four works just cited he spoke of this influence specifically. In "The Hall of Fantasy," as narrator-observer, Hawthorne has just greeted his old friends of Brook Farm and remarked upon their presence there. Then he says:

> Mr. Emerson was likewise there, leaning against one of the pillars, and surrounded by an admiring crowd of writers and readers of the Dial, and all manner of Transcendentalists and disciples of the Newness, most of whom betrayed the power of his intellect by its modifying influence upon their own. . . . No more earnest seeker after truth than he, and few more successful finders of it; although, sometimes, the truth assumes a mystic unreality and shadowyness in his grasp.[205]

Here Hawthorne sees the power of Emerson's intellect by recognizing his influence upon others.

In the preface to "Rappaccini's Daughter," Hawthorne related himself to the Transcendentalists, saying of M. de l'Aubépine, his stand-in:

> As a writer, he seems to occupy an unfortunate position between the Transcendentalists (who, under one name or another, have their share in all the current literature of the world) and the great body of pen-and-ink men who address the intellect and sympathies of the multitude. If not too refined, at all events too remote, too shadowy, and unsubstantial in his modes of development to suit the taste of the latter class, and yet too popular to satisfy the spiritual or metaphysical requisitions of the former. . . .[206]

Here Hawthorne emphasizes the influence of Transcendentalism on all the current literature as he places himself between two large groups of writers, the Transcendentalists and the "popular" writers.

In "The Old Manse" essay, Hawthorne acknowledges an Emersonian influence upon himself and others. Speaking of the study, into which he invites his readers, he writes: "It was here that Emerson wrote Nature; for he was then an inhabitant of the Manse, and used to watch the Assyrian dawn and Paphian sunset and moonrise from the summit of our western hill."[207] Echoing the very images from *Nature*,[208] Hawthorne seems to be saying more than that both Oriental and Greek thought enlightened the writer of *Nature* as he looked upon the physical world from his study; he seems to be symbolically suggesting that he, too, inherits from the past occupant of his study as well as from the old clergyman's orchard and the dark surrounding faces of the Puritans on the blackened wall. Sitting in that very study, Hawthorne wrote "The Artist of the Beautiful," a story one contemporary reviewer saw as the kind of story Emerson would have written, had he written stories.[209] Later, in "The Old Manse" essay, Hawthorne speaks of the "wide-spreading influence of a great original thinker," and pictures Emerson as a light revealing truth, a light to which a number of bats and owls are also drawn. Hawthorne evidently speaks for himself, as well as for all who are attracted to the Emersonian light, when he says: "It was impossible to dwell in his vicinity without inhaling more or less the mountain atmosphere of his lofty thought."[210] Such an acknowledgement of Emerson's influence upon himself is seconded in a later preface, "The Custom House," where Hawthorne talks of "living for three years within the subtile influence of an intellect like Emerson's."[211]

Thus Hawthorne the observer recognized and stated the wide-spreading influence of Emersonian Transcendentalism upon both the wise and foolish Truth-seekers of his day. The influence upon some of the wiser writers has been demonstrated earlier in this chapter. And Hawthorne acknowledged the subtle influence of the Emersonian ideas upon himself. It remains to investigate in Hawthorne's theory and practice the extent of that influence.

Hawthorne's Aesthetic Intentions

INTRODUCTION

MANY OF the concepts of Emerson, of other Transcendentalists, and of non-Transcendentalists who share some Transcendental beliefs are embodied in Hawthorne's aesthetics. What Emerson called the Over-Soul or Alcott referred to as "spirit," Hawthorne names a high Reality. This is Thoreau's breath of life, or Margaret Fuller's one presence that creates. It is the great central Truth for which the Melville Artist searches but which he can never fully know. For Hawthorne, the Artist is like Emerson's Representative Man, Alcott's prophet, or Thoreau's Poet living between spirit and matter and singing with a breath from the gods—singing what Margaret Fuller called the natural life of the soul. Hawthorne's Artist, like the Transcendental Poet, sees the Truth painted in Nature and makes his work of Art, as Margaret Fuller suggested, paint to the eye and show an architectural symmetry. What Emerson indicated as the thought level, Hawthorne attains by mingling Imagination with actualities until his central figure, Man, corresponds closely to Nature. And in his creation of characters in conflict with sin, he works out the Transcendental truth to one's own nature coincident with universal Truth. Thus he makes what Longfellow would call an image of the spiritual world or Emerson would see as a new and transcendent whole. Careful investigation

49

of Hawthorne's aesthetics will indicate not only these general correspondences to the Transcendental aesthetic but artistic views so specifically detailed that his aesthetic theories can only be called Transcendental.

When Hawthorne created a book for the world, he frequently saw fit "to pave the reader's way into the interior edifice"[1] with a preface. These prefaces, spanning a twenty-year period, offer invaluable insights into the author's aesthetic intentions, not only in specific books but also in the literary works to which he gave the best efforts of his life.

None of the four major novels or three collections of tales and sketches appeared without a preface, excepting *Twice-Told Tales*, to which, though publications in 1837 and 1842 appeared without such an introduction, a preface was appended in the 1851 edition. In addition to major works, "Rappaccini's Daughter" (1844) was introduced to the public with remarks on the writing of M. de l'Aubépine, a pseudonym Hawthorne here ingeniously used to criticize his own work. Even the three collections of children's stories are thoughtfully introduced, and the *Life of Franklin Pierce* is presented as a "species of writing" remote from the author's "customary occupations" and "tastes."[2]

A mere listing of Hawthorne's prefaces, chronologically arranged, offers impressive evidence of the author's consistent efforts to direct the reader into the interior of his works: These are prefaces to *Grandfather's Chair* (1840), "Rappaccini's Daughter" (1844, in *Democratic Review*), *Mosses from an Old Manse* (1846, introduction called "The Old Manse"), *The Scarlet Letter* (1850, introduction called "The Custom House," augmented by the Preface to the Second Edition), *Twice-Told Tales* (1851 edition), *The House of the Seven Gables* (1851), *A Wonder Book for Girls and Boys* (1851), *The Snow-Image* (1852), *The Blithedale Romance* (1852), *Life of Franklin Pierce* (1852), *Tanglewood Tales* (1853, introduction called "The Wayside"), *The Marble Faun* (1860), and *Our Old Home* (1863, introduction called "To A Friend").

Two problems are posed by such a listing: How specifically does each preface belong to the work it introduces? Is there any marked difference in Hawthorne's earlier and later aesthetic intentions? While these questions will not be overlooked in this study, several bits of evidence are here offered that concern with them does not need to govern the manner of handling the total problem. In 1852, in the midst of his writing career, when Hawthorne made his collection of earlier sketches for *The Snow-Image,* he found "the ripened autumnal fruit tastes but little better than the early windfalls."[3] He says:

> In youth, men are apt to write more wisely than they really know or feel; and the remainder of life may be not idly spent in realizing and convincing themselves of the wisdom which they uttered long ago. The truth that was only in the fancy then may have since become a substance in the mind and heart.[4]

Another indication of Hawthorne's "agreement with himself" over a period of years is the fact that his analysis of his writing which appeared in the preface to "Rappaccini's Daughter" as first published in 1844, though omitted from the first edition of the *Mosses from an Old Manse* (1846), was remembered and suggested to Fields for possible inclusion in the second edition of the *Mosses* (1854),[5] where it appeared. Finally, some of the most important evidence of Hawthorne's aesthetic views is found in the *Mosses* collection, with the first and second editions (the second carefully revised by the author) spanning an eight-year period including all major romances and collections except *Twice-Told Tales* and *The Marble Faun.*

In this collection are found some of the most important stories and sketches dealing with the Artist: "The Artist of the Beautiful," "Drowne's Wooden Image," "The Hall of Fantasy," and "A Select Party." "The Snow-Image" is perhaps the single most important story outside this collection where implicit meaning is coupled with explicit statement of aesthetic theory.

In addition to these prefaces and stories, the artist-observers in three of the four romances become part of an implicit meaning too, besides permitting their creator (even in *The Blithedale Romance,* with Coverdale as narrator) to make direct statements of theory.

Both setting and characters in *The Marble Faun* provide opportunity for views of the Artist's work. There is implied aesthetic theory in the techniques of the story-tellers of the children's books and of "The Antique Ring" and "Alice Doane's Appeal."

Together with all these relevant works there are the notebooks—American, English, French and Italian—where any page may record direct glimpses into the author's thought. And finally, the letters to James T. Fields and to William D. Ticknor, his publishers and friends; to Horatio Bridge, whose inspiration he deeply appreciated; and to Sophia, that so sensitive listener, are sources of occasional insight into his intentions as an artist.

With these materials the student of Hawthorne's aesthetic intentions begins—with these and the thought that what is revealed by the artist may well involve three areas: (1) something Hawthorne calls Reality, (2) something he recognizes as Romance, and (3) something he once names "circumstances . . . of the writer's own choosing or creation."[6]

HAWTHORNE'S AESTHETIC THEORIES

Reality

"Something truer and more real"

"There is something truer and more real than what we can see with the eyes and touch with the finger," Hawthorne clearly affirms in an authorial comment in "Rappaccini's Daughter."[7] This might also be called "the better sphere that lies unseen around us,"[8] or thought of as a truer world than this feverish one[9] where mere outward show has "nothing to satisfy the soul that has become acquainted with truth."[10] Distinguishing between an external and an inward life, Hawthorne says "the grosser life is a dream, and the spiritual life a reality."[11] This Reality is an Ideal Beauty "which Nature has proposed to herself in all her creatures, but has never taken pains to realize."[12]

There is a relation between this Reality and the individual, whether in Nature or Man. Though "our partial scope of vision" means that we can never judge "of the relations which we bear to our fellow-creatures and human circumstances," we are like "mighty mountains" that think "they have nothing to do with one another, each seems itself its own centre, and existing for itself alone; and yet, to an eye that can take them all in, they are evidently portions of *one grand and beautiful idea*, which could not be consummated without the lowest and loftiest of them."[13]

Hawthorne thinks of this Reality reflected in Man as he equates the flitting, transitory beauty he sometimes sees in his little daughter Una with her "real soul," and thinks "when she seems less lovely, we merely see something external."[14] It is this same spiritual essence, so uninhibited in the new Adam and Eve, that draws them toward the sky. Even in so negative a character as the Old Apple Dealer, Hawthorne sees the reflection of the spiritual:

> Yet, could I read but a tithe of what is written there, it would be a volume of deeper and more comprehensive import than all that the wisest mortals have given to the world; for the soundless depths of the human soul and of eternity have an opening through your breast. God be praised, were it only for your sake, that the present shapes of human existence are not cast in iron nor hewn in everlasting adamant, but moulded of the vapors that vanish away while the essence flits upward to the Infinite. There is a spiritual essence in this gray and lean old shape that shall flit upward too.[15]

Without that last inestimable touch of the Creator, Gervayse Hastings lives an unreal existence, completely out of touch with suffering humanity who pass before him like shadows, and his death only stops the flicker of his shadow on the wall.

Loss of faith in the high Reality, in the invisible, brings pride in the wisdom that rejects much that the eye can see and trusts confidently in nothing but what the hand can touch. To such depths the Artist of the Beautiful once falls.[16] But for the picture of a man whose spiritual part is dead, there is the Virtuoso: For a moment Hawthorne the observer hopes that "perhaps the ethereal spirit is not entirely extinct under all this corrupted or frozen mass of earthly life. Perhaps the immortal spark may yet be rekindled by a breath of Heaven." But the Virtuoso's answer destroys hope: " 'My destiny is linked with the realities of earth. You are welcome to your visions and shadows of a future state; but give me what I can see, and touch, and understand, and I ask no more.' " " 'It is indeed too late,' thought I. 'The soul is dead within him.' " And with this thought and the Virtuoso's icy handshake—"without a single heart throb of human brotherhood"—the observer is shown in departing "that the inner door of the hall was constructed with the ivory leaves of the gateway through which Æneas and the Sibyl had been dismissed from Hades."[17]

Thus it may be seen that Hawthorne's high Reality partakes of the characteristics of Emerson's Over-Soul or Thoreau's everlasting Something to which we are allied. It is the True, the Beautiful, the spiritual Essence in Nature and Man—what Alcott and Margaret Fuller called simply the "soul." This grand and beautiful Idea, of which diverse Nature seems to be parts, is the high Reality—invisible, intangible, but "truer and more real than what we can see with the eyes and touch with the finger."[18]

The "spiritual symbol continually beside us"

Hawthorne holds the Transcendental belief that the high Reality is shadowed in the things of earth. He stands on the river's brink near the Old Manse and reflects upon the images of "each tree and rock, and every blade of grass" as they assume "ideal beauty in the reflection." "All the sky glows downward at our feet" he thinks; "the rich clouds float . . . like heavenly thoughts." Although he knows that the river is gross and impure, he sees the picture of "the heaven that broods above it"; and remembering the tawny hue and the mud, says "let it be a symbol that the earthliest human soul has an infinite spiritual capacity and may contain the better world within its depths."[19] There is in these reflections an Ideal Beauty which satisfies the spirit "incomparably more than the actual scene" until Hawthorne is "half convinced that the reflection is indeed the reality—the real thing which Nature imperfectly images to our grosser sense. At all events, the disembodied shadow is nearest to the soul."[20] Crossing the Arno on the Ponte di Santo Trinita, he records that he was "struck by the beautiful scene of the broad, calm river, with the palaces along its shores repeated in it, on either side, and the neighboring bridges, too, just as perfect in the tide beneath as in the air above,—a city of dream and shadow so close to the actual one." "God has a meaning, no doubt," Hawthorne continues, "in putting this spiritual symbol continually beside us."[21]

Idea is shadowed in Nature. In "Footprints on the Sea-Shore" the huge rock with veins like inscriptions suggests a fancy that "Nature's own hand has here recorded a mystery, which, could I read her language, would make mankind the wiser and the happier. How many a thing," the author continues less fancifully, "has troubled me with that same idea!"[22] Here the ages "find utterance in the sea's unchanging voice, and warn the listener to withdraw his interest from mortal vicissitudes, and let the infinite idea of eternity pervade his soul."[23] When, looking out of the owl tower of Monte Beni, Donatello and Kenyon view a valley with several varieties of weather, Kenyon finds it " 'a page of heaven and a page of earth spread wide open before us!' " He advises, " 'Only begin to read it, and you will find it interpreting itself without the aid of words.' " He considers it a " 'great mistake to try to put our best thoughts into human language,' " because " 'when we ascend into the higher regions of emotion and spiritual enjoyment, they are only expressible by such grand hieroglyphics as these around us.' "[24]

"Something more" is shadowed in man's earthly enjoyments. On a glorious day, with love for Nature and thankfulness for breath, Hawthorne writes that "such a day is the promise of a blissful eternity; our Creator would never have made such weather, and have given us the deep hearts to enjoy it above and beyond all thought, if He had not meant us to be immortal. It opens the gates of Heaven, and gives us glimpses far inward."[25] In true happiness there is reflected "something more than the earth owns, and something more than a mortal capacity for the enjoyment of it."[26] Sometimes we interpret this sense wrongly: "We have strongly within us the sense of an undying principle, and we transfer that true sense to this life and to the body, instead of interpreting it justly as the promise of spiritual immortality."[27]

To see the spiritual in the shadows is not easy. "The trees reflected in the river;—they are unconscious of a spiritual world so near them. So are we."[28] Thinking of Sophia, Hawthorne wishes that he might see her spiritual reality—not Sophia Hawthorne, in actuality, whom he often pictured as a delightful but impertinent and earthly creature, but his "Dove." Capturing his whimsical yet serious mood, he tells her, "I sit writing in the middle of the chamber, opposite the looking-glass; and as soon as I finish this sentence, I shall look therein—and really I have something like a shadowy notion, that I shall behold mine own white Dove peeping over my shoulder." When he does not see her, he asks, "Is it merely the defect in my own eyes, which cannot behold the spiritual?"[29] The aspiring scientist Aylmer had not reached the profounder wisdom of seeing the spiritual or "he need not . . . have flung away the happiness which would have woven his mortal life of the self-same texture with the celestial." In his efforts to destroy earthly imperfection, he missed the reflection of the Perfect: "he failed to look beyond the shadowy scope of time, and, living once for all in eternity, to find the perfect future in the present."[30]

For "we dwell in the shadow cast by Time, which is itself the shadow cast by Eternity."[31] But the shadows have meaning. Hawthorne, the observer, had comforted the desperate bookworm when all his books had gone into the bonfire of Earth's Holocaust with this hope:

"Is not Nature better than a book? Is not the human heart deeper than any system of philosophy? Is not life replete with more instruction than past observers have found it possible to write down in maxims? Be of good cheer. The great book of Time is still spread wide open before us; and, if we read it aright, it will be to us a volume of eternal truth."[32]

Even some illusions are the "shadows of great truths."[33] And the author of "P.'s Correspondence," "after missing his object while seeking it by the light of reason," may very possibly "have stum-

bled upon it in his misty excursions beyond the limits of sanity."[34]
Out of these mists he writes:

> More and more I recognize that we dwell in a world of shadows;
> and, for my part, I hold it hardly worth the trouble, to attempt
> a distinction between shadows in the mind and shadows out of
> it. If there be any difference, the former are rather the more
> substantial.[35]

"A world of shadows"—"a volume of eternal truth."

"The black mud over which the river sleeps"

But the shadowing of the high Reality is a reflection in muddy
waters; the picture of heaven is shadowed in a gross and impure
river. "Mankind are earthern jugs with spirit in them."[36] Neither
Nature's Ideal butterfly nor a Georgiana without a birthmark is to
be found in this world. Beatrice, the heavenly angel, walks in a
poisoned garden though the "ugly mystery" is "but an earthly illusion." There is poison enough in Giovanni's nature to create a
"gulf of blackness" between their spirits.[37] When the physical
frame shadows forth the moral system, there may well be a serpent
there.[38] "But deeper still is the eternal beauty," Hawthorne declares in a notebook entry:

> The human Heart to be allegorized as a cavern; at the en-
> trance there is sunshine, and flowers growing about it. You step
> within, but a short distance, and begin to find yourself sur-
> rounded with a terrible gloom, and monsters of divers kinds; it
> seems like Hell itself. You are bewildered, and wander long
> without hope. At last a light strikes upon you. You peep towards
> it, and find yourself in a region that seems, in some sort, to repro-
> duce the flowers and sunny beauty of the entrance, but all per-
> fect. These are the depths of the heart, or of human nature,
> bright and peaceful; the gloom and terror may lie deep; but
> deeper still is the eternal beauty.[39]

That eternal Beauty, shadowed through earth's imperfections, is
Hawthorne's high Reality. The belief that Nature's language and
Man's inner soul shadow eternal Beauty through the evil is a tenet

shared by Emerson and Hawthorne. Or, as Alcott saw it, all unrest was the soul's struggle to recover what she had lost by her descent.

The Artist

"The last best touch" of the Creator

But if, as Hawthorne believes, the eternal lesson is written in all men's souls;[40] if, as he says, the Artist concerns himself merely with what is common to human nature;[41] if he appeals "to no sentiment or sensibilities save such as are diffused among us all,"[42] what exactly is the place of the genius? "Perhaps," Hawthorne suggests, "he whose genius appears deepest and truest excels his fellows in nothing save the knack of expression; he throws out occasionally a lucky hint at truths of which every human soul is profoundly, though unutterably conscious."[43] The knack of expressing the soul's profound, unutterable knowledge requires "the gift of discerning, in this sphere of strangely mingled elements, the beauty and the majesty which are compelled to assume a garb so sordid."[44] Artists have a "quick sensibility . . . apt to give . . . intimations of the true state of matters" that lie "beyond . . . actual vision."[45] The Creator has formed the man of genius "as the last best touch to his own handiwork," for "creation was not finished till the poet came to interpret, and so complete it."[46] To discern, to utter, to interpret what all men know—this is the work of the Artist. For this reason Hawthorne can humbly assure Sophia that in the immortal reality she is wiser and better than he, though "sometimes he may chance to interpret the flitting shadows around us more accurately."[47]

The gift of "imagination, sensibility, creative power, genius" is a gift to every human spirit; but it may or may not be developed in this world, depending on the circumstances. "Yet who can doubt that the very highest state to which a human spirit can attain, in its loftiest aspirations, is its truest and most natural state . . .?"[48] There is power in the imagination to make grand and beautiful things: "After all, the utmost force of man can do positively very little towards making grand things, or beautiful things; the imagination can do so much more. . . ."[49] Through art, little Benjamin

West could catch a look that appears and vanishes in a moment, and make it last for hundreds of years.[50] "Genius, indeed, melts many ages into one, and thus effects something permanent, yet still with a similarity of office to that of the more ephemeral writer." The age itself writes newspapers, which therefore have both a timely meaning and "a kind of intelligible truth for all times." "A work of genius is but the newspaper of a century, or perchance of a hundred centuries."[51]

Possessor of a gift in a sense common to all humanity, the Poet is the last best touch of the Creator; as the Imagination makes man most consistent with his highest and best self, so the Poet—the man of Imagination—makes his age and mankind. This is Emerson's Representative Man, Margaret Fuller's divine maker, Alcott's prophet.

"Faith is the soul's eyesight"

For the artist to be able to show the shadowing of the high Reality, there are several requisites; one of these is faith. To read the high truth revealed in Nature requires belief, a simplicity of faith. Owen Warland loses his ability to create when his faith wavers: "He had lost his faith in the invisible, and now prided himself, as such unfortunates invariably do, in the wisdom which rejected much that even his eye could see, and trusted confidently in nothing but what his hand could touch." Luckily, "in Owen Warland the spirit was not dead nor passed away; it only slept." When faith reawakens, this artist says, "Now for my task. . . . Never did I feel such strength for it as now."[52] The "haughty faith" with which artist Holgrave begins his life is a necessity, even though he comes to believe that it "would be well bartered for a far humbler one at its close, in discerning that man's best directed effort accomplishes a kind of dream, while God is the sole worker of realities."[53] Better that the Artist should believe he can create realities than that he should believe no reality exists. The little snow-sister created by Violet and Peony does not and cannot exist for a mere common-sensible man like their father. But the children have the faith of the Artist; Violet sees that Peony looks exactly like a snow-image except for his ruddy cheeks: This is belief in the shadowing of the Reality. Similarly their mother, with a "childlike simplicity and faith," "as pure and clear as crystal," "looking at all matters through this transparent medium, . . . sometimes saw truths so profound that other people laughed at them as nonsense and absurdity."[54]

Without belief in the Invisible, in himself, and in the shadowed Truth, Hawthorne's Artist fails as quickly as any Transcendental Poet. The lack of imaginative faith means missing the highest realities of the spirit. Hawthorne says of those who mistook "the castle in the air for a heap of sunset clouds to which the magic of light and shade had imparted the aspect of a fantastically constructed mansion":

> Had they been worthy to pass within its portal, they would have recognized the truth, that the dominions which the spirit conquers for itself among unrealities become a thousand times more real than the earth whereon they stamp their feet, saying, "This is solid and substantial; this may be called a fact."[55]

"The soul's instinctive perception"

The Poet must have not only faith but the "imaginative faith." He must have the power to perceive the shadowing of Reality in the Actual. In his imagination the creative work must be born. Hawthorne says, "An innate perception and reflection of truth gives the only sort of originality that does not finally grow intolerable."[56] What does he mean by "innate perception"? In an early idea for a story where a person discovers a truth in his dreams—though real life belies it—"the explanation would be—the soul's instinctive perception."[57] Earth-born visions are never to be confused with nor to obscure imaginative visions of the highest Reality. The inner soul knows truth the mind cannot get hold of. In his stern advice to Sophia against participation in the popular practice of spiritualism, Hawthorne says:

> What so miserable as to lose the soul's true, though hidden, knowledge and consciousness of heaven, in the mist of an earth-

born vision? . . . If thou wouldst know what heaven is, . . . then
retire into the depths of thine own spirit, and thou wilt find it
there among holy thoughts and feelings. . . .[58]

Such a view is "caused by no want of faith in mysteries, but from
a deep reverence of the soul, and of the mysteries which it knows
within itself, but never transmits to the earthly eye or ear. Keep
thy imagination sane—that is one of the truest conditions of com-
munion with Heaven."[59] Some seventeen years later, touching the
subject of spiritualism again, he listens to his own inner soul in
the face of facts which he accepts with his mind and asserts: "My
inner soul does not in the least admit them; there is a mistake
somewhere."[60]

Hawthorne, like Emerson—like Longfellow and Melville in one
phase of their aesthetics—suggests the involuntary nature of the
embodiment of the Artist's vision. Several times he suggests that
writing may occasionally take its own course. In an early *American
Notebook* this is made the idea for a story: "A person to be writing
a tale, and to find that it shapes itself against his intentions. . . ."[61]
Hawthorne's personal experience proved such a thing could happen. He wrote to Fields that *The Marble Faun* "has developed
itself."[62] Again he wrote, "The Devil himself always seems to get
into my inkstand, and I can only exorcise him by pensful at a
time."[63] The preference for realistic works which he was not able
to write[64] argues that Hawthorne recognized his imagination as
something beyond the control of his ingenuity. This was the reason
he could not profit by just censure, why he thought there was not
much use to attempt profiting: "There are weeds enough in my
mind, to be sure, and I might pluck them up by the handful; but
in so doing I should root up the few flowers along with them."[65]

So it is with Hawthorne's pictured artists: Not Kenyon but an
"unseen spiritual assistant" creates the "true image" of Donatello
through "some accidental handling of the clay," entirely inde-
pendent of Kenyon's will.[66] Drowne, ordinarily a mere craftsman,
is momentarily inspired to create, without his realizing how, a
miraculously beautiful wooden image. Those little miracle-
workers Violet and Peony, who took heaven's new-fallen snow to

make new beings of, were not "aware of their immortal play-mates," although they saw that "the image grew very beautiful while they worked at it," and thought that they themselves had done it all.[67] The poet in "The Great Stone Face" does not realize that he has incorporated in his poems words which give "the far-off echo of a heavenly song."[68]

The first sketchy rendition in some ways is better than a fuller embodiment which is less close to the inspiration. Hawthorne finds seeing the original drawings of Raphael and Michael Angelo "like looking into their brains, and seeing the first conception, before it took shape outwardly."[69] He speaks of pencil drawings in the Louvre as:

> . . . the earliest drawings of their great pictures, when they had the glory of their pristine idea directly before their mind's eye, —that idea which inevitably became overlaid with their own handling of it in the finished painting. No doubt, the painters themselves had often a happiness in these rude off-hand sketches, which they never felt again in the same work, and which resulted in disappointment, after they had done their best.[70]

"There is something more divine in these," he says elsewhere, "for I suppose the first idea of a picture is real inspiration, and all the subsequent elaboration of the master serves but to cover up the celestial germ with something that belongs to himself."[71] He re-words the idea in *The Marble Faun*, where he says, "There is an effluence of divinity in the first sketch; and there, if anywhere, you find the pure light of inspiration. . . ."[72]

Lacking instinctive perception, the Artist exercises all his skill in vain. The architect of the Houses of Parliament did not have a mind " 'before which the forms and fantasies that conceal the inner idea from the multitude vanish at once and leave the naked reality beneath.' "[73] As a result, "he reckoned upon and contrived all his effects, with malice aforethought, and therefore missed the crowning effect—that being a happiness which God, out of his pure grace, mixes up with only the simple-hearted best efforts of men."[74]

Seeing the artistic failure of the structure, Hawthorne quoted Emerson to account for it: "The reason must be, that the architect has not 'builded better than he knew.' "[75] He has failed, as Alcott would say, to discern by spiritual sight.

The toil of "catching butterflies"

Hawthorne never believed, however, that the intuitive perception of Truth was the end of the matter. Grant his Artist of the Beautiful his beautiful idea, quite evidently perceived from observation of the butterflies in Nature; yet that very observation is an effort of chasing and watching Nature's creatures to get hold of the beautiful idea. His created butterfly is a visible exercise of the spirit, and this exercise is conscious spiritual effort in conflict with practicality, delusion, and the loss of earthly hope.

Both Hawthorne's remarks about himself as artist and his notebooks taken generally and specifically indicate his conscious effort in observation and in reflection upon that which he observed. He refers to himself in the preface to *The Snow-Image* as "a person, who has been burrowing, to his utmost ability, into the depths of our common nature, for the purposes of psychological romance,— and who pursues his researches in that dusky region, as he needs must, as well by the tact of sympathy as by the light of observation."[76] His choice of the phrases "has been burrowing," "to his utmost ability," and "pursues his researches," indicates the effort. One senses the struggle to get at the meaning beneath the symbol as Hawthorne writes of the ragged scrap of cloth, the capital letter A:

> My eyes fastened themselves upon the old scarlet letter, and would not be turned aside. Certainly, there was some deep meaning to it, most worthy of interpretation, and which, as it were, streamed forth from the mystic symbol, subtly communicating itself to my sensibilities, but evading the analysis of my mind.[77]

The conscious effort involves both the "tact of sympathy" and the "light of observation." Hawthorne once fused these methods by imagining the self removed from and observing the self. In "Monsieur du Miroir," he says, "I will be self-contemplative, as Nature bids me,"[78] and he makes Monsieur the visible type of his own spiritual nature, a reflection of the truth in himself, both elusive and terrifying.

Even a casual reading of the notebooks gives copious evidence of his conscious efforts to observe and record for future use, but especially notable here are the frequent suggestions that something is "worth thinking over and studying out,"[79] or that a subject "offers hints of copious reflection,"[80] or "I must see it again; for it ought to be studied."[81] There is an emphasis on depth of thought, on letting the subject lie in his mind a day or two, as "too raw to be properly dealt with, immediately after coming from the scene."[82] Complaining of a hurried tour, he remarks, "I am slow to feel—slow, I suppose, to comprehend; and, like the anaconda, I need to lubricate any object a great deal, before I can swallow it and actually make it my own."[83] In an author's comment in *The Blithedale Romance*, he generalizes: "By long brooding over our recollections, we subtilize them into something akin to imaginary stuff, and hardly capable of being distinguished from it."[84] After the innate perception came the toil of chasing butterflies—the Transcendental pursuit of Beauty.

The Artist's power as interpreter, because he is seer of the "inmost soul,"[85] seems to give him almost a sense of commission, of saying because he "must." In "Passages from a Relinquished Work," the boy who decides to be a story-teller leaves his parson guardian for the wild life of a wandering teller of tales—he removes himself for what appears in New England to be a life of idleness; yet he insists that he must toil, though only in catching butterflies. With the fellow-traveller whom he meets, the perplexed itinerant preacher, he takes the position of guide. More emphatic is the statement in "The Artist of the Beautiful":

Alas that the artist, whether in poetry, or whatever other material, may not content himself with the inward enjoyment of the beautiful, but must chase the flitting mystery beyond the verge of his ethereal domain, and crush its frail being in seizing it with a material grasp.[86]

There is a hint of a commission to make Truth known in "The Old Manse," where Hawthorne pictures himself as inheritor of the old clergyman's orchard rather than of his library of heavy religious volumes and flighty tracts. Hawthorne treats this same idea in a somewhat comic vein, yet with a depth of seriousness, in "The Custom House," where the ghost of Mr. Surveyor Pue, in "the dignity of one who had borne his Majesty's commission," gives him a symbol and a charge.[87]

"To see wonders and to know that they are natural things"

It is through both the chase of butterflies and the "rays of divine intelligence which enable us to see wonders and to know that they are natural things,"[88] that is, both through active effort and intuitive perception that Nature reveals herself to the Artist. There are times when a set purpose to perceive, to understand, to see, will fail. Hawthorne develops this thought in terms of seeing landscapes, children, and external objects.

> Nature will not be understood on immediate demand: But, in truth, I doubt if anybody ever does really see a mountain, who goes for the set and sole purpose of seeing it. Nature will not let herself be seen, in such cases. You must patiently bide her time; and, by and-by [*sic*], at some unforeseen moment, she will quietly and suddenly unveil herself, and, for a brief space, let you look right into the heart of her mystery. But if you call out to her peremptorily—"Nature, unveil yourself, this very instant!"—she only draws her veil the closer; and you may look with all your eyes, and imagine you see all that she can show, and yet see nothing.[89]

Hawthorne lets Coverdale speak humorously of the Brook Farm labors: "Pausing in the field, to let the wind exhale the moisture from our foreheads, we were to look upward, and catch glimpses into the far-off soul of truth. In this point of view, matters did not turn out quite so well as we anticipated." But Coverdale goes on to echo views expressed in Hawthorne's notebooks:

It is very true that, sometimes, gazing casually around me, out of the midst of my toil, I used to discern a richer picturesqueness in the visible scene of earth and sky. There was, at such moments, a novelty, an unwonted aspect, on the face of Nature, as if she had been taken by surprise and seen at unawares, with no opportunity to put off her real look, and assume the mask with which she mysteriously hides herself from mortals.[90]

Once, rather casually, Hawthorne observes that "it is with children as Mr [sic] Emerson, or somebody else, says it with nature— you cannot see them so well when you look at them of set purpose. The best manifestations of them must take you at unawares."[91]

External objects reveal their meaning in a similar fashion:

There is a singular effect oftentimes when, out of the midst of engrossing thought and deep absorption, we suddenly look up, and catch a glimpse of external objects. We seem at such moments to look farther and deeper into them, than by any premeditated observation; it is as if they met our eyes alive, and with all their hidden meaning on the surface, but grew again inanimate and inscrutable the instant that they became aware of our glances.[92]

The revelation may be of variety. At Inversnaid, Hawthorne writes, "I strolled about the yard, in the intervals of rain-drops gazing up at the hill-sides, and recognizing that there is a vast variety of shape, of light and shadow, and incidental circumstance, even in what looks so monotonous at first as the green shape of a hill."[93] More important, it may be a unity in the variety. Looking at autumn woods

The effect is, that every tree in the wood, and every bush among the shrubbery, seems to have a separate existence, since, confusedly intermingled, each wears its peculiar hue, instead of being lost in the universal verdure of the summer. And yet there is a oneness of effect, likewise, when we choose to look at a whole sweep of woodland, or swamp shrubbery, instead of analyzing its component trees.[94]

He sees with an understanding of appropriateness; noticing swans, so beautiful in the water, so ugly walking on land, Hawthorne moralizes on the importance of seeing a person or thing "in the circumstances for which it is intended and adapted."[95] Thus Nature reveals herself in a revelation of the unity in variety and of the appropriateness of things to the circumstances which surround them. This is the Emersonian theory of the Poet's seeing the variety in Nature, seeing beyond to the unified meaning, the Oneness, and understanding the correspondences between character and surroundings.

The ideal Artist, then, for Hawthorne as well as Emerson or Alcott, can show the high Reality shadowed in the things of earth because he believes in the Reality and in the shadowing, because by intuition and conscious pursuit of Beauty he can perceive the Reality in the shadowing, and because he has the power, through his own Imagination and Nature's revelations, to interpret the shadows.

Romance: Actuality and Imagination

In "The Artist of the Beautiful" there are four kinds of butterflies: real butterflies in Nature, the mechanical butterfly created by the artist, the butterfly of the artist's idea to which he gave visible form, and Nature's ideal butterfly which he represented by his creation and to which his idea came nearer and nearer as his spirit mounted from earth to cloud and from cloud to celestial atmosphere. It is the blending of real butterflies with the artist's imaginative thought of butterflies that gives the beautiful idea form. Here in this story, Hawthorne's butterflies move up the Platonic scale of being in true Emersonian Transcendental style. The butterfly symbol of Artist Owen Warland is a moving, living, organic symbol. The picture on the box shows the Poet's movement up the scale toward the Ideal butterfly.

One figure that Hawthorne uses to explain the artist's work is suggested in a letter to Fields: "In writing a romance, a man is always, or always ought to be, careering on the utmost verge of a precipitous absurdity, and the skill lies in coming as close as possible, without actually tumbling over."[96] Hawthorne seems to feel that balance on the edge of the precipice is best maintained by mingling Actuality and Imagination; such a mingling is a means of revealing to readers the Reality shadowed in the Actual.

If the Artist fails to combine Actuality with the Imaginative, he is "too remote, too shadowy, and unsubstantial in his modes of development," content with "the faintest possible counterfeit of real life."[97] He writes stories that "have the pale tint of flowers that blossomed in too retired a shade,—the coolness of a meditative habit, which diffuses itself through the feeling and observation of every sketch. Instead of passion there is sentiment; and, even in what purport to be pictures of actual life, we have allegory, not always so warmly dressed in its habiliments of flesh and blood as to be taken into the reader's mind without a shiver."[98] Such writing is tame, lacks humanness and warmth, is weak in humor and pathos. Though such sketches "are not altogether destitute of fancy and originality," the author's "inveterate love of allegory . . . is apt to invest his plots and characters with the aspect of scenery and people in the clouds, and to steal away the human warmth out of his conceptions." Sometimes his stories have little reference to time or space,[99] and this is too much like spending all one's days in the Hall of Fantasy and seeing therefore the fulfillment of Father Miller's prophecy of the untimely end of the poor old earth, with the earthliness which Hawthorne loves. This failure in mingling more than "a breath of Nature, a raindrop of pathos and tenderness, or a gleam of humor," with the "fantastic imagery," takes us too much out of "the limits of our native earth"[100] and makes "blasted allegories" in which, at a later reading, Hawthorne was not quite sure he entirely comprehended his own meaning.[101]

The Artist will fail just as surely if, in the midst of realities, his Imagination will not reflect Actuality. Given all the actuality of his life in the Custom House, Hawthorne declared that he was unable to write for this reason: "My imagination was a tarnished mirror. It would not reflect, or only with miserable dimness, the figures with which I did my best to people it." His characters "would not be warmed and rendered malleable by any heat" from his "intellectual forge." They would not take on any feeling but stared back at him like dead corpses and seemed to say, "The little power you might once have possessed over the tribe of unrealities is gone!" While these "almost torpid creatures" of his fancy "twitted" him "with imbecility,"[102] there was a page of actual life spread out before him that seemed dull and commonplace only because he had not fathomed its deeper import, a book "written out by the reality of the flitting hour, and vanishing as fast as written," because his brain wanted insight and his hand the cunning to transcribe it. But he did not "diffuse thought and imagination through the opaque substance of to-day, . . . to make it a bright transparency; to spiritualize the burden . . . ; to seek . . . the true and indestructible value that lay hidden in the petty and wearisome incidents, and ordinary characters," with which he was conversant.[103] Hawthorne explains how little he cared for literature at this period. He did not care for books, and Nature—except human nature—was in a sense hidden from him; he continues, "and all the imaginative delight, wherewith it had been spiritualized, passed away out of my mind." The difficulty was that "a gift, a faculty if it had not departed, was suspended and inanimate within me."[104] During this same period he laments in his letters to Sophia that there is no labor or food in his Custom House life for his intellect, his heart and soul; "I *am* a machine," he asserts, "and am surrounded by hundreds of similar machines."[105] Again he says that his fancy has at the moment no command of external symbols,[106] or that his fancy is so torpid that he cannot sketch scenes that he could later weave into fiction,[107] and once he suggests how he means to personify the east wind, "if ever the imaginative portion of my brain recover from its torpor."[108] Fools thought the Hall of Fantasy was made of brick and mortar; Hawthorne knew it was not; he knew further that if the Imagination was a tarnished mirror, no reflection would succeed: there would, in fact, *be* no reflection.

To turn the attention from allegories Hawthorne disliked and from books he never wrote to his successes is to find his consistent statements that the Artist succeeds only by mingling the Actual and the Imaginative. This mingling is most artistically explained in the "moonlit room" passage in "The Custom House." He describes himself sitting "in the deserted parlor, lighted only by the glimmering coal-fire and the moon, striving to picture forth imaginary scenes." In his description the floor of the familiar room becomes "a neutral territory, somewhere between the real world and fairy-land, where the Actual and the Imaginary may meet, and each imbue itself with the nature of the other." The familiar room is filled with actualities: the chairs, each individual; the centre-table, with its workbasket, a book or two, a lamp not burning; a bookcase; the picture on the wall. A child's shoe; a doll, seated in a wicker carriage; and the hobby-horse are actual playthings as the chairs and table are useful things. There is a warm coal-fire suggesting actual human warmth. But into the room moonlight falls white upon the carpet, showing all its figures distinctly; it makes each object minutely visible. This moonlight is not a daytime light; it is an unusual, spiritualizing light—the moonlight of romance—by which all the details seem to lose their Actuality and become things in the mind. In thought, the Imaginary partakes of the Actual as well as the Actual of the Imaginary; and the familiar room has become the neutral territory. As the warm light of the fire mingles with "the cold spirituality of the moonbeams," snow-images are given "a heart and sensibilities of human tenderness"—they become men and women.[109]

In *The House of the Seven Gables* Hawthorne similarly mingles the Actual and the Imaginary. He attempts "to connect a bygone [imagined] time with the very [actual] present that is flitting away from us." The imagined legend of the past he hopes to carry "down into our own broad daylight . . . bringing along with it some of its legendary mist. . . ."[110] He worries about the difficulty of doing this, not only in the Preface but also in a letter to Bridge, wherein he wonders whether "the romance of the book shall be found somewhat at odds with the humble and familiar scenery in which I invest it."[111] He would rather have avoided the risk of having his reader "assign an actual locality to the imaginary events of this narrative"; yet his use of "the historical connection" does make this possible. The "personages of the tale . . . are really of the author's own making, or, at all events," his own imaginative combinations of qualities drawn from reality—"his own mixing."[112]

In *The Blithedale Romance*, since Hawthorne's Brook Farm experience was "essentially a daydream, and yet a fact," he found for his romance based upon his experiences "an available foothold between fiction and reality"—a sort of Faery Land such as the old countries provide the romancer. This place is "so like the real world, that, in a suitable remoteness, one cannot well tell the difference." At the same time, it has "an atmosphere of strange enchantment, beheld through which the inhabitants have a propriety of their own"; without such an atmosphere the "paint and pasteboard" of imagined beings is much too discernible. Since Faery Land was not provided ready-made in America, Hawthorne established his Brook Farm theatre, "a little removed from the highway of ordinary travel, where the creatures of his brain may play their phantasmagorical antics, without exposing them to too close a comparison with the actual events of real lives."[113] Such was his mingling of Actuality with the Imagined in this book.

For *The Marble Faun* Italy afforded "a sort of poetic or fairy precinct, where actualities would not be so terribly insisted upon." The "broad and simple daylight"[114] of his native land could never provide the atmosphere for the American romance writer. The characters are on the one hand meant to be related to human life and human nature but on the other hand "so artfully and airily removed from our mundane sphere, that some laws and proprieties of their own should be implicitly and insensibly acknowledged." The idea of the modern Faun loses its poetry and beauty "if we bring it into the actual light of day."[115] The author wanted to locate him between the Real and the Fantastic. Hawthorne had wanted to avoid the word "Faun" in the title (before he seems to have considered prefixing "Marble") because he did not want the fantastic aspect to become too prominent.[116]

Even in writing biographical sketches for children, Hawthorne uses the adventures of "the substantial and homely reality of a fireside chair" for the "machinery of the work" because he sees no better method "by which the shadowy outlines of departed men and women can be made to assume the hues of life more effectively than by connecting their images" with such a reality.[117] In the *Wonder Book*, too, the boy story-teller and the children, in settings as real as porches and playrooms, provide an imaginative frame, very near Actuality, for the romantic retelling of the classic myths.

In "Passages from a Relinquished Work" the youthful story-teller stands on a hill looking back through the mist at the village: "Half of the parson's dwelling was a dingy white house, and half of it was a cloud."[118] Actuality and Imagination blend in the vision, just as they do in "The Snow-Image," where "Violet and Peony wrought together with one happy consent." Violet, "the guiding spirit,"[119] "looked like a cheerful thought more than a physical reality; while Peony expanded in breadth rather than height, and rolled along on his short and sturdy legs as substantial as an elephant, though not quite so big."[120] This working together of two related elements may be taken symbolically as a blending of Imagination and Actuality.

Hawthorne's assertions that Actuality and Imagination must be mingled to create Romance correspond to Emerson's view of the Work of Art as partaking of both the Actual world and Truth. When the Emersonian Poet reaches from a point nearer the sky than the surrounding objects down into the dark wet soil of the earth, he uses the symbol, created when Imagination acts upon the Actual object, moving it up the scale of being from object to thought. The Emersonian conjunction of Ideal and Real in the symbol is Hawthorne's mingling of Imagination and Actuality in the symbol. The symbol is the twin-born thought of Longfellow's Flemming or Melville's admixture of material and poetry.

The Artist's Means

"A high truth"

One purpose of such a mingling of Actuality and the Imagined, for Hawthorne, was to attract readers who would be repelled by a story weak in either element.[121] A more vital purpose, for Hawthorne, was the opportunity such a mingling gave for developing a truth. In *Doctor Grimshawe's Secret* Hawthorne describes the rudiments of a poetic and imaginative mind as "a brooding habit taking outward things into itself and imbuing them with its own essence until, after they had lain there awhile, they assumed a relation both to truth and to himself, and became mediums to affect other minds with the magnetism of his own."[122]

The Hall of Fantasy, where the actual world is viewed through windows, merits "an occasional visit, for the sake of spiritualizing the grossness of this actual life, and prefiguring to ourselves a state in which the Idea shall be all in all."[123] Hawthorne criticizes an art work in Crawford's studio, saying that it does not impress him "as having grown out of any great and genuine idea in the artist's mind, but as being merely an ingenious contrivance enough."[124]

A "lover of the moral picturesque,"[125] Hawthorne insisted on idea, truth, moral, soul, meaning—not only as an essential of a work of art but as the work's excuse for being and as its beginning point. He insists that either a novel or a romance "sins unpardonably so far as it may swerve aside from the truth of the human heart."[126] And he specifically mentions truths in his own works: "I write the book for the sake of its moral";[127] "I resolved . . . to achieve a novel that should evolve some deep lesson";[128] "I remember that I always had a meaning, or at least thought I had."[129] He worries because *The Scarlet Letter* is so concerned with an idea: "Keeping so close to its point as the tale does, and diversified no otherwise than by turning different sides of the same dark idea to the reader's eye, it will weary very many people and disgust some."[130] He certainly agreed with Emerson's "veracity first of all and forever."[131]

His Artist of the Beautiful works from the beautiful idea. Hilda, the copyist, selects some "high, noble, and delicate portion" of a great picture, the culmination of its spirit and essence, and following the original painter's procedure, paints the soul—while inferior copyists attempt "only a superficial imitation," "working entirely from the outside, and seeking only to reproduce the surface." "These men are sure to leave out that indefinable nothing, that inestimable something, that consitutes the life and soul through which the picture gets its immortality," but "Hilda was no such machine as this; she wrought religiously, and therefore wrought a miracle."[132] Hawthorne admires the Dutch Masters because they "get at the soul of common things, and so make them types and interpreters of the spiritual world."[133] "In all my stories, I think," Hawthorne says, "there is one idea running through them like an iron rod, and to which all other ideas are referred and subordinate."[134]

But knowing that when a romance does anything like teaching, "it is usually through a far more subtle process than the ostensible one," Hawthorne thinks it hardly worth while "relentlessly to impale the story with its moral as with an iron rod,—or, rather, as by sticking a pin through a butterfly." It is better that "a high truth" should be "fairly, finely, and skilfully wrought out, brightening at every step, and crowning the final development of a work of fiction." This may "add an artistic glory, but is never any truer, and seldom any more evident, at the last page than at the first."[135] So the butterfly, the beautiful idea, the truth, is there from beginning to end but instead of being stiffened "in an ungainly and unnatural attitude," is "finely, and skilfully wrought out . . . and crowning the final development."[136] This is the Artist's "better wisdom, which draws the moral while it tells the tale."[137] This is getting more of various modes of truth than could have been grasped by a direct effort.[138] This is moving from a material trifle to a lofty moral, putting the spirit of beauty into form and giving it motion.[139]

Mellowed lights and deepened and enriched shadows

Essential to the development of meaning is the artist's management of his atmospheric medium. To some extent the nature of the idea determines this management. It was said of the painter of "The Prophetic Pictures" that he painted "not merely a man's features, but his mind and heart." He caught "the secret sentiments and passions," and threw them "upon the canvas, like sunshine—or perhaps, in the portraits of dark-souled men, like a gleam of infernal fire."[140] In "The Custom House," Hawthorne complained of the "stern and sombre aspect" of *The Scarlet Letter*, "too much ungladdened by genial sunshine; too little revealed by the tender and familiar influences which soften almost every scene of nature and real life, and, undoubtedly, should soften every picture of them."[141] As the painter used sunshine and infernal fire to suggest meaning, so Hawthorne found the "dark idea" of *The Scarlet Letter* would not take "cheering light." "I found it impossible to relieve the shadows of the story with so much light as I would gladly have thrown in," he says.[142] He called it a hell-fired story, into which he found it "almost impossible to throw any cheering light."[143] This recalls the words of the humorous little showman of "Main Street," to the viewers of his puppets who think his scenes "all too sombre." " 'So, indeed, they are,' he admits; 'but the blame must rest on the sombre spirit of our forefathers, who wove their web of life with hardly a single thread of rose-color or gold, and not on me, who have a tropic-love of sunshine, and would gladly gild all the world with it, if I knew where to find so much.' "[144]

Hawthorne early wished for some method of using light to express meaning. He wrote to Sophia:

> I wish there was something in the intellectual world analogous to the Daguerrotype (is that the name of it?) in the visible— something which should print off our deepest, and subtlest, and delicatest thoughts and feelings as minutely and accurately as the above-mentioned instrument paints the various aspects of Nature.[145]

He set about finding an answer for that need, stating it as the author's prerogative so to manage his medium "as to bring out or mellow the lights and deepen and enrich the shadows of the picture."[146] The Hall of Fantasy, with windows like old-world Gothic cathedrals, will "admit the light of heaven only through stained and pictured glass, thus filling the hall with many-colored radiance and painting its marble floor with beautiful or grotesque designs; so that its inmates breathe, as it were, a visionary atmosphere, and tread upon the fantasies of poetic minds."[147] The Man of Fancy's castle in the air is gilded with a flood of evening sunshine and lit within by meteors covered in evening mist that glow "like the brilliancy of a powerful yet chastened imagination."[148] The light of heaven through pictured glass suggests the bringing out of the lights into many-colored radiance; the misty meteors of the powerful yet chastened imagination suggest the deepening and enrichment of contrasting and meaningful shadows.

The broad light of day is not an artistic medium for Hawthorne; he prefers the moonlight of romance which will change the character of lingering daylight, will soften and embellish, will make the shadows fall deeper and more brooding; will, as it grows more powerful, transfigure and make picturesque with a dark obscurity.[149] The visions—the ideal conceptions—of all authors are shelved in the moonlit room of the castle in the air. If a man cannot write romance in a moonlit room, he may as well give over the attempt. As his vision is a moonlit vision, so he may well write "moonshiny Romance,"[150] with an atmosphere intended to effect a golden gloom through which flit shadowy, weird, fantastic shapes.[151]

Hawthorne admires the Gothic architects because they "seem first to imagine beautiful and noble things, and then to consider how they may best be partially screened from sight. A certain secrecy and twilight effect belong to their plan."[152] This twilight effect is a deepening and enriching of shadows. The Artist may attain a remarkable effect by harmonizing the shadows, even the absence of light, with the whole work. Hawthorne and the sculptor Powers spent some time discussing the use of shadow in Michael Angelo's "Lorenzo di Medici," where the arrangement of the visor "throws the upper part of the face into shadow," and the niche in which the statue sits evidently throws a still deeper shadow. Hawthorne thinks it very possible that the sculptor "calculated upon this effect of sombre shadow," and that "he wrought the whole statue in harmony with that small part of it which he leaves to the spectator's imagination, and if he had erred at any point, the miracle would have been a failure; so that, working in marble, he has positively reached a degree of excellence above the capability of marble, sculpturing his highest touches upon air and duskiness."[153] There are painters, however, who "leave out some medium—some enchantment that should intervene, and keep the object from pressing so baldly and harshly upon the spectator's eyeballs." This lifelikeness leaves no illusion, Hawthorne continues. "I think if a semi-obscurity were thrown over the picture, after finishing it to this nicety, it might bring it nearer to Nature. . . . Perhaps these artists may hereafter succeed in combining their truth of detail with a broader and higher truth."[154] Some things can be better seen by artificial light which removes somewhat from the region of bare reality.[155]

Firelight, too, is a medium, and a better one than "the vulgar daylight"; in firelight shadows can be seen in the "glimmer and pleasant gloom."[156] A warmer, more human medium, the firelight may throw its ruddy blaze into the moonlit room to touch its ghostly images or to light by a dusky gleam the Vision of the Fountain, that spirit of radiance of an unborrowed light.

A mist sets a scene "beyond the limits of actual sense and makes it ideal,"[157] and a dense fog will almost spiritualize materialism.[158] Hawthorne spoke of the legendary mist of the past, floating almost imperceptibly about the characters and events in *The House of the Seven Gables*, a mist used for the picturesque effect. The narrator of "Alice Doane's Appeal" throws a veil of deep forest over the land and intends "to throw a ghostly glimmer round the reader, so that his imagination might view the town through a medium that should take off its every-day aspect, and make it a proper theatre for so wild a scene as the final one."[159] In the indistinctness of twilight he summons up a blacker horror to reach the hearts of the listeners.

Sunlight, moonlight, firelight, mist, and fog—the author manages his atmospherical media for contrasts of light and shadow. As Emerson said, "Light is the first of painters." The artist should see where the brighter light falls on the idea and where the lesser. For Hawthorne, in general, it is moonlight that makes Romance; moonlight and the semi-obscurity of twilight and mists is the medium for shadows. In all the intricate management of the medium, the lights and shadows enhance, never contradict, meanings, though the shadows of intentional ambiguity and imaginative suggestion will also be components of the picture.

The Neutral Territory

"*A faint and not very faithful shadowing.*"—In the neutral territory of the moonlit room is a looking-glass which pictures a repetition of the gleam and shadow of the room, the glow of the fire, the white moonbeams—all "one remove further from the actual, and nearer to the imaginative."[160] The mirrored picture is the Artist's work, a blending of Actual and Imaginative in the objects and in a scene which images Truth. The mirror, a favorite figure not only for Hawthorne, but, as Emerson said, for the age,[161] served to compose a work something like the eye's composition and to suggest reflection as both thought and expression.

In some of his works Hawthorne makes quite clear this blending of Actual and Imaginative. In *The House of the Seven Gables* his humble scenery is not of local manners or community characteristics; it has a street—which the author laid out, a piece of land—which he appropriated, a house—of materials used for castles in the air; it has the name Pyncheon, chosen for appropriateness of tone.[162] In *The Blithedale Romance* preface he insists that Blithedale is "a faint and not very faithful shadowing" of Brook Farm. Though he says that he had the Brook Farm community in mind and that "actual reminiscences" have been used to give "a more life-like tint to the fancy-sketch," he insists on a fictitious handling. He has borrowed the community to establish a theatre for the creatures of his brain.[163] He insists in the preface to *The Marble Faun* that his "fanciful story" "did not propose attempting a portraiture of Italian manners and character," but he remarks on the extent of his descriptions of "various Italian objects, antique, pictorial, and statuesque."[164] In "Drowne's Wooden Image" the Imagination works on the actual object, the oak log. In "The Antique Ring" the story is developed from observation of the ring to which a dream is added. The faun as a creature mingles the fanciful and the real.[165]

But when the actualities are blended with the Imagination, or reflected through and by the Imagination, in the mirror, Truth results; for "the looking-glass, . . . you are aware, is always a kind of window or doorway into the spiritual world."[166] As arches translate the sky,[167] or as a lake opens an eye to heaven,[168] so the mirror frames the mimic representation of the ideal and kindles the imagination more than the reality (that is, actuality) would. Watching boys sail miniature vessels on Frog Pond, Hawthorne accounted for the imaginative pleasure of imitation:

> There is a full-rigged man of war, with, I believe, every spar, rope, and sail, that sometimes makes its appearance; and when on a voyage across the pond, it so identically resembles a great ship, except in size, that it has the effect of a picture. All its motions—its tossing up and down on the mimic waves, and its sinking and rising in a calm swell, its heeling to the breeze,—the whole effect, in short, is that of a real ship at sea; while, moreover, there is something that kindles the imagination more than the reality would. If we see a real, great ship, the mind grasps and possesses, within its real clutch, all that there is of it; while here, the mimic ship is the representative of an ideal one, and so gives us a more imaginative pleasure.[169]

Thinking of the truth in a mirror, Hawthorne could write, "What a pity that one of the stately mirrors has not preserved a picture of the scene, which, by the very traits that were so transitory, might have taught us much that would be worth knowing and remembering!"[170] This is what the Artist does: he gives the mirrored picture permanence. Seeing the ghosts of ourselves in all reflecting surfaces, we forget them because they vanish; but the Artist's mirror gives the portraits duration;[171] he can make a look last for hundreds of years.

As Hawthorne indicated to Sophia in advising her about her sketches, unity can be built into a picture by choice of meaningful details; once he writes: "all around must be tokens of pestilence and mourning" and again: "On the table and scattered about the room must be symbols of warfare."[172] In his notes on *Dr. Grimshawe's Secret* he suggests to himself: "Give vivid pictures of the society of the day, symbolized in the street scenes."[173] Beginning with idea, Hawthorne relates minutiae to it; just as he admires the million touches necessary to the effect of the Dutch Masters—"not one too little or too much"—[174] so he wishes to finish *The House of the Seven Gables* "with the minuteness of a Dutch picture."[175] Within the romance itself he comments: "The author needs great faith in his reader's sympathy; else he must hesitate to give details so minute, and incidents apparently so trifling, as are essential to make up the idea of this garden-life."[176] The minute details and apparently trifling incidents are *essential* to make up the *idea*. In "The Gray Champion" the author states: "The whole scene was a picture of the condition of New England,"[177] and he continues by indicating his meaning. In "The Wedding Knell" he indicates detailed use of images for making a scene emblematic: "the whole scene expressed, by the strongest imagery, the vain struggle of the gilded vanities of this world, when opposed to age, infirmity, sorrow, and death."[178] In notes he reminds himself, "Make the following scene emblematic of the world's treatment of a dissenter," or again, "There should be symbols and tokens, hinting at the schoolmaster's disappearance, from the first opening of the scene."[179] Hawthorne was also attracted by scenes where people would naturally pass by, as the gate of a city for a locality,[180] or the meeting of distinguished characters at a tavern and the register of their names.[181] These suggestions give some idea of the artist's intention to unify the meaning of individual scenes, symbolizing by parts and by the whole, and his intention to choose scenes belonging to a larger idea.

Hawthorne wrote, "When God expressed himself in the landscape to mankind, He did not intend that it should be translated into any tongue save his own immediate one."[182] This may well suggest his appreciation for imitation. He had seen some pictured landscapes that were "full of imaginative beauty, and of the better truth etherealized out of the prosaic truth of Nature," but he says, "I do not think I can be driven out of the idea that a picture ought to have something in common with what the spectator sees in Nature."[183] If Sibyl is right and " 'everything . . . has its spiritual meaning, which to the literal meaning is what the soul is to the body,' "[184] if even the Indian relics picked up on the Old Manse battleground are each individual, if each squash plant in the Old Manse garden gets a separate interest, it would appear that a scene could be artistically constructed by an imaginative use of individual actualities, chosen and unified for spiritual meaning.

Personages of the author's own making or mixing.—Since actual characters too have a kind of untranslatable meaning, the exercise of Imagination on actualities provides characters for the Romance, if not of the author's own making—completely imagined—at least of his own mixing,[185] imaginatively combining traits of characters known to him. Hawthorne once noted of a little seamstress with whom he was acquainted that she never said anything worth hearing in itself, "but she herself is an expression, well worth studying."[186] He and the painter Thompson "talked of physiognomy and impressions of character—first impressions—and how apt they are to come right, in the face of the closest subsequent observation."[187] But not everyone has a turn for observation of character; Thomas Green Fessenden's "former companions had passed before him like images in a mirror, giving him little knowledge of their inner nature."[188] This is what happens to the Poet when he cannot mingle imagination with the actualities; the ordinary characters of the Custom House seemed dull to Hawthorne because the torpor of his imagination prevented his fathoming their deeper import.

In *The Scarlet Letter* preface Hawthorne insists on the authenticity of Hester Prynne, the particulars of whose life and conversation are purportedly recorded on the roll of dingy paper; but he further insists that in "imagining the motives and modes of passion that influenced the characters," he has allowed himself nearly as much license as if the facts had been entirely his own invention.[189] The working of the author's imagination is suggested in his concern lest he had refined a little too much for popular appreciation on the principal character in *The House of the Seven Gables*.[190] In his analysis in the preface to *The Blithedale Romance*, Hawthorne categorizes his four main characters—the self-centered Philanthropist, the high-spirited Woman, the weakly Maiden, the Minor Poet—as persons who might have been looked for at Brook Farm but had never appeared there. To whatever extent they are based on real persons, they have their basis in Actuality. Even Ellen Langton, of the despised *Fanshawe*, was to have been "something not more than mortal, nor, indeed, quite the perfection of mortality, but charming men the more, because they felt, that, lovely as she was, she was of like nature to themselves."[191] In *The Marble Faun*, as already mentioned, Donatello was intended as a mystical, anomalous creature between the Real and the Fantastic. The characters were designed to bear a certain relation to human nature but to be artfully removed from the Actual. As explained in the preface, he imagined a sculptor, for whom he stole a bust of Milton and a statue of a pearl-diver from Paul Akers, and a magnificent statue of Cleopatra from William W. Story. Hawthorne advises himself on the creation of the old Hospitaller in *The Ancestral Footstep*: "The character must not be allowed to get vague, but, with gleams of romance, must yet be kept homely and natural by little touches of his daily life."[192] Actuality must be blended with the Imaginative. In a bit of advice to Sophia, Hawthorne suggests that Master Cheever is a very good subject for a sketch of a boy getting punishment; he describes his appearance in the picture, including the imaginative details to blend in a unified meaning: "The Master . . . must be calm, rigid, without anger or pity, the very personification of that unmitigable law, whereby suffering follows sin."[193]

There are other instances where the imaginative element is particularly emphasized. Meeting an old gentleman who "inquired very freely" about his "character, tastes, habits, and circumstances," Hawthorne felt his freedom sanctioned by his character and remarks on the importance of the manner and motives of saying a thing.[194] The imaginative grasp of motives is here suggested in meeting an actual personage; this is the same imagination that functions in "imagining the motives and modes of passion that influenced the characters" of *The Scarlet Letter*. In the notes for *Dr. Grimshawe's Secret*, several hints show the imagination symbolizing: "Introduce the Doctor early as a smoker, and describe"; "The result of Crusty Hannah's strangely mixed breed should be shown in some strange way"; the boy and the girl are to have certain specific qualities; the boy is to be dark, the girl, light.[195] The imaginative handling of the character is in a sense as unrestricted as the Main Street showman's operation of his puppets. It is a making of shadows, as Grandfather does, as all artists do, by Hawthorne's theory—shadows with meaning.

Incidents—A pathway through glorified mist and fog.—The Artist's work is a mirror reflecting Reality or Truth, and such reflection implies not only selection of that which is to be imaged in the mirror but progression of the otherwise static images according to some pattern. To evolve a thoughtful moral,[196] a truth which is "fairly, finely, and skilfully wrought out, brightening at every step, and crowning the final development of a work of fiction,"[197] the author selects and orders the incidents. How Hawthorne as artist does this becomes clear only when incidents or events are seen in relationship to scene, character, and atmosphere.

In Hawthorne's view, plot and scene have a closer relationship than what might be termed "action and setting" or "plot and spectacle." When Hawthorne speaks of "striving to picture forth imaginary scenes, which, the next day, might flow out on the brightening page in many-hued description,"[198] he obviously is using the word *scene* to imply action conjoined with scenery. In stretches of narration between dramatic passages in his stories, he sometimes uses an expression like "a scene occurred."[199] When he says that the love of allegory "is apt to invest his plots and characters with the aspect of scenery and people in the clouds,"[200] he seems to imply that "plots" and "scenery" may be, to some extent, synonymous terms. In an attempt to get hold of a real beginning point for writing *The Ancestral Footstep*, though he indicates the interweaving of scene, characters, and events, he says, "If I could but write one central scene in this vein, all the rest of the Romance would readily arrange itself around that nucleus."[201] A few days later, he talks in a similar way about an incident in this romance: "This incident is very essential towards bringing together the past time and the present, and the two ends of the story."[202] *Scene*, and even *scenery* at times, then, may suggest much more than appropriate background for happenings.

Interrelationships of characters, for Hawthorne, provided action in "scenes." The words he uses in voicing his admiration of "The Laocoön" in the Vatican sculpture-galleries indicate that he saw the static expression in terms of action: "It is such a type of human beings, *struggling* with an inextricable trouble, and *entangled* in a complication which they cannot *free themselves* from by their own efforts, and out of which Heaven alone can help them." He admires the artistic picturing: "It was a most powerful mind, and one capable of reducing a complex idea to unity, that imagined this group."[203] In such a static scene, characters are made to reveal themselves in relation to one another and to an underlying idea. Hawthorne's admiration of this group may be related to his analysis of *The Scarlet Letter* where he speaks of "turning different sides of the same dark idea to the reader's eye."[204] His use of "different sides" here may imply both the use of characters representative of different "sides" or "phases" of Truth and a series of scenes, all related to the same idea.

Had Hawthorne been picturing altogether actual characters or purely allegorical shadows, the probability or line of causation for the action would have been more sharply limited. Actual characters must act in line with psychological motives; allegorical characters must act in line with the philosophical concept embodied in the name. Hawthorne's characters were, however, "made" or "mixed" of the Actual and Imagination and were obliged to act on both levels at the same time, relating the line of action both to the character motivation and to the reader's understanding of the Truth. The artist's search for probability, then, begins in the character's "soul." When Hawthorne explains his artistic practice in "The Old Manse," recounting a visit to the grave of two British soldiers, one slain by the axe of a nervous boy who came upon him lying wounded by the corpse of his companion, Hawthorne indicates that his own thought, his imagination, follows the torture of the boy's soul by the blood stain, through the boy's subsequent career. When the artist knows the motives, he creates corresponding outward acts. Hawthorne called Septimius Felton's walk "this writing of his body, impelled by the struggle and movement of his soul."[205] In his notes on *Dr. Grimshawe's Secret*, Hawthorne advises himself to put something into the character which will be concretely revealed by incident: "Put into the Doctor's character a continual enmity against somebody, breaking out in curses of which nobody can understand the application"; again, of another character, "Represent him as a refined, agreeable, genial young man, of frank, kindly, gentlemanly manners."[206] From enmity against a person come curses; from refinement and amiability, gentlemanly manners—incident directly arising from characteristics. Since, however, the characteristics given Hawthorne's characters are often in line with a single truth or meaning which that character represents, incidents must also make this truth clear to the reader. When Hawthorne analyzes his characters at Blithedale, he does not call them Hollingsworth, Zenobia, Priscilla, and Coverdale; he calls them "the self-concentrated Philanthropist," "the high-spirited Woman," "the weakly Maiden," and "the Minor Poet," indicating that each represents to some extent an idea or concept not merely individual. In his analysis he further shows that the action of these characters is appropriate to them as representatives of those ideas. Given the idea of a "high-spirited Woman," incidents will picture her "bruising herself against the narrow limitations of her sex"; given "the weakly Maiden, whose tremulous nerves endow her with Sibylline attributes," incidents must show her foreseeing. The "self-concentrated Philanthropist" must be pictured through incidents that make clear the idea of selfish philanthrophy. Hawthorne sees his Minor Poet "beginning life with strenuous aspirations which die out with his youthful fervor," and must provide incidents indicating this reversal.[207] In Hawthorne's criticism of Lewis W. Mansfield's allegorical poem, he said, "There should be a distinct pathway to tread upon—a clue that the reader shall confide in, as being firmly fastened somewhere." He seems to have felt that Mansfield's poem failed to show both character motivation and connection between incidents; for Hawthorne advises the interpolation of three scenes, showing character interrelationships, in a chronological picturing of the hero's changing understanding of the story of the "land without a night." Hawthorne promises that then "the story will be true (that is, allegorically true) as the history and experience of many souls." The clue, then, is in the "mixed" character; the pathway is provided by the series of incidents appropriate to the "mixed" character.[208]

Actions of a character both Actual and Imagined will develop at two levels, the real and the unreal. The mingling of Actuality and Imagination in plot is, for Hawthorne, both desirable and inevitable. It requires, however, that the artist prevent the reader from holding the incidents against Actual life without regard for the Imaginative. Therefore, Hawthorne puts his characters in a remote setting so that his "fancy pictures" will not be brought into "positive contact with the realities of the moment."[209] He says that he moves his little Blithedale theatre away from the highway; here "the creatures of his brain may play their phantasmagorical antics, without exposing them to too close a comparison with the actual events of real lives."[210]

In the remote setting, Hawthorne purposes to manage the atmospheric medium so that the two-level incidents may be accepted by the reader on either level without affecting his belief in the meaning. Hawthorne told Mansfield that it was "allowable, and highly advisable, . . . to have as much mist and glorified fog as possible, diffused about on all sides."[211] In the preface to *The House of the Seven Gables*, Hawthorne explains that the author "may so manage his atmospherical medium as to bring out or mellow the lights and deepen and enrich the shadows of the picture." Then he defines his particular atmospherical medium in this book as the "legendary mist," and goes on to say that "the reader, according to his pleasure, may either disregard, or allow it to float almost imperceptibly about the characters and events for the sake of a picturesque effect."[212] This is Hawthorne's clear suggestion that the reader may either take the legends for "reality" (in the remote setting, of course) or may know them for "unreal" and enjoy the author's playing with the fancies. Whichever the reader chooses, the artist will have secured the true and indestructible value that lies hidden in incidents.[213]

CONCLUSION

Hawthorne, like Emerson, saw Reality shadowed in the Actual; the Perfect in the Imperfect—in Nature and Man. Hawthorne's Artist, like Emerson's, was the last best touch of the Creator, enabled by Faith, Intuition, the pursuit of Beauty and by Nature's revelations to him to create an image of the Ideal. The Work of Art, for Hawthorne and for Emerson, is an expression of Unity, Truth, Beauty by Variety; that is, by the Symbol, made possible by mingling Imagination with the Actual. Actuality, acted upon by thought, provides a unified Truth for the purpose of the Work, a Truth which governs all its details. The Artist[214] sees by means of light and reflects his vision in the mirror by means of light. He sees Man in correspondence with Nature, or appropriate to his background scene, in the Imagined picture; that is, at the thought level. Man's inner character, at this level, is spoken outwardly, even more than is true in Actuality. For both Hawthorne and Emerson, the Artist must order the incidents in a succession of events governed causally by a character who acts at two levels at the same time: the partial and the universal. The partial level is close to Actuality; the universal level is close to Reality—but the two are mingled.

Finally, the most significant difference felt in Emerson and Hawthorne is accounted for partially by the point of view, particularly as relates to the problem of evil. Emerson pointed up the difference when he explained that at the level of intellection there is nothing for us but praise and joy, but at the level of action there must be the strife with sin. In his essays Emerson chose the level of intellection—of praise and joy; in his pictures of the human heart Hawthorne chose the level of action—of strife with sin.

Hawthorne's Aesthetic Practices: The Tales

INTRODUCTION

It is now evident that Hawthorne held Transcendental aesthetic views. As a conscious artist and a thorough self-critic, Hawthorne, in practice, must have given artistic embodiment to those views. A detailed and careful consideration of the same specific facets of his Transcendental aesthetic as they took shape in his work is now in order. Postponing to a later chapter the criticism of his longer works, the study will look first at the tales. It will center upon a group of eight tales chosen to give a fair representation of the variety of Hawthorne's artistry in this form and to represent, to a great extent, tales most frequently criticized. These tales are: "The Celestial Railroad," "Ethan Brand," "The Gentle Boy," "The Maypole of Merry Mount," "The Minister's Black Veil," "Rappaccini's Daughter," "Roger Malvin's Burial," and "Young Goodman Brown." The criticism will move from artistic method to artistic method rather than from story to story, drawing together the specific studies of the Actual, the Imaginative, the Truth, light, scenes, characters, and incidents, in order to see the richly varied way in which Hawthorne practices his Transcendental aesthetic.

ARTISTRY IN THE TALES

Hawthorne repeatedly asserted that Romance was written by mingling Actuality and Imagination. It should be possible to see this mingling taking place throughout the tales, to discover evidences of intentional emphasis on the Actual, interspersed with elements of the Imagined, so that a reader is drawn at times toward Actuality, again toward the Imagined, making the Romantic result of any story a combination of both elements.

Intermingling the Actual

First, how does Hawthorne intermingle the Actual? One of his most obvious methods is by citation of historical fact. "The Maypole of Merry Mount" (with its introduction emphasizing facts recorded in New England history) develops in some expository detail the transportation of hereditary pastimes of Old England to Merry Mount, as well as the characteristics and attitudes of the Puritans, and refers to both as "authentic passages from history."[1] Governor Endicott and churchman Blackstone are historical personages figuring in the tale, and Hawthorne's footnote on the specific Blackstone mentioned increases rather than diminishes the historical emphasis. "The Gentle Boy" is introduced by several paragraphs recounting certain Quaker history between 1656 and 1659 and takes its beginning point on the evening of the day when two Quaker men were martyred. Then Hawthorne inserts a slight remark about the locked door when Tobias comes home—a remark that goes far toward effecting Actuality: "for at that early period, when savages were wandering everywhere among the settlers, bolt and bar were indispensable to the security of a dwelling."[2] "Young Goodman Brown" is set in Salem in witchcraft days, and the "devil" and others throughout the story make more or less definite references to persons and events of the time. The "devil" speaks of the Puritans, of lashing the Quaker woman through the streets of Salem, of King Philip's war; of deacons, selectmen, members of the Great and General Court, the governor. A voice like the deacon's talks of persons from Actual locations, Connecticut and Rhode Island. Hawthorne's note on "The Minister's Black Veil" reports that a clergyman of York, Maine, Mr. Joseph Moody, who had died about eighty years before, had worn a black veil, thus claiming a kind of historical basis for the eccentricity. "Roger Malvin's Burial" is related to "Lovell's Fight" in 1725, and Hawthorne says that some of the incidents will be recognized by persons who have heard the story of the few men left to retreat. There is an effective citation here of the "almost superstitious regard" "paid by the frontier inhabitants to the rites of sepulture" and indefinite reference to "many instances of the sacrifice of life in the attempt to bury those who had fallen by the 'sword of the wilderness.' "[3] Actual historical citation (using both recorded history and tradition) is so evident in Hawthorne that it is perhaps not surprising to find readers making extensive study of Hawthorne's knowledge and use of New England history and intensive studies (for example of the relation between Lovewell's fight and Hawthorne's tale).[4]

There is another element of Actuality, however, that might simply be called "common sense" Actuality. Such a picturing of places or persons is accepted by the reader's common sense as "real" or "actual." He assumes, without recognizing it as an assumption, that there was such a "real" person or place, because the picture accords with the "real" world he himself knows. Hawthorne employs this Actuality very frequently. The small town Milford, where Mr. Hooper lives and preaches, is any small town; the lime-kiln where Ethan Brand once tended the fire is like any lime-kiln; Hawthorne's forests are "real" forests first—though they become something more, it is true. In his handling of characters, it is often in specific psychological accuracies that Hawthorne does most toward mingling the Actual in his Romance. For instance, in "The Maypole of Merry Mount" Edith's pensive sadness in the midst of the merriment has an accuracy many a reader will appreciate before Hawthorne gives it an interpretation. The softening of the iron man Endicott at the spectacle of early love is psychologically believable, particularly as he has just gained the victory over the masquers. The superstitous fears of Tobias when he hears the unidentified wailing from beneath a lonely fir tree, his sudden release of Ilbrahim's hand when he discovers him a Quaker, are actions one knows by common sense belong to such a "real" man. Ilbrahim, himself, is pictured again and again in terms of a common sense "real" child, though a strange one: he cries when reviled by other children, he runs to his mother as soon as she steps down from the pulpit, he longs for the companionship of other children, he tells highly imaginative stories. Or Faith, in "Young Goodman Brown," reacts in a very "real" way to her husband's absence: she is fearful that she may be troubled by bad dreams. And Brown, walking through the forest solitude, like many a traveler, begins to think of the possibility of an unseen multitude. His hiding at the coming of Goody Cloyse to keep her from asking about his companion and his destination is also highly believable. In "Rappaccini's Daughter" there is the conflict between Baglioni and Rappaccini, recorded in the black-letter tracts in the medical department of the University of Padua; very plausible it is that there should have been such a conflict and equally likely that it should have been managed in learned fashion. The reader easily grants belief to the poison-antidote situation in the same tale. More will be said of this use of Actuality in specific study of character motivation, but these few examples suffice to show that common sense Actuality is at least as important to Hawthorne as historical Actuality.

Intermingling the Imagination

With Actuality, Hawthorne mingles the Imaginative. Sometimes he simply asserts the non-factual as non-factual: he explains in the first paragraph of "Roger Malvin's Burial" that the tale is built on an incident "naturally susceptible of the moonlight of romance," that imagination casts "certain circumstances judiciarily into the shade,"[5] and that there has been a substitution of fictitious names. In "Young Goodman Brown" he states of the staff that seems to wriggle like a serpent, "This, of course, must have been an ocular deception, assisted by the uncertain light."[6]

More frequently, Hawthorne so manages the atmosphere of the tale as to make it difficult to check the facts. This is sometimes done by making the setting remote. In "Rappaccini's Daughter" both time and place are distantly and vaguely removed from here and now; the time is "very long ago," the place in "a high and gloomy chamber of an old edifice" in Padua. The house is made even more remote and vague by "the armorial bearings of a family long since extinct."[7] In "Young Goodman Brown" as in "Roger Malvin's Burial" the remote spot in the forest is chosen for the background of certain of the more imaginative events.

As a flavor, Hawthorne mingles the Marvellous. The "little shower of withering rose leaves" that fall upon Edith and Edgar as they struggle with the mystery of sadness in the midst of merriment is "as if a spell had loosened them."[8] More marvellous is the immediate withering of the wet twigs the "devil" strips from his walking stick in "Young Goodman Brown," the staff that "actually seemed to wriggle in sympathy"[9] with its owner, and the fall of the pink ribbon from the air. In "Ethan Brand" there is "the shape of a human heart"[10] appearing in the kiln with Ethan's skeleton. Taken out of context these happenings sound truly marvellous, but it must be remembered that flavoring without substance is likely to be "strong"; and in Hawthorne, the Marvellous is used so sparingly as to be only a flavor and serves its purpose *within* the context.

Truth

Besides being effected by the mingling of Actuality and Imagination, Romance, according to Hawthorne, has Truth for its purpose. In the tales Hawthorne characteristically states meanings of stories or parts of stories, sometimes making restatements through a story, so holding the reader to the Truth until he makes it his own, and meantime working out the Truth by the developing details.

In "The Maypole of Merry Mount," Hawthorne's third sentence states symbolically his Truth: "Jollity and gloom were contending for an empire."[11] In the middle of the tale, he repeats the conflict in terms of the relation to the young couple: "From the moment that they truly loved, they had subjected themselves to earth's doom of care and sorrow, and troubled joy, and had no more a home at Merry Mount."[12] Having said that the success of "the grizzly saints" or "the gay sinners"[13] would affect the nation, Hawthorne pictures the destruction of the Maypole by a statement of that the Maypole is "symbolic of departed pleasures."[14] Hawthorne concludes with a statement of Truth in his last graph:

> As the moral gloom of the world overpowers all systematic gayety, even so was their home of wild mirth made desolate amid the sad forest. . . . But as their flowery garland was wreathed of the brightest roses that had grown there, so, in the tie that united them, were intertwined all the purest and best of their early joys.[15]

Thus the Truth of jollity and gloom contending for an empire, while no more true at the conclusion of the story than at its beginning, has been wrought out parallel with Hawthorne's restatements of phases of that Truth. This is clearly holding the reader to the Truth until he makes it his own.

In "The Minister's Black Veil," subtitled "A Parable," Hawthorne lets the minister state the meaning: "Know, then, this veil is a type and a symbol, and I am bound to wear it ever." "If I hide my face for sorrow, there is cause enough, . . . and if I cover it for secret sin, what mortal might not do the same?"[16] And a little later Hawthorne says of him, "Mr. Hooper smiled to think that only a material emblem had separated him from happiness, though the horrors, which it shadowed forth, must be drawn darkly between the fondest of lovers."[17] Soon after this, Hawthorne himself makes a kind of summary statement: "Thus, from beneath the black veil, there rolled a cloud into the sunshine, an ambiguity of sin or sorrow, which enveloped the poor minister, so that love or sympathy could never reach him."[18] At the conclusion of the story, Hawthorne lets the minister state the meaning again:

> "What, but the mystery which it obscurely typifies, has made this piece of crape so awful? When the friend shows his inmost heart to his friend; the lover to his best beloved; when man does not vainly shrink from the eye of his Creator, loathsomely treasuring up the secret of his sin; then deem me a monster, for the symbol beneath which I have lived, and die! I look around me, and, lo! on every visage a Black Veil!"[19]

Here Hawthorne has stated his Truth both directly, as narrator, and indirectly through the minister who, making himself the representative, is well qualified to explain the meaning of the veil.

In "The Gentle Boy," the most significant statement of Truth is made in the middle of the tale, and made in terms of three characters, Dorothy, Catharine, and the boy: "The two females, as they held each a hand of Ilbrahim, formed a practical allegory; it was rational piety and unbridled fanaticism contending for the empire of a young heart."[20]

Hawthorne does not declare his Truth so early in the tale of "Young Goodman Brown," but makes instead a statement in the last paragraph; after he has worked out the happenings and handled the ambiguity by indefinitely relating the events to a dream, he says simply "it was a dream of evil omen for young Goodman Brown," and concludes by picturing him as "a stern, a sad, a darkly meditative, a distrustful, if not a desperate man," whose "dying hour was gloom."[21] In this manner he says that what happened to young Goodman Brown through the tale made him the character described at the end of the tale, and implies that he has wrought out this truth of the human heart.

In "Rappaccini's Daughter," after the story has moved along for a little time, Hawthorne gives a rather lengthy analysis of what Giovanni *should* do, because of the effect Beatrice has on his emotions, and he concludes his statement with a sort of "text": "Blessed are all simple emotions, be they dark or bright! It is the lurid intermixture of the two that produces the illuminating blaze of the infernal regions."[22] Since Giovanni knew, Hawthorne says, that he had "put himself, to a certain extent, within the influence of an unintelligible power," "the wisest course would have been, if his heart were in any real danger, to quit his lodgings and Padua itself at once; the next wiser, to have accustomed himself, as far as possible, to the familiar and daylight view of Beatrice—thus bringing her rigidly and systematically within the limits of ordinary experience." The worst thing for him to do was to avoid her sight but remain near enough to allow his imagination to produce "wild vagaries," or "the lurid intermixture."[23] The dark view would send Giovanni out of the influence of the unintelligible power;

the bright view would encourage him to see Beatrice in daylight and might give him a chance to appreciate her true spiritual self. But enjoying the mixture of love and horror was sure to create an infernal blaze. This truth is closely related to Hawthorne's analysis of the relation between Giovanni and Beatrice just before his harsh words to her near the conclusion of the story. In her presence he has "recollections" of the "benign power" and "many a holy and passionate outgush of her heart,"[24] recollections, which, Hawthorne says, "had Giovanni known how to estimate them, would have assured him that all this ugly mystery was but an earthly illusion, and that, whatever mist of evil might seem to have gathered over her, the real Beatrice was a heavenly angel." Hawthorne's Truth here is clearly one of the attitudes or mixed emotions of Giovanni toward a "heavenly angel" overshadowed by the "earthly illusion" of a "mist of evil."[25]

In "The Celestial Railroad" Hawthorne handles the Truth differently, as is obviously necessary in this sort of writing. What he does is call up the total Truth of Bunyan's *Pilgrim's Progress* by mention of "the famous City of Destruction"[26] in the first sentence. Thus he may work out through the parody a relationship to Bunyan's Truth, in whole and in parts, and the extent to which he accepts or rejects Bunyan's Truth indirectly states his own.

"Roger Malvin's Burial" concludes with Hawthorne's statement of the meaning of the action, that is, the Truth of the tale, in terms of the protagonist: "His sin was expiated,—the curse was gone from him; and in the hour when he had shed blood dearer to him than his own, a prayer, the first for years, went up to Heaven from the lips of Reuben Bourne."[27]

In "Ethan Brand" after Hawthorne has had Ethan define his sin as "The sin of an intellect that triumphed over the sense of brotherhood with man and reverence for God, and sacrificed everything to its own mighty claims,"[28] he seats him before the kiln and has his thoughts trace the intellectual development of The Idea and the withering of the heart until he "lost his hold of the magnetic chain of humanity," and "was no longer a brother-man" but merely a cold observer. And Hawthorne turns immediately to a statement of his Truth: "Thus Ethan Brand became a fiend. He began to be so from the moment that his moral nature had ceased to keep the pace of improvement with his intellect."[29]

It is evident, then, that Hawthorne presents a Truth in each tale; it is also evident that he does not leave the reader to search out this Truth without any help from the author; it is finally evident that he uses varied methods in his statement of the truths and should never be accused of simply "tacking on" a moral to every tale.

Light

As Hawthorne most frequently referred to "light" imagery—even equating moonlight with Romance—it is not remarkable to find him using light as a device to bring out the meaning in characters and to develop phases of the structure of tales.[30]

In "The Maypole of Merry Mount," Hawthorne creates one of his most colorful tales in terms of the contrast between "jollity" and "gloom." Here light, darkness, and color are used for both characterization and narrative method. The story opens with the word "bright": "Bright were the days at Merry Mount," and Hawthorne paints the opening scene in "vivid hue" "at sunset on midsummer eve." The silken banner streaming from the Maypole is "colored like the rainbow";[31] there is "liveliest green," with "silvery leaves," and ribbons with "fantastic knots of twenty different colors, but no sad ones." The "seven brilliant hues" of the banner are enhanced by the "wreath of roses," some from "the sunniest spots of the forest," others "of still richer blush"[32] from the colonists' homes. Standing in "the broad smile of sunset"[33] are the "people of the Golden Age,"[34] in fantastic dress of pink, red, green, surrounding the "glistening"[35] youth with rainbow scarf and gilded staff and a maiden equally gay. "Bright roses" glow in contrast with the "dark and glossy curls" of this "lightsome couple."[36] But their "golden time" has a "pensive shadow"[37] though they are not like the older ones who follow "the false shadow wilfully,"[38] because her garments glitter brightest. Thus Hawthorne has pictured the young couple as a part of the brightness, which, for the older ones, is a mere mummery of brightness; yet they have a real glow of love which is more than a part of the fantastic picture. The shadow upon their brightness foreshadows the darkening of the tale, which Hawthorne manages both by the fading of a last "solitary sunbeam" from the summit of the Maypole, relinquishing the whole domain to "evening gloom," and by the instantaneous rush "from the black surrounding woods," of the "black shadows"[39] of the Puritans. When Endicott cuts down the Maypole, "tradition says, the evening sky grew darker, and the woods threw forth a more sombre shadow."[40] The "shining ones,"[41] now stand "pale," their "glow . . . chastened by adversity."[42] But in "the deepening twilight," though the iron man insists upon more decent garments for the youthful pair, "instead of their glistening vanities,"[43] he throws about the couple the wreath of roses, the brightest ones like "the purest and best of their early joys."[44] With fine brush touches Hawthorne has painted contrasting scenes, indicating by color, light, and shadow both the interrelationship of Edith and Edgar to the glittering masquers and the gloomy Puritans and the story's structural advance from scene to scene.

The Gentle Boy has a "pale, spiritual face," and eyes that seem "to mingle with the moonlight,"[45] when he is found one autumn evening as "the lingering twilight" is "made brighter by the rays of a young moon."[46] Dorothy calls him a "pale and bright-eyed little boy,"[47] and Hawthorne characterizes his countenance as "pale and spiritual"[48] and speaks of his "white brow,"[49] and "his long, fair locks."[50] At his happiest, he is "like a domesticated sunbeam, brightening moody countenances, and chasing away the gloom from the dark corners of the cottage,"[51] but the injury to his spirit destroys "the dance of sunshine . . . by the cloud over his existence."[52] The key to the character Hawthorne gives in the pale spirituality combined with both moonlight and sunlight brightness. The moonlight spiritualizes the boy until he might be thought of as "The Gentle Spirit" or "The Christian Spirit," but the sunlight hints at more reality until he is made something nearer Ilbrahim. Hawthorne has located the "Boy" between the purely

Actual and the purely Imaginative by the light. Contrasted with him is Catharine, the irrational fanatic, with the "blackness" of her "raven hair" "defiled by pale streaks of ashes"; her "dark and strongly defined" eyebrows adding to "the deathly whiteness"[53] of her countenance. Here the black-white contrast seems overtly to suggest the inner character of the fanatic's extremes. But Dorothy is first seen in the "red blaze"[54] of firelight, suggestive of homelike warmth and friendliness. Pearson, whose color comes and goes as he stands before Catharine, so evidences his inner spirit of confusion and indecision, while his wan, pale countenance at the end of the story marks the change in him.

"The Minister's Black Veil" opens with a contrast: in the "Sabbath sunshine" where children with "bright faces"[55] may be seen appears Mr. Hooper in his "black veil."[56] His "pale-faced congregation"[57] hear a sermon "tinged, rather more darkly than usual, with the gentle gloom," on a subject that has reference to "secret sin."[58] The "horrible black veil" adds "deeper gloom" to a funeral, and from beneath it a cloud rolls "duskily" and dims "the light of the candles" at the wedding. Its blackness is intensified by the bride's "deathlike paleness"[59] and the minister's white lips, when he rushes forth into the darkness. The "dismal shade"[60] which darkens his eyes forever throws its terrors "like a sudden twilight" around Elizabeth, and she leaves him in his "miserable obscurity."[61] Its gloom enables him "to sympathize with all dark affections"; his converts sometimes figuratively suggest that before being brought to "celestial light," they have been with him "behind the black veil."[62] In the "shaded candlelight"[63] of the death chamber, it seems to "deepen the gloom . . . and shade him from the sunshine of eternity."[64] Here Hawthorne has equated blackness with sin, gloom, obscurity, and terror, using contrasts of the sunshine brightness of the everyday world or deepening the darkness by deathlike pallor. Very significant, however, is the glimmering, flickering, smile of the minister, repeatedly mentioned, for it suggests the individual personality of the minister (behind a veil that marks him symbolically as everyman). The faint, sad smile flickers forth a message of the minister's personal goodness, under-standing, and—at the same time—eccentricity.

Rappaccini is pictured as "a tall, emaciated, sallow, and sickly-looking man, dressed in a scholar's garb of black." He has "gray hair, a thin, gray beard."[65] Hawthorne speaks too of his "pale intelligence,"[66] and calls him "the pale man of science."[67] Here the paleness suggests overtones of heightened intellect and intense dedication, but it is coupled with the emaciation and sallowness to show the unhealthiness of his intellectual pursuits. The light and color that surround both the garden and Beatrice are made too rich and too profuse. The sunshine in the garden seems to the homesick boy not quite as cheerful as that of southern Italy; yet the "purple blossoms, each of which had the lustre and richness of a gem . . . made a show so resplendent that it seemed enough to il-luminate the garden, even had there been no sunshine."[68] The plant glows in the air and makes the pool "overflow with colored radiance from the rich reflection."[69] Beatrice's voice is "as rich as a tropical sunset," making Giovanni think of "deep hues of purple and crimson." She has "a bloom so deep and vivid that one shade more would have been too much."[70] She glows with such brilliance that she seems positively to illuminate "the more shadowy intervals of the garden path."[71] The reptile she kills is "orange-colored";[72] the beautiful insect that dies by her breath is a "winged bright-ness," whose "bright wings"[73] shiver in its death. Something about all the gorgeousness seems "fierce, passionate, and even unnatu-ral."[74] But at the same time there is "a fervor" that glows in Bea-trice's whole aspect and beams upon Giovanni "like the light of truth itself."[75] But Giovanni prefers the "lurid intermixture"[76] of his emotions to the sunlight view of Beatrice and the garden; he thinks too little of the "familiar and daylight view"[77] by which he could bring her within the limits of ordinary experience, and by his character he loses the "pure whiteness"[78] of her image and creates the "gulf of blackness"[79] between them.

In "Young Goodman Brown" Hawthorne uses lurid light against forest blackness to picture the "dream of evil omen"[80] which brought Young Goodman Brown to gloom. And the gloom contrasts with the cheerful color of Faith's pink ribbons and the heavenly, hopeful blue of the light of the sky. Since Brown starts at sunset, the forest gloom will deepen and increase both by his progress along the way and by the natural coming of the night, so that when it is "deep dusk in the forest," it will be "deepest in that part of it where these two"[81] are journeying. But for a period of time there is still some light from heaven. "The faint gleam from the strip of bright sky athwart which" the owners of the voices should have passed, does not reveal them. The fact that they are not visible by the sky's light indicates their dark origin; yet even in the midst of Brown's doubts "the blue arch, and the stars brightening in it,"[82] show a heaven still above him. But after Young Goodman Brown has lost his Faith and testified to his conversion to doubt and evil, the blue sky is no longer visible; he plunges into "the heart of the dark wilderness,"[83] until he sees a "red light" that throws up a "lurid blaze against the sky," and a rock surrounded by "four blazing pines, their tops aflame."[84] The light rises and falls, making the congregation shine forth, then disappear into shadow again. Hawthorne then increases the light to "a loftier flame," and makes "the fire on the rock" shoot "redly forth"[85] to arch the figure of the speaker; "the dark figure" shows "the fiend worshippers"[86] and identifies the whole earth as "one stain of guilt, one mighty blood spot."[87] And Brown sees Faith "by the blaze of the hell-kindled torches."[88] Out of so deep a darkness lit by so lurid a light, Brown emerges into "the early sunshine"[89] to see Faith of the pink ribbons without greeting her, he having become so "darkly meditative"[90] a man.

In "The Celestial Railroad" Hawthorne again uses a lurid, hellish light which flames from the engine and Apollyon's very breath, which lights the valley of the shadow by "a radiance . . . created even out of the fiery and sulphurous curse . . . a radiance hurtful, however, to the eyes, and somewhat bewildering,"[91] a radiance that compares with "natural daylight" as falsehood compares with truth. Through "walls of fire on both sides of the track" the mouth of the infernal region is reached whence dart "huge tongues of dusky flame,"[92] and where the "dark, smoke-begrimed" inhabitants have "a glow of dusky redness in their eyes as if their hearts had caught fire and were blazing out of the upper windows."[93] And Mr. Smooth-it-away's final laugh is accompanied by "a smoke-wreath . . . from his mouth and nostrils, while a twinkle of lurid flame darted out of either eye, proving indubitably that his heart was all of a red blaze."[94]

In "Ethan Brand" the most interesting use of light is in the indicated movement from scene to scene as related to the opening and closing of the door of the limekiln, its infernal light related to the fiend named "Brand." In the first four scenes, Hawthorne's management of the door of the limekiln indicates both change of scene and development of the idea, and throws necessary light on the happenings. Scene one pictures Bartram and his son at the limekiln listening to Ethan's laughter as he approaches. The door of the kiln, "with the smoke and jets of flame issuing from the chinks and crevices" is closed; and it resembles "nothing so much as the private entrance to the infernal regions, which the shepherds of the Delectable Mountains were accustomed to show to pilgrims."[95] When opened at intervals "the reflection of the fire quivered on the dark intricacy of the surrounding forest, and showed in the foreground a bright and ruddy little picture of the hut, the spring beside its door, the athletic and coal-begrimed figure of the lime-burner, and the half-frightened child, shrinking into the protection of his father's shadow."[96] Thus Hawthorne has used the kiln both as symbolic of the infernal regions (especially as reached from the heights of the Delectable Mountains near the Celestial City) and as a lighting device for his scene, showing up both the forest blackness and the bright picture beside the hut. "And when, again, the iron door was closed, then reappeared the tender light of the half-full moon, which vainly strove to trace out the indistinct shapes of the neighboring mountains; and, in the upper sky, there was a flitting congregation of clouds, still faintly tinged with the rosy sunset, though thus far down into the valley the sunshine had vanished long and long ago."[97] These words end the scene, indicating the admixture of moonlight with its romance and indistinctness when the door is closed; they also picture the last tinges of sunset, bringing with it both moon-light and darkness. Hawthorne has opened the door for the reader to see the setting, he has related moonlight to the whole, and the indication has been given that the intervals of opening the door for light from the kiln will have meaning.

In scene two Ethan arrives at the kiln and Bartram throws open the iron door, "whence immediately issued a gush of fierce light, that smote full upon the stranger's face and figure."[98] Ethan fixes his very bright eyes intensely upon the brightness of the furnace. Again Hawthorne has used the kiln light for scene lighting and for symbolic indentification with something in Ethan.

Bartram is alone with Ethan in scene three. While the door is shut, with Ethan sitting there looking steadfastly at it, his crime, "in its indistinct blackness" seems to overshadow the lime-burner—his own sins commune with Ethan's—he remembers vague stories of Ethan's converse with Satan in "the lurid blaze of this very kiln," of his evoking a fiend to confer with about his search until at the first gleam of daylight, "the fiend crept in at the iron door."[99] In the midst of these ambiguous horrors, Ethan flings open the door of the kiln and Bartram almost expects "to see the Evil One issue forth, red-hot, from the raging furnace."[100] Ethan is only trimming the fire. So Hawthorne has suggested ambiguous shadows of blackness, followed by a closer identity of Ethan with the fire as the fierce glow reddens on his face while he stirs the vast coals and thrusts in more wood. When he has closed the door, he explains having seen many a human heart "seven times hotter with sinful passions"[101] and in pride identifies the creation of his own great sin. In the furnace light this time Ethan has seen himself and left Bartram thinking him a sinner very likely but a madman too.

In scene four the villagers arrive, and, laughingly boisterously, "burst into the moonshine and narrow streaks of firelight"; and Bartram opens the door again, "flooding the spot with light, that the whole company might get a fair view of Ethan Brand, and he of them."[102] In the open space before the kiln, the first incident of the scene is pictured, but the second part of this scene is removed from the spot immediately in front of the kiln, into the "cheerful light"[103] in front of the hut and near the spring, artistically effecting a play within a play, and setting up the scene as an immediate contrast.

The villagers gone, the firelight glimmers on the forest with here and there a gigantic corpse of a dead tree, "decaying on the leaf-strewn soil."[104] Ethan appropriately puts more wood into the fire and for the last time closes the door. When Bartram and Joe have left Ethan to feed the fire for the night, he remembers how he "lost his hold of the magnetic chain of humanity," and "became a fiend." Ethan having risen by his Idea to "a star-lit eminence,"[105] it only remains to complete the symbolism by climbing to the top of the kiln, standing while "the blue flames" play upon his face with "wild and ghastly light," embracing the deadly element of fire, and "plunging into his gulf of intensest torment."[106] The final scene is lit with the day's sunshine; and, appropriately, Ethan has let the fire go out.

So Hawthorne uses light and color, in varied ways, to shine through his characters and evidence meaning and to illuminate the structural design of his work.

Scenes

There are several considerations involved in Hawthorne's scenery. His Transcendental intentions make clear that he purposes to picture in the mirror mingled Actuality and Imagination for a more ideal representation of Truth. To discover the working out of this purpose the reader may well look in Hawthorne's mirror expecting to find Actual and Imaginative *details* used for the *unified picture* of Truth, and Nature as Actuality so touched by Imagination that correspondences between outer and inner worlds become more noticeable.

In "Roger Malvin's Burial," to tell the story of a man whose failure to keep a vow blights his life but drives him back to the scene where he finds expiation, Hawthorne, for the development of the idea, chooses particular objects to make up his picture, objects which will signify—with necessary changes over the years— in the opening and closing scenes of the story. He sets the scene in the forest, near a group of oak trees surrounded by pine, giving the background a double separation from the rest of the world: in the forest, in a unique spot. The grey rock which provides Roger Malvin's tombstone has veins that seem "to form an inscription in forgotten characters,"[107] and the grey rock alone remains unchanged through the eighteen years that intervene between Reuben's appearances beside it. It stands to assure the entombment of Roger Malvin's bones. With all the permanence and meaning of Nature, suggesting Reuben's inner sense of law, it awaits Reuben's return and draws him back to the scene; and it will remain, like Nature's law, equally unmoved through generations upon generations. But the oak sapling, towering above withered oak leaves, has Nature's qualities of change, death, and renewal. It will grow and die, perhaps be blighted, like human nature; and Hawthorne chooses the blight to parallel the maturing of Reuben. Some sign is needed to mark the spot from afar: the bloody bandage from Reuben's wound is fastened high up on the tall young oak as Reuben stands upon the rock and makes his vow in blood. But this sign will appropriately disappear as the days go by, to be remembered, however, when the boy—Reuben's own blood—lies bleeding beneath the blighted oak. A branch of the blighted oak parallels this precisely as, waving in the breeze, it draws Dorcas to the scene of her son's and father's deaths. Of the blight that struck the topmost branch of the oak, Hawthorne asks, "Whose guilt had blasted it?"[108] implying such correspondence in Nature to the condition of Reuben's soul that the loosening of that bough to scatter in "soft, light fragments upon the rock, upon the leaves, upon Reuben, upon his wife and child, and upon Roger Malvin's bones"[109] is the natural corresponding picture of the expiation. So, in corresponding particulars of Nature, Hawthorne pictures physically the scene of Reuben's vow and his spiritual expiation, making a highly Transcendental use of Nature in correspondences between the physical world and the human soul.

Similar corresponding details are used in "The Maypole of Merry Mount." The setting for Hawthorne's maypole is outside the town, beyond the law of the heart regarding systematic pleasures. He chooses for the time of the tale, midsummer, when the "mirthful spirit"[110] of May should have developed into summer maturity. The maypole is a pine tree from the American forest, with the slender grace of youth combined with the height of the old wood monarchs, suggesting an interrelationship of the youth and age of the nation. It is decked with two kinds of flowers, the wreath of roses also interwoven of both garden flowers (some grown from English seed) and forest flowers—suggesting the country's heritage from England and the wilderness. The golden seed time signifies not only the springtime of life, but of a nation. Here Hawthorne chooses physical details to symbolize his Truth about the nation's life and growth and all human life and growth.

When Hawthorne wishes to picture the man who returns successful from his quest for the Unpardonable Sin, the choice of the limekiln setting makes possible numerous correspondences between Ethan and the setting. A limekiln will burn with intense heat, corresponding to Ethan's burning, passionate intensity. The kiln is on a hill; Ethan has his hilltop, starlit superiority. The kiln has a door at the base and an opening at the top and burns the substance of the hills; so Ethan melts his dark thoughts into one thought, burns out by infernal fires the substance of his existence, though his heart was once open to the sky. The kiln will be tended in loneliness; Ethan has his loneliness and final complete isolation. At night the light of the fire will contrast with the surrounding blackness; Ethan provides a momentary brilliance in contrast with his surroundings. Finally, the kiln will burn the limestone to the highly infusible solid, lime; with his heart as hard as marble, the half bushel of the infusible fragments of his earthly body is Ethan's only gift to humanity. As Hawthorne parallels the kiln and Ethan, he gets a physical picture of Ethan's soul. Ethan remembers a different correspondence between his soul and Nature before the change in him; then the dark forest whispered to him and the stars gleamed upon him. But now the boy Joe imagines "that the silent forest" is "holding its breath until some fearful thing should happen."[111] With Ethan gone, the morning sunhine pours gold upon the mountain tops and the valleys smile cheerfully "in the promise of the bright day."[112] Before he gets other evidence, Joe knows: "That strange man is gone, and the sky and the mountains all seem glad of it!"[113]

The choice of the garden setting for "Rappaccini's Daughter" contrasted with the room looking into the garden takes symbolic overtones as Hawthorne multiplies specific details. Any garden may very easily be beautiful with a fountain in the middle; Hawthorne makes this garden unnaturally luxuriant with a ruined fountain in the midst. The gorgeously magnificent plants which people the soil surround the central plant in its marble vase in the midst of the pool. From the shattered fountain runs water, as cheerful as ever, till Giovanni feels "as if the fountain were an immortal spirit that sung its song unceasingly and without heeding the vicissitudes around it." Though one century embodies it in marble and another may scatter "the perishable garniture on the soil,"[114] yet the water, the spirit, keeps the plants, the people, alive even in this Eden of poisonous flowers. So Hawthorne details the garden of depraved fancy—in its center the one plant representing the height of sensuality, yet growing in the fountain of immortal spirit. Does the garden belong to the house? "Heaven forbid,"[115] says withered old Lisabetta. But the garden looks like the pleasure-place of an opulent family—and one of the ancestors of the now extinct family was pictured by Dante in the Inferno. Since the house does not belong, it provides a vantage point; through the window, the inexperienced, unenlightened youth may look into the garden. As it becomes a pleasure-place for him, he too may learn of an Inferno of depraved fancies which miss spiritual beauties. In the garden the reader sees the physical picture of such depraved fancies.

In "Young Goodman Brown" Hawthorne uses the town-forest setting to represent outwardly Brown's journey into darkness. In the depths of the forest while Nature corresponds to the darkest things in Brown's soul, yet all the frightful sounds seem to laugh him to scorn. He later hears "all the sounds of the benighted wilderness pealing in awful harmony together," and his cry is "lost to his own ear by its unison with the cry of the desert."[116] Here Hawthorne has used Nature both un-Transcendentally to mock Brown's madness and Transcendentally to blend with—or, correspond to—his final lost state.

The railroad is an especially happy choice of "outward" setting to correspond with the soul's travel by a modern, easy, speedy, "wholesale" mode of transportation to Bunyan's Celestial City. Certain pictured particulars symbolize the soul's avoidance of all difficulties: the bridge over the Slough of Despond, the simple purchase of a ticket, the engine to do the work, the baggage car for burdens, the tunnel through the Hill Difficulty, the elimination of the Valley of Humiliation.

By his choice and arrangement of details of scenery, Hawthorne uses actualities to represent ideas, so making by the symbol his mirrored picture of Truth. And this is Transcendental symbolism.

Characters

Hawthorne purposed to mingle the Actual and Imaginative in characters in such a way that "real" characters meant something or spoke an idea. In the tales he uses varied methods to fulfill this intention. In "Young Goodman Brown," for instance, he presents actually a respectable young man and a girl. Then by giving them the closest of human relationships and naming them Young Goodman Brown and Faith, he suggests their meaning. Sometimes he is more specific, saying what certain characters represent as he does in "The Maypole of Merry Mount" for the Puritans and masqueraders, or at least hinting the meaning level by making the young couple real "partners for the dance of life."[117] When he assigns meaning to Dorothy and Catharine in terms of their relation to the Gentle Boy, he indicates both that each character speaks a Truth and that the interrelationships will show sides of a single Truth. Now since all characters reveal themselves (whether or not the author assigns meaning) by appearance and actions which become the imagery and incidents of the story, both areas develop the Actual-Imaginative personages. First, the investigation will center on characters largely divorced from incident.

The character of the minister in "The Minister's Black Veil" is imaged—as already suggested in the study of light and dark—by the veil and the smile so that his relation to other characters is always twofold. He is himself, a good eccentric, smiling behind a veil that materializes the mystery of sin and makes him everyman. He is the most Transcendental single character in Hawthorne, as he is under both universal and individual law and acts for both universal and partial character at one and the same time. This being true, Hawthorne of necessity keeps all the other characters vague—and with the single exception of Elizabeth—all others appear in groups, with the minister as center. Hawthorne provides in this way a universal view of the minister without detracting from his centrality and completeness, for he is the whole Truth and meaning in this tale.

Though Hawthorne says clearly in "The Gentle Boy" that certain of his characters are representative of ideas, Catharine of fanatic enthusiasm and Dorothy of rational piety, yet he gives them ordinary names that could even be interchanged without much harm to the tale (except for the appropriately quieter sound of "Dorothy"). The Gentle Boy, however, is called sometimes by his strange name Ilbrahim and sometimes by the name appropriate for "a sweet infant of the skies" that has "strayed away from his home."[118] While he is no mere shadow, yet he clearly symbolizes a true Christian spirit, so that each character's attitude toward him as actual boy is representative of the manner in which that character receives or rejects such a spirit. The Puritan boy with the "slight distortion of the mouth, and the irregular, broken line, and near approach of the eyebrows," the "almost imperceptible twist of every joint, and the uneven prominence of the breast," "a body, regular in its general outline, but faulty in almost all its details,"[119] evidences physically not only his own moral irregularities but those of the Puritans. Hence this boy's reception of the Gentle Boy becomes typical. Hawthorne describes Dorothy by saying that "her mild but saddened features, and neat matronly attire, harmonized together, and were like a verse of fireside poetry"; and he insists that "her very aspect proved that she was blameless, so far as mortal could be so, in respect to God and man."[120] She alone has a true appreciation for the Gentle Boy. In the same manner he pictures

Catharine and Tobias, intending to let their attitudes toward the boy speak sides of the Truth through the incidents. Mixing his characters in this tale of Actual persons and Ideas they represent, Hawthorne names the tale by the allegorical name of the principal character and works out the various sides of the Truth through the characters.

"The Celestial Railroad" characters are clearly allegorical by names alone: Mr. Stick-to-the-right, Mr. Foot-it-to-heaven, Mr. Smooth-it-away, Mr. Take-it-easy; one might quote Hawthorne: "I need only mention the names of the Rev. Mr. Shallow-deep, the Rev. Mr. Stumble-at-truth, that fine old clerical character the Rev. Mr. This-to-day, who expects shortly to resign his pulpit to the Rev. Mr. That-to-morrow; together with the Rev. Mr. Bewilderment, the Rev. Mr. Clog-the-spirit, and, last and greatest, the Rev. Dr. Wind-of-doctrine."[121] But Hawthorne, for the more important of the characters, makes their meaning exceedingly evident by imagery of their inner selves. Mr. Smooth-it-away, with his "dry cough" and his "hearty laugh,"[122] shows finally the "same disagreeable contortion of visage"[123] observable in the inhabitants of the Dark Valley. Mr. Take-it-easy belongs to this group, "dark, smoke-begrimed, generally deformed, with misshapen feet, and a glow of dusky redness in their eyes."[124] But the two dusty pilgrims, "with cockle shell and staff," "mystic rolls of parchment in their hands and their intolerable burdens on their backs"[125] have woeful and compassionate faces, and Mr. Stick-to-the-right speaks in "a sad, yet mild and kindly voice," when he asks, "Sir, . . . do you call yourself a pilgrim?"[126] Because of the comic nature of this dream allegory parody, Hawthorne purposefully overindulges his use of imagery to reflect inner being. Such symbolizing makes, by means of both characters and scenes, an extreme contrast of the two opposing views.

In "Ethan Brand" Hawthorne represents in the scene of the three old villagers three levels of the lowest kind of human sympathy. By character delineation he develops the specific picture and the related idea. The stage-agent is wilted, smoke-dried, wrinkled, red-nosed, "in a smartly cut, brown, bobtailed coat, with brass buttons";[127] seemingly puffing the same cigar he lighted twenty years ago; his person and his dry jokes are permeated by a flavor of brandy-toddy and tobacco smoke. Lawyer Giles, "an elderly ragamuffin," is on a lower social level: now a soap-boiler, he has lost part of one foot and a hand, and appears in "soiled shirtsleeves and tow-cloth trousers." His having slid into the soap-vat from a higher intellectual level of work by means of "flip, and sling, and toddy, and cocktails, imbibed at all hours,"[128] is typified by his maimed appearance and dirty dress. On a still lower level is the village doctor, now "a purple-visaged, rude, and brutal, yet half-gentlemanly figure, with something wild, ruined, and desperate in his talk, and in all the details of his gesture and manners." "Grumbling thick accents at the bedside"[129] of the sick, smoking his everlasting pipe (said, in allusion to his swearing, to be always alight with hell-fire), this man is still driven to try to exercise healing powers upon society. By the representation of physical appearance, Hawthorne has pictured the three men, in descending order of their usefulness to society. The stage-agent's humor is actually worth something; the lawyer's spirit to fight the battle with his one hand is worth observing; at least the ruined doctor's efforts continue, though he probably kills more than he saves. These three act together in their friendly offer of the black bottle to Ethan and create a moment of meaningful contrast by *their* superiority to the proud intellectual who knows no human sympathy.

The character of Reuben Bourne, in "Roger Malvin's Burial," is depicted for the most part as Actual, but when he loves his son Cyrus, largely "as if whatever was good and happy in his own nature had been transferred to his child, carrying his affections with it," then the boy symbolizes the best in Reuben like a "reflection or likeness of his own mind,"[130] and his death has symbolic meaning paralleling Reuben's destruction of the best in himself.

In "Rappaccini's Daughter" the characters are developed to symbolize phases of the idea of human affection. Rappaccini, in a sense, is the simplest character for he has no mixed emotions, no wavering, no change; in fact, no human sympathy. He cares more for science than for mankind; his theory is said to be that medicinal

virtues derive from vegetable poisons. He is a pryer into secrets not
for men, an irreverent manipulator and controller of the human
soul and spirit, finally a cold fiendish scientist who actually seeks
his good in evil (his virtues in poisons). Because of him the garden
is depraved and Beatrice's earthly nature is poisoned. She is his
earthly child as the central shrub is his intellectual. But though as
his daughter she partakes of the earthly poison, Beatrice has a
quality that is something more, beyond his control, for she is a
"heavenly angel,"[131] with an "expression of simplicity and sweetness"[132] and a spirit shocked by many of her father's flowers. In
an earthly body contaminated by poison, she is drawn to her "sister," the flowering shrub whose breath is hers; she lives and
breathes in the poisonous air. Yet she is "simple, natural, most af-
fectionate, and guileless."[133] She is dangerous, not because of moral
evil in her nature, but because she does not understand (nor is she
morally responsible for) her power for evil; in her innocence she
trusts wholly to the spiritual essence and to Giovanni's understanding. The name Beatrice—recalling Beatrice Cenci—pictures,
by allusion, a suffering innocence that looks like evil.

Baglioni is as genial and jovial as Rappaccini is serious. His
mixed affections produce a curious set of outward actions. He has
some appreciation for Giovanni's father—an emotion that does not
really seem living but only the memory of something—but while
he purports to act for Giovanni, he is to some extent amused at
the entanglement of the young man with the beautiful Beatrice.
For Rappaccini he entertains great admiration coupled with a
desire to outwit him. Beatrice, for him, is only a pawn. Baglioni's
final response is a mixed one: it is a combination of horror and
triumph at "the upshot" of Rappaccini's experiment. His acting
from a mixture of emotions, none of them deep and none of them
"spiritual," indicates a kind of insincerity as bad in one direction
as Rappaccini's intentness is in another.

Giovanni, as protagonist, clearly has to make choices regarding
Beatrice. Is she angel or demon? Shall he believe his eyes or only
what she tells him? Beautiful or terrible? He murmurs and trem-
bles. With all his freedom to act, Giovanni wavers between doubt

and faith in the spiritual goodness of Beatrice. If he is to believe his senses, she is terrible; if her words from her heart, she is beautiful and good. Beatrice poisons him with neither love nor horror but the offspring of both, that burns like one and shivers like the other. Beatrice is terrible and she is heavenly; Giovanni never accepts her completely as either, but lets his depraved fancies enjoy the mixture of horror and love. Hope and dread war within him. He remains near her and lets the wild vagaries come to seem real. It is finally the poison of his own mixed emotions that entraps him.

Here Hawthorne has developed characters through imagery of light and dark combined with imagery of color, of warmth and coldness, of physical appearance, and of sound of voice; and he has related all to the sensuous yet spiritual image of an odor. The characters are imaged to give outward evidence of inner beings representing various (and, in Giovanni, shifting) mixtures of emotion—except for Beatrice—who evidences the simple love of a heavenly nature in her expression but the poison of her earthly body in her general appearance and her breath. But this unnatural, this adulterous mixture, is the fiendish Rappaccini's doing. The un-Transcendental characterization of Beatrice (deplored as "false symbolism" by Austin Warren)[134] in reality emphasizes the unnatural character of Rappaccini. Nature would not have done this; Rappaccini did.

Hawthorne evidently sensed that in his characters, as he tried to intermix the Actual and the Imaginative, he might create people in the clouds. They might easily become too allegorical and seem unreal. For this reason he used "a raindrop of pathos and tenderness, or a gleam of humor," to "make us feel as if, after all, we were yet within the limits of our native earth."[135] Such humor, pathos, tenderness draws the people back from the clouds into the Actual world as the reader's sympathies are engaged.

In "The Minister's Black Veil," Hawthorne develops humor in minor characters. Little boys in church and on the street provide pictures of humorous incidents. In church, "several little boys clambered upon the seats, and came down again with a terrible racket."[136] On the way to school, "one imitative little imp covered his face with an old black handkerchief, thereby so affrighting his playmates that the panic seized himself, and he well-nigh lost his wits by his own waggery."[137] This is Hawthorne's comic rendering of just what had happened to the minister—on the day, and in the paragraph, preceding—when he rushed out from the wedding party. When the deputation sits before the minister, Hawthorne drolly remarks, "The topic, it might be supposed, was obvious enough"; then he proceeds to describe seriously the effect of the veil on their imaginations, leaving them "speechless, confused, and shrinking uneasily" before the minister's glance. The contrast between these frightened men and the stiff dignity with which they report the matter "too weighty to be handled, except by a council of the churches, if, indeed, it might not require a general synod,"[138] creates humor. With the minister himself, Hawthorne creates for the reader occasional pathos: there is his rush away from the wedding into the darkness; there is the moment when Elizabeth leaves him; there is his grief that the children flee from him. But his finally gaining the name Father Hooper has in it a suggestion of tenderness.

In "Ethan Brand" Hawthorne is successful at getting a gleam of humor with the stage-agent, Lawyer Giles, and the Doctor; with the old Dutchman calling everybody Captain; with the dog chasing his tail—the diorama and the dog incidents both acting as parallels, the former with the narrator showing his pictures, the latter with Ethan's unreasonable, foolish search. But there is pathos in Old Humphrey too, and in the boy's sense of Ethan's "bleak and terrible loneliness."[139] Yet the lime-burner's rough conclusion that his "kiln is half a bushel the richer"[140] for Ethan's bones strikes the reader humorously because at this point there is a sense in which Ethan has cut himself off from all human sympathy, including the reader's.

Readers are likely to sympathize in "The Gentle Boy" with the pathetically warped fanatics and the little outcast Ilbrahim, with the wavering Tobias, and with Dorothy in her losses. The scene where the cruel boy strikes Ilbrahim in the mouth with his staff is handled without the sentimentality that might so easily have resulted and creates a high degree of pathos. There are gleams of humor in the story too: the picture of the Puritan trying the apparition of the boy by "the test of a short mental prayer,"[141] and even in the awkward attempt of the old Quaker to "cheer" Catharine with news of her boy's death—"Sister! go on rejoicing, for his tottering footsteps shall impede thine own no more."[142]

There is pathos and tenderness enough in "Roger Malvin's Burial"—in the conversation between Reuben and Roger as Roger persuades the youth to leave him to die; in the scene where Reuben is prevented from telling of Roger's death, prevented not alone by physical and moral weakness but by Dorcas' interruption, "He died"; and certainly pathos enough in the conclusion.

To see Hawthorne using humor in a somewhat different fashion, one turns to "The Celestial Railroad." Here the characters are almost pure allegories with very little of the Actual about them. As a kind of balance, Hawthorne makes the narrator a comic character, appropriate to both parody and dream. The narrator is less intelligent than the reader; his fears and tremblings are amusing; he is so completely taken in by the farce that he points up error by his insistence in the face of the obvious on the great advantages of the modern way. His fears and assurances provide opposite answers possible for a dream-character (and symbolically provide the normal shakiness of a character trying to convince himself of a non-existent easy way). While admitting the seeming shakiness of his mode of travel at times, out of his very fear he seizes upon Mr. Smooth-it-away's comfortable assurances and excuses himself because of his fear. He asserts at the most unlikely times that this "would have done Bunyan's heart good,"[143] or that Christian will "rejoice to hear of this"[144] or that "every good heart must surely exult at so satisfactory an arrangement" as the employment of the "prince's subjects"[145] about the station-house. He is quite as capable, however, of harming his cause by superlatives like his comment on the travelers' conversation: "Even an infidel would have heard little or nothing to shock his sensibility."[146] He tries a reasonable view and speaks in absurdities—"our friend Bunyan—a truthful man, but infected with many fantastic notions."[147] Sometimes he makes straight-faced arguments against the railroad, as in his description of how the pilgrims, "worthy simpletons," made Vanity Fair "look wild and monstrous, merely by their sturdy repudiation of all part in its business or pleasures."[148] At other times he joins heartily in enjoying the practical jokes of Apollyon at the pilgrims' expense or goes a step beyond in pride and snobbery as he decides the travelers by railroad will make real examples to draw meaner men to religion and real adornments in the Celestial City. A thoroughly inconsistent character, he creates constant incongruities by his narration of events. And Hawthorne—particularly through the comic narrator—draws his allegory back toward the Actual.

Incidents

In the investigation of Hawthorne's theory of incidents in my Chapter III, in the section entitled "Incidents—a pathway through glorified mist and fog," three specific theories are shown to be related to his development of a tale: Hawthorne saw plot largely as scenes in a series, each scene showing character interrelationships; he saw the progression of scenes as proceeding from outward actions revealing inner character; and this revelation was of characters compounded of Actuality and Imagination, resulting in some improbable actions for which the artist must account. Thus the areas of investigation are: scenes in a series, causation at two levels, and resultant "ambiguity."

"The Celestial Railroad" as one of the more simply plotted stories makes a good beginning point. Here the rapid passage of scenes effects two useful phases of the artistry: it makes possible the brief enumeration of many places, and it emphasizes the hurry and haste by means of the railroad as compared with the dusty footpath. Both effects increase the satire, the first making it possible for it to cut in many directions, the second emphasizing shallowness with the endeavor to ignore truth by a hurried smoothing over, and the too rapid arrival at the Valley of the Shadow of Death. The places where the engine stops are also—by this very hurry—brought into sharp contrast with the places it does not stop. In the Valley of the Shadow, there is a stop for refueling at the cavern that looks like the infernal regions; they stop at Flimsy-Faith's castle; they stop finally, with one last horrible scream of the engine, in the land of Beulah, where they hear the music of the reception of the dusty pilgrims arriving in the city beyond the river. But they have rushed by the Interpreter's House, by the place where Christian lost his burden at the sight of the Cross; they have rushed by Giant Transcendentalist without knowing his yea or nay; they have missed the Palace Beautiful with Miss Prudence, Miss Piety, and Miss Charity. They could not arrive at the Celestial City. Since there is no sufficient Actual reason why they could not have crossed the river but an excellent Allegorical reason why they cannot arrive at the city, the conclusion of the tale has to satisfy both demands. Here the dream framework stops the tale without the necessity of solving the question in any Actual way though it leaves the Allegorical meaning clear.

Frequently Hawthorne's stories are developed with a few scenes, each showing character interrelationships. In "Roger Malvin's Burial" Hawthorne indicates typographically his division of the story into five parts. The first is introductory. The four scenes follow: (1) Beneath the oak trees the two men talk, Roger leaning against the grey rock, Reuben hesitantly taking his leave, after having tied the blood-stained bandage from his wound to the top of an oak sapling and vowed by it to return; (2) Reuben at home, wounded, does not admit his vow (there follow the account of his marriage, his remembrance of the picture of Roger, his deterioration, his love of his son); (3) After the forest journey, come the shot and again the blasted tree, and (4) By the rock again, the son dead, the mother senseless, Reuben is at last freed from the curse by shedding blood dearer than his own—and upon them all and upon Roger's bones fall the soft fragments of the withered topmost bough of the blighted oak. It is noticeable in this tale that a circular pattern of action is followed; Reuben's vow drives him back to the rock where he made the vow; within the forest he travels in a circle (as well he might from having no definite plan); when he leaves the camp within the forest to hunt, he travels in a circle, coming back near the opposite side from which the boy had left to hunt. This pattern is more important for the interpretation than are the successive scenes taken merely as a series of pictures, for this pattern emphasizes the importance of the first and last scenes, both for the interrelationship of characters and for the relationship of the two scenes. The circle pattern, paralled by the special area within the forest, drives Reuben inexorably back and back to his beginning point, demanding, by the laws of Nature and by his inner nature, the keeping of his vow. The artistic lack of vivid pictures in the middle of the story further emphasizes the first and last scenes. The motivation of Reuben provides causation for the happenings. Neither Hawthorne nor the reader blames the young man for leaving Roger; nonetheless he leaves with a sense of guilt, a sense sufficient to make him take advantage of the opportunity to suppress the fact by silence and indefiniteness. Having started his concealment of the truth and increased the sense of guilt he already feels, he is most likely to find it increasingly difficult to "confess" and at the same time increasingly tormenting. After eighteen years it will take a tremendous shock to make him speak the words which break the pattern of concealment. Because of the high degree of Actuality in the character of Reuben and Hawthorne's handling of the symbolism of the boy, no improbability develops in the incidents of this tale.

"The Gentle Boy" provides four vivid pictures, all with the Gentle Boy as central in accord with Hawthorne's plan to develop the story by characters representing sides of an idea: (1) Ilbrahim, on a stormy night, moaning over his father's grave, found and taken home by the sympathetic Tobias, (2) Ilbrahim, in a Puritan church, being deserted by his mother Catharine, while Dorothy earnestly befriends him and Tobias hesitantly steps forward—against a background of Puritans still somewhat stunned by Catharine's fanatical outbreak at the sacred desk, (3) Ilbrahim, making his way through the vicious Puritan children who attack him on all sides, toward his "friend"—who strikes him in the mouth with his staff, (4) Ilbrahim dying, while Tobias laments his lot to the old Quaker, Dorothy remains by his side, and Catharine arrives out of the stormy night to see him on his deathbed. Causation in "The Gentle Boy" largely involves him as passive character; that he would be a passive character is provided for by his Quaker training to accept persecution. The actions of all other characters towards him are probable at the Actual level and meaningful at the Imaginative level, so that there is no resultant ambiguity in action. It is interesting to conjecture how different the problem would be were he active protagonist.

In "Rappaccini's Daughter," the picture of Giovanni is developed through the scenes, scenes which shift from garden to room to street, with five specific scenes in the garden—the first three with Giovanni looking down into the garden, the last two picturing him there. The final relationship of the characters is vividly pictured in the last scene in the garden: Beatrice, the beautiful, innocent spirit, is dying; Giovanni, the sensuous, selfish lover is looking on with more concern for his own well-being than hers and failure to reach across the "gulf of blackness";[149] Rappaccini stands detached from any emotional or sympathetic involvement, probably making mental calculations on his experiment; and Baglioni, lacking insight into the spiritual, looks into the garden from without and maintains his narrow view of the conflict as being merely a personal one in a material world. The causes of Giovanni's actions are in his character—an ardent temperament, a shallow heart. The ambiguous incidents in this tale arise from the character of Beatrice. Does she poison insects and wilt flowers with her breath or does she not? Is she angel or devil—to be loved or feared? The incidents get a double removal—they are seen through Giovanni's eyes, and he sees them from a distance. Each time Giovanni thinks he sees the miraculous—the lizard's death by a drop or two falling from the broken flower stem, the bright insect dying from Beatrice's breath, the withering of the bouquet as she holds it—Hawthorne suggests that the distance was too great for him to see anything so small or that his eyes deceived him. This means that the reader can agree with Hawthorne and at the same time get the hint of what Beatrice seems to Giovanni and why the best thing for him to do would be to leave.

In "Young Goodman Brown," though one may think of the scenes as (1) in the town, (2) into the forest, (3) in the forest's depths, and (4) in the town again, the movement into the forest is particularly significant. The arguments which begin as Brown and the "devil" reason with each other are developed with psychological accuracy through arguments about good people, then more personally about Faith and the Good as related to himself; the climactic change comes just after he applauds himself on his escape. In this tale several events are highly Imaginative. And Hawthorne clearly gives the reader permission to treat it as a dream—where the old man can be devil easily enough, the staff can wriggle like a serpent, the pink ribbon can fall from the clouds. One can emphasize the wavering image of the lurid fires and the wakening in the chill and damp and call it a dream. Hawthorne probably would not object to a reading which saw it as a journey taken only in Brown's mind where the "devil" stands for his darker, doubting self, and where, as the tormented would testify, vivid visions are not uncommon. The reason Hawthorne would not object to such a reading is that his Truth remains whether one reads the ambiguous incidents as Actual or Imaginative.

CONCLUSION

In his intermingling of the Actual and the Imaginative, his presentation of Truth, his use of light, his arrangement of scenes, his creation of character, and his development of incidents, Hawthorne is a Transcendental symbolist when studied as a writer of tales. It remains now to consider Hawthorne as artist of the Romance.

V

Hawthorne's Aesthetic Practices:
The Scarlet Letter and *The Marble Faun*

INTRODUCTION

In consideration of the artistry of Hawthorne's longer works, an investigation centering, as in the previous chapter, in the phases of symbolism will not be satisfactory. Such a study would fail to define as coherently as possible the unity of Hawthorne's blending of all phases of his art in larger pictures. For this reason the romances will be discussed book by book; in each instance, however, the study will investigate Hawthorne's Transcendental mingling of the Actual and the Imaginative, his statements of Truth, his use of light, his arrangements of scenes, his creation of characters, and his handling of incidents.

Again the criticism will be selective, centering upon two of the four romances, *The Scarlet Letter* and *The Marble Faun*. These two romances, however, give a fair representation of Hawthorne's success in this art form, including as they do his first and most famous romance, *The Scarlet Letter* (1850) and his last finished romance, *The Marble Faun* (1860).

THE SCARLET LETTER

Mingling the Actual and the Imaginative

In *The Scarlet Letter* Hawthorne succeeded in so mingling Actuality and Imagination that the created image is a masterful fusion of those elements in the picture of his Truth.

He says in his preface that "the main facts" of the story were "authorized and authenticated by the document of Mr. Surveyor Pue,"[1] and he mentions the manuscript again in the conclusion of the novel. Asserting "the authenticity of the outline,"[2] he puts his imagination to work on Hester's story.

It is not difficult to marshal historical facts to indicate Hawthorne's insistence on Actuality. The names of Governor Bellingham and John Winthrop immediately occur; in fact, the specific citation of Winthrop's death perhaps "dates" the story more exactly than Hawthorne wished. The mention of other names gives a "historical ring" to the account: Endicott, Bradstreet, Increase Mather, Sir Thomas Overbury. The practices and customs of the Puritans of Boston in the seventeenth century are detailed: the crimes they punished, the methods of punishment, the connection the important magistrates had with minor crimes, Puritan enjoyments, their use of fine gloves and ruffs, their Election Day holiday, their sermons, their superstitious beliefs. Together with facts that could to some extent be historically documented, Hawthorne builds in highly probable Actuality which could not be historically documented: the story told Chillingworth of "Hester's husband" at the scaffold; the plan to take Pearl from her mother; the particular house, with its Biblical tapestries, in which Dimmesdale and Chillingworth live.

Mingled with this Actuality, by Hawthorne's insistence, is the Imaginative. At one point Hawthorne asserts that Pue's record is set forth on "half a dozen sheets of foolscap." Hence he insists that he has allowed himself, in dressing up the tale, in "imagining the motives and modes of passion that influenced the characters who figure in it," "nearly or altogether as much license as if the facts had been entirely" of his "own invention."[3] Throughout the work, he builds on superstitious beliefs, cites alleged traditions when their significations will help make clear his Truth, and similarly ascribes meaningful ideas and actions to Mistress Hibbins, the witch. He removes the story to a remote time two centuries ago where it will be difficult or impossible to document specific facts.[4] There he mingles the Marvellous as a flavor only, connecting the marvellous origin of the rosebush with some indefinite authority and not fully accepting it, presenting the picture of Pearl patting the head of a wolf as improbability even in the doubly removed forest setting—but still presenting it to suggest the kindred wildness of the child and wild Nature.

It is not germane to the present purpose to discover the precise extent to which the tale is devoted to historical accuracy, nor precisely which facts are imagined; but it is significant to notice Hawthorne's *mingling* of the Actual and the Imaginative in the opening chapter of the work as both promise and fulfillment of his customary method. The very first sentence pictures a group of persons, attired in earlier costumes than those of Hawthorne's time, standing before what appears to be a very actual, oak-timbered, iron-spiked door. Hawthorne immediately indicates that these persons were founders of a new colony, following this up with the place name Boston and an assumption that the first prison was built almost as soon as the first burial ground, which he specifically locates. He concludes the second paragraph with a detailed description of the jail and the wild rosebush at its threshold. In the third and last paragraph of the chapter, he asserts the historical accuracy of the rosebush, which he then mingles with Imagination as he cites the possibility of the marvellous origin of the bush, it having been said to spring up "under the footsteps of the sainted Anne Hutchinson." Hawthorne maintains his position "on the edge of the precipice," by saying that "we shall not take upon us to determine" whether the bush had such a marvellous origin or had merely survived out of the wilderness. Having initiated this mingling of Actual and Imaginative, he chooses one of the flowers "to symbolize some sweet moral blossom that may be found along the track, or relieve the darkening close of a tale of human frailty and sorrow."[5] This is Hawthorne's method throughout the work: Actuality (often historical) mingled with Imagination to create a symbol.

Truth

Since Hawthorne promises a single rose or moral, and since he saw this story as presenting different sides of the same dark idea to the reader,[6] one is justified in looking for a single statement of his Truth within the work. Such a statement related to a principal character occurs in the conclusion: "Among many morals which press upon us from the poor minister's miserable experience, we put only this into a sentence:—'Be true! Be true! Be true! Show freely to the world, if not your worst, yet some trait whereby the worst may be inferred!' "[7] In order to see this Truth completely, one must examine Hawthorne's specific statements about the various "sides" of the Truth. Such "sides" will necessarily be related to the characters as representative of phases of the same dark idea.[8]

The sin of Dimmesdale with which Hawthorne is primarily concerned is not the sin of passion which precedes the story, but the minister's divergence from Truth. Hawthorne asserts of the minister that "it was his genuine impulse to adore the truth, and to reckon all things shadow-like, and utterly devoid of weight or value, that had not its divine essence as the life within their life."[9] Again he says, "By the constitution of his nature, he loved the truth, and loathed the lie, as few men ever did."[10] Thus when Dimmesdale as minister speaks the Truth while in his personal life he transforms it into falsehood, he alienates himself from Truth, from God. Though the people still hear Truth from his lips, everything becomes false to him and his own real existence is endangered. Hawthorne says:

> It is the unspeakable misery of a life so false as his, that it steals the pith and substance out of whatever realities there are around us, and which were meant by Heaven to be the spirit's joy and nutriment. To the untrue man, the whole universe is false,—it is impalpable,—it shrinks to nothing within his grasp. And he himself, in so far as he shows himself in a false light, becomes a shadow, or, indeed, ceases to exist. The only truth that continued to give Mr. Dimmesdale a real existence on this earth was the anguish in his inmost soul, and the undissembled expression of it in his aspect.[11]

Hawthorne also asserts the mockery of the midnight scaffold scene, in which Dimmesdale's "soul trifled with itself." This is "heaven-defying guilt and vain repentance."[12] He lets Dimmesdale say, "Of

penance, I have had enough! Of penitence, there has been none!"
If something like the scarlet letter could make him known as a
sinner, even this much truth would save him. "But, now," Dimmesdale says, "it is all falsehood!—all emptiness!—all death!"[13] Only
after his final appearance on the scaffold, with his dying words, can
the minister hope that he is not cut off from God forever. In Dimmesdale, Hawthorne sees a sin against Truth and God, a sin
against the minister's own constitutional love of Truth; this sin
cuts him off from God and Truth, leaving falsehood, emptiness,
death. Until the last moment of his life, Dimmesdale exercises
penance but only a mockery of penitence. Though his death is—as
he calls it—one of "triumphant ignominy,"[14] providing hope that
his soul is not lost forever, it is too late for an earthly reconstruc-
tion of a true life, and he teaches the story's moral by his earthly
tragedy.

Hester presents another side of the Truth of the tale. Hawthorne
says of Hester that she contrasts with the image of Divine Materni-
ty, the "sacred image of sinless motherhood, whose infant was to
redeem the world." "Here," he asserts of Hester, "there was the
taint of deepest sin in the most sacred quality of human life, working such effect, that the world was only the darker for this woman's
beauty, and the more lost for the infant that she had borne."[15]
Later her rejecting the pleasure of making beautiful things to
make coarse garments for the poor is shown to be a sort of penance; "this morbid meddling of conscience with an immaterial
matter betokened, it is to be feared, no genuine and steadfast penitence, but something doubtful, something that might be deeply
wrong, beneath."[16] Her loss of faith in any good in humanity "is
ever one of the saddest results of sin." However, Hawthorne holds
out some hope for Hester: "Be it accepted as a proof that all was
not corrupt in this poor victim of her own frailty, and man's hard
law, that Hester Prynne yet struggled to believe that no fellow-
mortal was guilty like herself."[17] But later Hawthorne still asserts,
"The scarlet letter had not done its office."[18] Only years after Dimmesdale's death, after Pearl is grown, does Hester show any change.
Of her return to Boston, Hawthorne says, "Here had been her sin;

here, her sorrow; and here was yet to be her penitence."[19] Thus Hawthorne sees a deep sin depriving Hester of the life she should have had beside a fireside, and he sees a penance enforced by others and then by Hester herself with real penitence. By her sin, she is cut off from society, and only after many years does her real penitence give her a place again in the world as comforter and counselor of the sorrowful and perplexed.

Roger Chillingworth, Hawthorne says, "was a striking evidence of man's faculty of transforming himself into a devil, if he will only, for a reasonable space of time, undertake a devil's office." He is given one view of himself that Hawthorne calls his "moral aspect . . . faithfully revealed to his mind's eye." Chillingworth says of himself with respect to Dimmesdale, "A mortal man, with once a human heart, has become a fiend for his especial torment!"[20] This is a man who has nothing to do with either penance or penitence, who takes his highest gift of intelligence to revenge himself upon a human brother, partly for art's sake alone, and so becomes a devil.

Since as a child Pearl is not subject to moral laws beyond her comprehension, she begins her life outside the chain of humanity. Hawthorne sees her as "a lovely and immortal flower,"[21] a gift of God. Yet he says "the child's own nature had something wrong in it which continually betokened that she had been born amiss."[22] In the account of the forest walk, Hawthorne says of her: "She wanted—what some people want throughout life—a grief that should deeply touch her, and thus humanize and make her capable of sympathy. But there was time enough yet for little Pearl."[23] Only after her great grief is she brought into the human family of responsible adults; her tears upon her father's cheek are "the pledge that she would grow up amid human joy and sorrow, nor forever do battle with the world, but be a woman in it."[24]

Hence without oversimplifying too much, perhaps it can be said that these four characters represent sides of the idea: "Be true." Each character represents a single phase as an individual, yet each works out the universal problem. Dimmesdale's best self loves Truth, loves God; he—a minister—turns Truth to falsehood (with respect to his individual life) and destroys his unity with God and his own Reality of existence. Hester's union with society should come through her own best gift to be a wife and a mother in a home; her sin against this gift has cut her off from society's acceptance. Further, her divided faithfulness to Chillingworth and Dimmesdale prevents complete Truth to either and cuts her off specifically from each by her promises of secrecy. Chillingworth's best self, which searches out Truth scientifically, takes a devil's direction, destroying his humanity and cutting him off from his best self, in fact, withering him completely. Pearl's isolation from everyone is a result of sin, but not her sin; through great grief she comes to a knowledge of Truth and is brought into the Unity. Hence, Hawthorne's dark idea of sin's destruction of Unity with God, fellow-men, and one's own best self is viewed from different sides, and the simplest possible statement of moral meaning is "Be true."

It must be noted that the total view is seen against the Puritan society, which Hawthorne neither totally approves nor totally rejects. As a society, the Puritan group identify law and religion as one; yet their moral grasp is incomplete, for they excuse the rough sailors who are outside their society. Incompetent to judge Hester, those men—undoubtedly good in many respects—act with a sternness that shows too little heart, too little human sympathy; they need "the mighty and mournful lesson, that, in the view of Infinite Purity, we are sinners all alike. . . . The holiest among us has but attained so far above his fellows as to discern more clearly the Mercy which looks down, and repudiate more utterly the phantom of human merit, which would look aspiringly upward."[25]

Light

Both the title, *The Scarlet Letter*, and the story's concluding motto, "*On a field, sable, the letter A, gules*,"[26] suggest that color, light, and shadow figure importantly in this legend. Hawthorne uses light both to indicate the meaning of his characters and to contrast scenes within the structure of the story. Dimmesdale's pallor, referred to again and again, is more than a pallor of the moderately introspective; it hints "the black secret of his soul."[27] There are two contrasts. Once his face undergoes "a dark transfiguration"; "never was there a blacker or a fiercer frown than Hester" encounters when she tells him who Chillingworth is and the "violence of passion . . . the portion of him which the Devil claimed,"[28] flashes forth. And once he gains a glow of "flickering brightness"[29] in the forest. But usually he is pale. During his triumphant Election Sermon, how pale he looks; and when the glow of inspiration which has burned upon his cheek is extinguished, his face even has "a deathlike hue."[30] Hawthorne pictures him giving outward evidence which speaks his heart despite his efforts to maintain secrecy.

Hester first appears adorned by the fantastically embroidered letter, the brilliance of red cloth and gold thread. Hawthorne speaks of her "deep black eyes," and the sunlight gleaming on her dark and glossy hair. "Those who had before known her, and had expected to behold her dimmed and obscured by a disastrous cloud," are "astonished, and even startled, to perceive how her beauty" shines out, and makes "a halo of the misfortune and ignominy" in which she is "enveloped."[31] Though she continues to wear the scarlet letter that seems to "scorch" beneath the finger of Chillingworth as if it were "red-hot,"[32] yet her dress becomes habitually "sombre,"[33] and her "pale cheek"[34] only on occasion flushes crimson. So Hester emphasizes through her enforced penance the unholy light of her impenitent soul while in her sombre greyness she outwardly conforms to society's requirements. When in the forest Hester rids herself of the scarlet letter, she takes off the formal cap that confines her hair and lets the hair fall "upon her shoulders, dark and rich, with at once a shadow and a light in its abundance." Beaming from her eyes and playing around her mouth is "a radiant and tender smile," and "glowing on her cheek, that had been long so pale," there is "a crimson flush."[35] For a moment she becomes the rich and beautiful woman she might have been but cannot be now—except in the lawless forest. With Pearl's insistence, however, and the return of the scarlet letter, she binds up her hair, and "as if there were a withering spell in the sad letter, her beauty, the warmth and richness of her womanhood," depart "like fading sunshine; and a gray shadow" seems "to fall across her."[36] She appears in her coarse gray garment on Election Day. But years later when she returns, "a tall woman, in a gray robe,"[37] at last she does more than conform to outward rules. Now she has been made wise "through dusky grief."[38]

Chillingworth, remembered first by Hester as "a pale, thin, scholar-like" man "with eyes dim and bleared by the lamplight" (though the "bleared optics"[39] had a penetrating power to read the human soul), appears at the scaffold for Hester's punishment with a "face darkened with some powerful emotion."[40] His eyes glow intensely upon Hester in the prison in attempts to read her secret. As he bores into the minister's soul, a change comes over his features; "his dark complexion" grows "duskier."[41] His visage begins to grow sooty with the smoke of "infernal fuel"[42] and sometimes "a light" glimmers out of his eyes, "burning blue and ominous . . . like one of those gleams of ghastly fire that darted from Bunyan's awful doorway in the hill-side."[43] The smile with which Roger seems to try to mask his expression and hide his real self comes to flicker over his visage derisively, so that the spectator can "see his blackness all the better for it." And there is "a glare of red light" that comes at times out of his eyes, as if his "soul were on fire, and kept on smouldering duskily within his breast."[44] Such is the man who has become a fiend. But the last picture of him is with "a blank, dull countenance, out of which the life seemed to have departed."[45] His fiend's work is ended, and his hellish light extinguished.

Pearl is given the same brilliance bestowed on the scarlet letter and given that brilliance by the same person—Hester. She gets both her moral coloration and the brilliance of her physical adornment from her mother. "However white and clear originally," "the rays" of the infant's "moral life" "had taken the deep stains of crimson and gold, the fiery lustre, the black shadow, and the untempered light of the intervening substance," that is, of Hester herself. The "cloud-shapes of gloom and despondency" are in Pearl, but they are "illuminated by the morning radiance of a young child's disposition."[46] Her magnificent dress and decoration let the splendor of her beauty shine through to make "an absolute circle of radiance around her, on the darksome cottage floor."[47] Appearing in the Governor's mansion with her luxuriant beauty, shining with "deep and vivid tints; a bright complexion, eyes possessing intensity both of depth and glow, and hair already of a deep, glossy brown" which later will be nearly black, there is "fire in her and throughout her." Her "crimson velvet tunic" "embroidered with fantasies and flourishes of gold-thread" makes her "the very brightest little jet of flame that ever danced upon earth."[48] Such an emphatic analogy between Pearl and the scarlet letter has been the creation of Hester's morbid ingenuity. Dressed for Election Day by Hester, Pearl looks like "the many-hued brilliancy from a butterfly's wing, or the painted glory from the leaf of a bright flower," blending with Nature to suggest her childlike irresponsibility. Or, again, she resembles the "shimmer of a diamond that sparkles and flashes,"[49] a gem to suggest Hester's responsibility for her appearance. Realized aside from Hester's coloration, Pearl's character, with all its brilliance, has "a hard, metallic lustre"[50] which only grief can soften.

Hawthorne also uses light imagery in the development of the narrative structure. Beginning with the dark prison door and the single rosebush, he sets the first scene on a summer morning. Into the bright morning sunlight emerges the black shadow of the town beadle. Then the winking child is brought into "the too vivid light of day" from the "gray twilight"[51] of the prison, brought by the brilliant Hester, with the illuminating letter. Thus "iniquity is dragged out into the sunshine."[52] There is a kind of necessity in this as Hawthorne indicates that Truth will be known, but at the same time there is a kind of inappropriateness in man's taking such judgment so harshly into his own hands. The hot midday sun burns down on Hester and lights up her shame. This is a Hester who should instead have been seen in the quiet gleam of the fireside. Into this sunlight comes the Governor with clergyman John Wilson, who also winks "in the unadulterated sunshine,"[53] and whose sermon makes the symbol take on new terrors, seeming to derive its hue "from the flames of the infernal pit," till those who look after Hester as she vanishes again into the prison think it throws "a lurid gleam along the dark passage-way."[54] So the first big scene, beginning and ending in prison darkness, is set in too bright sunlight, illuminating too vividly the letter's lurid light.

The scene in the Governor's Hall has different lighting. Sparkling outside as the sunshine glitters upon the broken-glass stucco, illuminated within by two tower windows and an embowed hall window, the hall's most brilliant picture is the suit of mail, "especially the helmet and breastplate, so highly burnished as to glow with white radiance and scatter an illumination everywhere about upon the floor."[55] Thus the cheerful exterior of the mansion is deceiving, and the windows which admit the light of day throw their light upon cold and warlike objects. These objects become convex mirrors, exaggerating the scarlet letter out of all proportion and reflecting the naughty antics of Pearl until she seems not a child at all but an imp. Here Hawthorne has given by the reflected stern and warlike light of helmet and breastplate a picture of the evil as interpreted by the heads and hearts of the cold, stern Puritans—exaggerated until no good is left; reflecting the sin back to the sufferers who, seeing the distortion, find no hope.

Midnight upon the scaffold, too, has its particular lighting. An "obscure night" it is, with "an unvaried pall of cloud" muffling "the whole expanse of sky"—the "dark gray of the midnight."[56] The white-nightcapped, white-gowned, ghostly figure of the old Governor looks out a window; the lamp of the witch-lady appears at another window; then the darkness returns. A "glimmering light"[57] approaches along the street—that of Father Wilson. The "lurid playfulness" of the minister's mind pictures the coming of morning: "dim twilight," "dusky tumult," "red eastern light."[58] Then Hester and Pearl appear out of the darkness and stand with the minister upon the scaffold. Just as the minister refuses ever to stand there at noontide, and says that only before the judgment seat shall they three stand together ("the daylight of this world shall not see our meeting"), "a light" gleams "far and wide over all the muffled sky," with so powerful a radiance that it thoroughly illuminates "the dense medium of cloud betwixt the sky and earth." The great vault brightens "like the dome of an immense lamp." Then all objects show up strangely with the "awfulness" imparted "by an unaccustomed light."[59] The minister in his disordered mental state thinks he sees "the letter A—marked out in lines of dull red light."[60] And that same meteoric light discovers the minister to Roger Chillingworth as he passes along the street. The lighting in this scene is particularly interesting by contrast with earlier scenes. It must be remembered that here Dimmesdale is acting the mockery of penitence, making Truth into falsehood, in such a way as to bring himself near madness. It is his mad and grimly humorous view of the horrors that causes him to laugh aloud and attracts the attention of Pearl. Only in a scene like this would the appearance of a meteor be appropriate lighting (with all the superstitious meanings gathering around it). The minister's mind is already "lighted" by the sense of his sin; Chillingworth has probed his soul to keep that knowledge alive just as Pearl and the scarlet letter have burned in Hester's soul. Egotistically, Dimmesdale interprets this light as for himself alone. Artistically, it takes a universal interpretation. The light shows what is already there.

The forest scene has a different kind of lighting from any Hawthorne has used thus far. As Hester and Pearl enter the forest, "a gleam of flickering sunshine"[61] plays along the path but withdraws as they come near, leaving greater dreariness because they had expected to find those sunny spots remaining bright. Pearl is able to catch the sunshine, but Hester cannot stretch out her hand "and grasp some of it."[62] This, of course, is just what Hester intends to do, grasp some of the sunshine by persuading Arthur to go away with her. Deep in the wood is the little brook flowing through scenes heavily shadowed with gloom. In the dim wood it is difficult for Arthur and Hester to realize each other's actual and bodily existence. But they glide "back into the shadow of the woods"[63] and sit to talk. Now the gloom of the dark forest is more precious than golden light. Here for one moment Arthur, though false to God and man, as seen by Hester alone, may be true. Here, to correspond with Dimmesdale's momentary Truth of character, Hawthorne allows the wild, heathen Nature of the forest to throw upon them a flood of sunshine, as with a sudden smile of heaven, "gladdening each green leaf, transmuting the yellow fallen ones to gold, and gleaming adown the gray trunks of the solemn trees." "The objects that had made a shadow hitherto" embody "the brightness" now. For Love "must always create a sunshine, filling the heart so full of radiance, that it overflows upon the outward world."[64] Pearl, too, stands "in a streak of sunshine"[65] but "on the other side of the brook,"[66] and when finally they leave, the dell is "left a solitude among its dark, old trees."[67] Given a moment of sunshine—outside convention where they can for a moment be true—they see Nature smile on Love; but as Hawthorne indicated early in the scene, this is ungraspable sunshine. For there are still Pearl, still the scarlet letter, still some sort of society and law to which they must return.

The New England Holiday is colorful with Indians, mariners, even the dark Puritans displaying gayer finery than usual. The sunshine shimmers on the weapons and armor of the military company, and Pearl flits and sparkles here and there like a diamond. Mistress Hibbins in her showy magnificence insists that the scarlet letter which all can see in the sunshine "glows like a flame in the dark."[68] And Dimmesdale speaks "as if an angel, in his passage to the skies, had shaken his bright wings over the people for an instant,—*at once a shadow and a splendor*,—and had shed down a shower of golden truths upon them."[69] But his final appearance is not in a glaring sunlight, but in the clear, open daylight that etches his picture clearly: "The sun, but little past its meridian, shone down upon the clergyman, and gave a distinctness to his figure, as he stood out from all the earth, to put in his plea of guilty at the bar of Eternal Justice."[70]

Such is the sombre legend, "relieved only by one everglowing point of light gloomier than the shadow:—

'On a field, sable, the letter A, gules.' "[71]

Scenes

Before looking more carefully at Hawthorne's scenes and his characters within the scenes, it will be interesting to notice how, in chapter headings alone, he centers his attention and the reader's on scenes and character interrelationships rather than on action. There are twenty-four chapters in the work, but not one title contains a verb. Four name specific places: The Prison Door, The Market-Place, The Governor's Hall, and (significantly) The Interior of a Heart. Eight include character names: three are named singly—Pearl, The Leech, Another View of Hester; five name characters in relation—The Elf-Child and the Minister, The Leech and His Patient, Hester and the Physician, Hester and Pearl, The Pastor and His Parishioner. Three titles name a single character in a given place or situation: Hester at Her Needle, The Child at the Brookside, and (again significantly) The Minister in a Maze. One names a time: The New England Holiday. Seven name happenings: The Recognition, The Interview, The Minister's Vigil, A Forest Walk, A Flood of Sunshine, The Procession, The Revelation of the Scarlet Letter. And the final chapter is simply called Conclusion. Hawthorne, as is clear from his letters, gave considerable thought to his titles, and here is the suggestion by chapter titles alone of his narrative method: there will be static scenes, characters will be viewed within the scenes alone and in interrelationships (with inner states symbolized outwardly), and the progression of scenes will tell the story.

In each scene Hawthorne achieves a unification of details to point a single truth. I have already indicated how he does this in the opening chapter. For another excellent example of unification, the second chapter may be cited, "The Market-Place." Here it is necessary for the reader to see what sort of person Hester seems to those who look on, and Hawthorne needs to give a fair cross-section of opinion. He does this by a little scene within the larger one, a scene of five women, each of whom speaks once only, with four of the five briefly characterized by Hawthorne. The first, "a hard-featured dame of fifty," thinks it would be well if the five of them there in a knot together could give the total judgment; they would not let Hester off so easily. Another mentions the minister's grief at the scandal. "A third autumnal matron"[72] thinks Hester should have had the brand on her forehead. A young wife with a child realizes that the pang of the letter will be always in Hester's heart. The ugliest and most pitiless thinks Hester ought to die. Only one of the five shows pity; the others are even crueler than the magistrates. By their comments, however, Hawthorne has done more than give a cross-section of opinion; he has introduced themes as well as facts—the themes of sin, of judgment and religion (with especial reference to Dimmesdale), of a mark upon a gown and a pang within the heart, and of death. Finally, this tight little circle already has excluded Hester from their society as completely as she will be isolated from all society. Another excellent arrangement of details is effected in the placement of the scaffold beneath the church eaves, so that the unity of law and religion in the Puritan mind is made evident, while the platform situated *above* the scaffold provides clergymen and magistrates a position from which to *look down upon* the suffering sinners.

If Nature includes external objects, these details suggest the correspondence between outward Nature and inner Man. When Hawthorne deals specifically with landscapes, he frequently represents, in Transcendental fashion, a correspondence between Man and Nature. He shows Hester, as if by a new birth through her sin, belonging to the forestland, a wilderness where her mind can wander undirected. He shows her choosing an abandoned cottage on the shore, "looking across a basin . . . at the forest-covered hills,"[73] and continually longing for the "forestland." And she chooses a dwelling concealed by scrubby trees. Transcendentally speaking, it is as though she had built her own world in outward Nature. Pearl builds her own world as well, like any child, making the pine trees Puritan elders, the ugliest weeds their children, always creating enemies with whom she rushes to do battle. Just as these materials become "spiritually adapted to whatever drama occupied the stage of her inner world,"[74] so Hawthorne makes the drama of man's inner world reveal itself by its correspondence to Nature. Chillingworth's study of weeds becomes emblematic of his search for sin in the minister, and Hester looks expectantly as Chillingworth goes stooping along the earth, "to see whether the tender grass of early spring would not be blighted beneath him, and show the wavering track of his footsteps, sere and brown." She wonders whether the sun really falls upon him or whether, as it seems, "a circle of ominous shadow"[75] moves with his deformity.

When Hester goes to meet Dimmesdale, the Nature of the forest "to Hester's mind" images "not amiss the moral wilderness" in which she has "so long been wandering."[76] There the brook speaks the sorrow the heart already knows; it cannot talk to Pearl who has no great grief. The forest pictures the blackness of sin and sadness:

> The forest was obscure around them, and creaked with a blast that was passing through it. The boughs were tossing heavily above their heads; while one solemn old tree groaned dolefully to another, as if telling the sad story of the pair that sat beneath, or constrained to forebode evil to come.[77]

For a moment their love creates a flood of sunshine in that wild, heathen forest. Pearl, totally in sympathy with that wild, lawless Nature, finds that the forest answers her with kindest moods. It pleases her with fruits, with friendly animals, with flowers; she is "in closest sympathy with the antique wood."[78] The sunshine sympathizes with her. Here in the forest Hawthorne has showed an outer correspondence in Nature to the inner spirit of Man. Where Hester and Dimmesdale are outside the law and thereby find Nature stern, Pearl has no moral law and corresponds with "antique" Nature. The flood of sunshine, like the scarlet letter, is a point of light that makes the shadows deeper. For it too is the outward revelation of their love. When Dimmesdale returns from the forest, having "yielded himself, with deliberate choice, as he had never done before, to what he knew was deadly sin,"[79] outer Nature seems to have changed; the pathway seems wilder; familiar objects are different. Hawthorne says, "The minister's own will, and Hester's will, and the fate that grew between them, had wrought this transformation."[80] It would appear that Hawthorne has suggested in several ways a correspondence between Nature and Man and that he has Transcendentally pictured Man creating his own outward world by his inner will.

Characters

Hawthorne's characters, in *The Scarlet Letter* as elsewhere, are mingled of the Actual and the Imaginative. They stand for both individual and idea. It is probably the complexity of the ideas for which Dimmesdale and Hester stand, together with the extended psychological development of actual personages, that makes these two characters among those most fully realized by Hawthorne. Had Hester been made representative merely of "the figure, the body, the reality of sin,"[81] as she seemed to the Puritan accusers, she could never have been sympathetically realized and would have lost her Actuality. Had Dimmesdale revealed his total "meaning" only by the hand upon the heart, he too would have become merely a hated allegory. Even the misshapen Chillingworth, with his devilish gestures upon discovering the minister's secret, because of his need long ago for Hester's youth and warmth at his fireside, seems not merely a devil but a man who made himself a devil, which is a more complicated idea, necessarily involving a development not found, for instance, in Ethan Brand.

Pearl has suffered much from critics who find in her only an Idea, too often pointed up as an Idea, and who fail to see her as Actual. It may be that such criticism fails to take into consideration the complexity involved in the representation of Pearl. She necessarily lacks a completely Actual existence throughout the work because she is never personally morally accountable until the final scaffold scene. Pearl's vision of herself in the pool tells her that "either she or the image" is "unreal."[82] The very fact that she cannot tell—does not know herself—indicates her immaturity and, therefore, incompleteness. Further, Pearl necessarily receives an undue emphasis as Idea because Hester insists upon it in her clothing. Again, Pearl is necessarily the "living hieroglyphic,"[83] a constant remembrance (and a good gift to that extent) whose existence points and points and points to Meaning. And with the aid of the Puritan society, the Idea is forever brought to mind.

On the side of Actuality, critics sometimes ignore the purely childish characteristics of Pearl. Again and again and again she does things an Actual child would do. As a child she is capricious, moving from discontent to rage or grief or sudden tenderness. She feels the scorn of the little Puritans and hates them for it. Having been early attracted to the bright letter, she senses her mother's hesitancy to answer her questions about it. She acts extraordinarily naughty (when Hester most wishes her to be good) in the Governor's Hall; and having been already upset because she could not have a rose, answers the minister's "Who made thee?" with the fantasy that her mother picked her off the rosebush. She senses the minister's kindness and takes his hand, but the sentiment lasts only a moment. She asks questions about mysterious things, "Why does the minister keep his hand upon his heart?" "What does the Scarlet Letter mean?" "Have you ever met the Black Man?" Like any child, she senses when she is being hesitantly answered; this increases her curiosity—and the questions. Instances could be multiplied to show that Pearl is an Actual child as well as the representative of an Idea—even without dwelling on the abnormalities that would necessarily suggest themselves because of her strange isolation from everyone but Hester and because of Hester's own attitude toward her. To all this add the somewhat grim humor of Pearl's wild fights with real or imagined Puritan children; then add the pathetic loneliness of a child cut off from other children, and Pearl takes on even more Actuality.

In general, Hawthorne could do very little with humor in this work; the book, as he said, would not take cheering light. Except for Pearl's antics, there is little but Dimmesdale's mad laughter on the scaffold, a laughter not humorous but awful like Ethan Brand's. There are, it is true, depths of pathos in the tragedy of Dimmesdale and in that of Hester. Probably it is this engagement of the reader's sympathy that most gives the characters Actual life.

Incidents

In *The Scarlet Letter* the repeated tableau figures in the action as Hawthorne thrice gathers his four main characters at the scaffold, symbol of punishment and penitence. The relation of each of the characters to the scaffold and to each other is pictured in progress through these three scenes. Careful study of these symbolic pictures imprints a total meaning on the mind. In the first scene proud Hester takes her punishment without penitence; Arthur Dimmesdale stands above her on the balcony, pale and disturbed;

Chillingworth, with darkening face, signals his direction from a distance; and baby Pearl holds up her little arms towards Dimmesdale. This in a summer morning—while the crowd looks on. The second scene at midnight shows a weakened Arthur taking his punishment without penitence, a still proud Hester, Pearl wanting the minister to stand with them in the daytime, and Roger Chillingworth at the foot of the platform, quite capable of drawing the minister away with him. The final scene on Election Day pictures the spiritually victorious and at last penitent minister dying on the scaffold, Hester drawn there only because he is there, Pearl becoming a normal child, and the dull-countenanced Chillingworth defeated.

If these pictures were arranged to tell the story, between the first and second should be placed the scene in the Governor's mansion and between the second and last the scene in the forest. Significantly, these two scenes emphasize the basic symbol of sin in the letter and in Pearl by mirrored reflection. The four main characters are present in both scenes, with the exception of Chillingworth from the forest scene—we discover only that he knows such an interview has taken place. In the convex mirrors of the breastplate and headpiece hanging in the Governor's mansion, the scarlet letter is exaggerated out of all proportion and so is the naughtiness of Pearl—distorted in both breastplate and headpiece like the unsympathetic reasoning of the Puritans. In the forest brook, that boundary between two worlds, the angry image of Pearl expresses its shadowy wrath with a pointed finger. Distortions in the town but no escape in the forest—Hawthorne's dark idea necessarily returns his characters again and again to the scaffold.

It is interesting to trace the psychological causation of Dimmesdale's acts. His first words, in his speech to Hester on the scaffold, indicate his weakness and his strength. He appeals to her with the idea that if it will help her, she should speak out the guilty name. (For that she will protect him.) Yet he goes on to insist with his consistent ability to *say* the Truth, that it would be better not to tempt the unknown partner in her crime to add hypocrisy to sin; he may not have the courage to take the bitter, wholesome cup that is now presented to her. It is with great relief that he accepts her strength and generosity when she will not reveal the name. As he begins to lose his sense of discernment between the true and false in his own life, he is so "conscious that the poison of one morbid spot" is "infecting his heart's entire substance," that he attributes "all his presentiments to no other cause."[84] This explains his taking Chillingworth for his physician despite a deep antipathy he feels for him. Always of studious, introspective nature, now his thoughts —with Chillingworth's help—torture him. This torture of the mind he works out by the bloody scourge, the fasts, the vigils in darkness, and the viewing of his face in the glass by powerful light. He is unable to purify himself by his intense remorse, and his lack of courage prevents anything more than a mockery of confession, so that all his talk about his sinfulness is only interpreted to bring him greater veneration. Such a position with respect to the people makes the needed courage even greater and simultaneously increases his suffering as the distance between his true self and his reputation widens. Finally, he is so weakened by his suffering that death is too definite a thing to wish for, and he will be unable to take action without some outside intervention. In a sense this has already been provided in the person of Chillingworth. Then Hester, with her confession that Chillingworth is her husband, brings the minister momentarily to life with that truth. But he sinks down again to ask for her strength. It is her strength that plans their escape, but it is his concurrence that breaks the many years' pattern of false action and remorse. Recognizing, however, the poison of his first wilful act of sin (a deliberate choice this time— not an act of passion), he becomes a wiser man, but as Hawthorne says, with a bitter kind of knowledge. He rejects Chillingworth's help, writes an inspired Election Sermon, and goes out next morning a different man who impresses both Mistress Hibbins and Hester with his separation from them. At the last moment he has the strength to do what he should have done seven years before. Without the wisdom and strength gained from the forest walk, Dimmesdale, psychologically, would have been powerless to act.

The two major points of ambiguity in this story center in happenings affecting the minister: the meteoric "A" in the sky and the appearance of an actual mark upon the minister's breast. As pointed out earlier, Hawthorne relates the minister's interpretation of the meteor to his mental state at the time. By supporting such a specific view with varied specific views of others, he not only prevents a too marvelous interpretation but interrupts with comment just when the reader might otherwise be tempted to ask whether even a meteor at that precise moment were not too beautifully timed. Where Hawthorne handles the meteoric "A" in this way at the Actual level, at the Meaning level he gets a suggestion of Truth's universal denunciation of the minister's falsehood. When the suffering minister bares his breast on the scaffold, Hawthorne steps back from assertive description in reverence; then he reports various explanations, all conjectural. He next includes those who denied that there was any mark at all, who made the minister a parable, and he adds up all the opinions to form a single truth. Actually, some of the opinions might be questioned; at the Meaning level, the suffering of the minister was there—whether or not in a visible mark. So in both instances the reader may take his choice of specific answers, while Hawthorne has enhanced his Truth by the combination of opinions. Hawthorne's picture of Pearl patting the head of the wolf may be seen in a similar way. Mingling the Actual and the Imaginative at this point, Hawthorne builds like the sculptor he admired, actually on air, telling more by the shadow which obscures something than he could by the bare fact.

THE MARBLE FAUN

Actuality and Imagination

The Marble Faun, though in some ways unique among Hawthorne's works, is still a romance in which he mingles Actuality and Imagination. Structurally this is a novel in which his created artists imaginatively develop outward expressions of inner states of character, with Hawthorne remaining present as narrator; hence the mingling becomes a little more complicated. This complication is suggested in the double title, *The Marble Faun; or The Romance of Monte Beni*, for both the "Faun" of Praxiteles and the Count of Monte Beni have Actuality, though the statue has tangible historical meaning and the count is created to resemble (to some extent) any believable Italian of his rank. The Imagination of Praxiteles has already been given shape; the Imagination of Hawthorne takes shape in his creation of Monte Beni—the keynote being the suggested resemblance between the statue and the count. With such a keynote it is not surprising that throughout the work Hawthorne makes his artists create by mingling Actuality and Imagination, giving often a once removed view of his own Imagination at work. The story has a close parallel with "The Artist of the Beautiful," in which Owen creates his specific butterfly while Hawthorne creates his "butterfly" in the total story.

In such a work as *The Marble Faun* there is a double reference, then, for drawing toward the Actual, for Hawthorne may use the city of Rome, naming its streets and buildings; the Italian people, detailing their characteristics; historical personages, by reference to places that call to mind their names; and at the same time he may use the works of art which now have also purely Actual existence. In titles for chapters he cites specific places: the Pincian, the Medici Gardens, the Apennines, Perugia, the Campagna, the Corso. He discusses in some detail certain customs and characteristics of the Italians. There is a vagrant band of musicians to whose music Donatello and Miriam dance—a band, "such as Rome, and all Italy, abounds with."[85] There is the amiable Italian concern over Hilda's disappearance; they "overflow with plausible suggestions" and are "very bounteous in their avowals of interest," though this really promises little but "good wishes."[86] There is their handling of truth that makes it almost impossible to discover from their faces whether to believe or disbelieve them, "it being the one thing certain, that falsehood is seldom an intolerable burden to the tenderest of Italian consciences."[87] Among the ruins of Rome appear, for instance, the Coliseum, the Arch of Constantine, the Palace of the Caesars, and the Arch of Titus. Picturing a Roman triumph, with its "gorgeous pageantry of earthly pride," Hawthorne cuts short his historical allusion by adding yet two more names as he says, "Nor, if we would create an interest in the characters of our story, is it wise to suggest how Cicero's foot may have stepped on yonder stone, or how Horace was wont to stroll near by."[88] Among art works to be seen in and around Rome, Hawthorne mentions six in the very first paragraph of the story; and he makes one part of his story turn about the discussion of Guido's "Archangel." It is as though, as the story travels through the ruins of the Roman world, the narrator's passing comment upon specific historical fact will draw the reader's mind toward the actualities. And while Hawthorne frequently indicates that the specific pictures or statues or places have symbolic significance within the work, he also recognizes, both in preface and conclusion, "the extent to which he . . . introduced descriptions of various Italian objects, antique, pictorial, and statuesque,"[89] or, as he says in conclusion when he looks down upon Rome from the top of St. Peter's, "It is not my purpose further to describe," "having already sinned sufficiently in that way."[90]

Yet Hawthorne clearly indicates in the preface that he has no intention of portraying "Italian manners and character,"[91] and within the work he moves through the wealth of ruins which provided him the vague romantic atmosphere, pointing first to one, then another, or emphasizing some particular one that becomes symbolic—on which the reader can exercise his imagination as Hawthorne has exercised his own by the choice of the "Faun" of Praxiteles for a key symbol. It was the very antiquity of the Roman ruins that provided shadows so necessary to the romance writer, and Hawthorne insists upon the shadows. Immediately after he has pictured the four characters in the gallery with a view out the window, he says: "We glance hastily at these things,—at this bright sky, and those blue distant mountains, and at the ruins, Etruscan, Roman, Christian, venerable with a threefold antiquity, and at the company of world-famous statues in the saloon,—in the hope of putting the reader into that state of feeling which is experienced oftenest at Rome." Because this "vague sense of ponderous remembrances" makes "our individual affairs and interests . . . but half as real here as elsewhere," the narrative can be woven with "some airy and unsubstantial threads, intermixed with others, twisted out of the commonest stuff of human existence."[92] It probably is with such an idea in mind that Hawthorne names one chapter "Fragmentary Sentences," and another "Myths"; with such an idea that he asserts "no sober credence" had for some years been given "the mythical portion"[93] of the Count's pedigree; or says, in another connection, that "we will imagine"[94] that Hilda during her mysterious absence from Rome spent some time with the great departed masters she so much admired. It is with this in mind that Hawthorne gives many of his specific settings a second removal—into the catacombs, or towers, or studios, or galleries, or cathedrals; into the forest, or off among the mountains; upon the dreamlike, moonlit precipice, or amidst the dreamlike hilarity and confusion of the carnival.

Hawthorne hovers on the edge of the precipice: he invites a look into the blue distance and heights that appear scarcely real because, dreamed of so much, they take tints "which belong only to a dream." But he adds, "These, nevertheless, are the solid framework of hills that shut in Rome . . . no land of dreams, but the broadest page of history." Almost at once he moves away from history again, "But, not to meddle with history,—with which our narrative is no otherwise concerned than that the very dust of Rome is historic, and inevitably settles on our page and mingles with our ink,—we will return to our two friends."[95] The delight for the sensitive reader must be like Kenyon's. He read the musty documents of the Monte Beni family, but he liked Tomasco's legends better. And "what especially delighted the sculptor was the analogy between Donatello's character, as he himself knew it, and those peculiar traits which the old butler's narrative assumed to have been long hereditary in the race."[96] It is on the edge of the precipice that the Actual and the Imaginary may meet and the symbol become richly suggestive.

The Marvellous in this work centers in the idea—forever left, as it must be, ambiguous—of the furry ears. And it is precisely here that Hawthorne introduces a highly playful, humorous handling of the thought. In such fashion he can mingle the highly Imaginative with enough humor to increase Actuality; but the humor must be managed by attitudes of others and of Donatello—as well as Hawthorne—regarding this similarity between the count and the "Faun." The idea is first introduced in a scene of gayety with Miriam's playful request and is handled throughout the work and in the conclusion with playfulness and so used to suggest the location of the Faun between the Fantastic and the Real. Even in the midst of his remorse in his tower, Donatello smiles when he speaks of not uncovering his ears for Kenyon to model his bust.

Hawthorne uses humor throughout the work to draw his Imaginative characters and the work as a whole back toward the Actual. Miriam has a fitful, uncontrollable wit that makes her speak humorously even in the midst of great suffering or upon most serious matters. When she meets Kenyon in the marble saloon and explains her awful brooding, he says, "This is very sad, Miriam," and Hawthorne shows her humor breaking into Kenyon's dead seriousness as she says "with a short, unnatural laugh," "Ay, indeed; I fancy so."[97] Or Miriam, upon viewing the sculptured hand of Hilda and discussing her self-sufficiency with Kenyon smilingly breaks into Kenyon's sad thoughts with "Well, . . . perhaps she may sprain the delicate wrist. . . . In that case you may hope."[98] Donatello, by contrast, is capable early in the work of only great playfulness, never of intellectual wit, but his gambols and frolics, his attentions to Miriam reminding one of a pet spaniel, produce another kind of humor. Kenyon's humor is that of the appreciative but realistic observer who can be amused at the story of the nymph in the fountain or at Hilda's simple statements of belief in which he sees "pretty absurdity."[99] Hilda, on the contrary, lacks humor, particularly early in the work before her suffering; the detachment from reality is evidenced in her by this very lack. At the same time it is partly this lack that places her oftener than Hawthorne intended beyond the reader's deepest sympathy. Hawthorne as narrator has a humor similar to Kenyon's and has several enjoyable moments inserting comment upon the smell of monks (living or dead), the noseless statues, or the ceremony expected by the English on their private balcony (who looked as "English people of respectability would, if an angel were to alight in their circle, without due introduction from somebody whom they knew, in the court above."[100]) One of the finest touches of Actuality is the discovery, in the Pantheon, upon the altar, of "a very plump and comfortable tabby-cat."[101]

Truth

Hawthorne's statements of Truth in *The Marble Faun* tend, of course, to be related to the outward expression of that Truth in works of art. In the very first paragraph of his work, as he gathers his four individuals together, he pictures "a symbol . . . of the Human Soul, with its choice of Innocence or Evil close at hand, in the pretty figure of a child, clasping a dove to her bosom, but assaulted by a snake." More important in this connection than the picture is Hawthorne's inserted comment; he says it is "a symbol (as apt at this moment as it was two thousand years ago)."[102] Hawthorne cites a number of related, specific truths, but this idea is his "iron rod." He later asserts the universality of his symbol when he says: "Every human life, if it ascends to truth or delves down to reality, must undergo a similar change; but sometimes, perhaps, the instruction comes without the sorrow; and oftener the sorrow teaches no lesson that abides with us."[103] Since he indicates that his keynote is the resemblance between Donatello, the young Italian, and the "Faun" of Praxiteles, Donatello is most immediately connected with the main truth. Again Hawthorne states a number of specific truths, one of which must be cited. He says: "In the black depths, the Faun had found a soul, and was struggling with it towards the light of heaven."[104] Detailed statements of Truth about Donatello and other characters, as these meanings relate to the iron-rod meaning, will not be discussed here but will be seen in their connection with the phases of the artistry as analyzed. As a single clue, however, one sentence near the story's end should be quoted. In it, Hawthorne recalls his characters as seen early in the story, picturing Miriam as a sort of protagonist: "She flung herself upon the world, and speedily created a new sphere, in which Hilda's gentle purity, the sculptor's sensibility, clear thought, and genius, and Donatello's genial simplicity, had given her almost her first experience of happiness."[105]

Light

When Hawthorne created *The Marble Faun* he depended once again on that "special excellence of pictured glass," with the light "interfused throughout the work," illuminating the design and investing it "with a living radiance." As "the unfading colors transmute the common daylight into a miracle of richness and glory in its passage through the . . . shapes,"[106] so Hawthorne develops his characters by means of light and color.

Miriam is the most brilliant and colorful of the characters in the work, another of Hawthorne's darkly beautiful women. She is pictured with a "pale and tear-stained" face in a mood which passes "like a thunder-shower" leaving all "sunshine again."[107] Later Hawthorne says in a general comment that her nature has "a great deal of color," and that she resembles "one of those images of light, which conjurers evoke and cause to shine before us."[108] He pictures her again as "pale" in the "irregular twinkling" of her torch in the catacomb,[109] or hints at her seriousness "belied by a laughing gleam in her dark eyes"[110] when she speaks of the specter. He talks of her throwing the shadow of the model into the light which she "diffused around her."[111] But a detailed description is not given until Hawthorne lets Donatello see Miriam's self-portrait, Hawthorne admittedly having foreseen this occasion to bring Miriam's beauty "perhaps more forcibly before the reader."[112] The portrait shows a complexion with "no roseate bloom, yet neither was it pale"; dark eyes with a depth beyond sounding; and "black, abundant hair, with none of the vulgar glossiness of other women's sable locks," but looking rather like "a dark glory"[113] crowning her head. Watching Donatello's rapture as he observes the picture, "a smile of pleasure"[114] brightens on her face though her eyes gleam with something of scorn. When "a bright

natural smile" breaks over her face, Donatello wants it to "shine
upon the picture," though he insists, "Shroud yourself in what
gloom you will, I must needs follow you."[115] So in Hawthorne's
lighting of the character of Miriam he has kept her shadowy and
mysterious—then let her paint herself. In the suburban villa, a "ray
of sunlight" glimmers "among the moody meditations that encom-
passed Miriam," and lights up "the pale, dark beauty of her
face."[116] Here she brightens up "as if an inward flame, heretofore
stifled, were now permitted to fill her with its happy lustre, glowing
through her cheeks and dancing in her eye-beams,"[117] but her
"dark emotion"[118] returns when the model interrupts the sylvan
dance. So the model destroys the momentary sunshine she finds in
Donatello. The model hints that her "white hand had once a
crimson stain."[119] And later she herself admits that her secret is
her "dark-red carbuncle—red as blood."[120] She thinks it a sin "to
stain" Donatello's "joyous nature with the blackness"[121] of a woe
like hers, admits her doubts of God's providence by telling Hilda,
"just now it is very dark to me,"[122] and comes very suddenly to the
"fiery intoxication" and "dark sympathy"[123] that follow the bloody
crime which cements her life with Donatello's. But next day "the
wild ecstasy . . . has faded away, and sunk down among the dead
ashes of the fire that blazed so fiercely."[124] Now because her face
will bring memories to darken all his life, she tells Donatello to
leave her and forget her. When he does reject her, and when she
appears sometime after to Kenyon in the marble saloon, she is
not "beaming with even more than the singular beauty that had
heretofore distinguished her" but is "very pale, and dressed in deep
mourning."[125] Then only the hope that Donatello loves her still
brings "a flush of color . . . over the paleness of her cheek,"[126] and
the interview leaves her with a "new, tender gladness" beaming out
of her eyes and an "appearance of health and bloom."[127] Totally
dependent upon Donatello's love, seemingly penitent because he
is pentitent, while Donatello makes his pilgrimage, she becomes
"a figure in a dark robe"[128] haunting the pathway, a person who
finally lifts a face "pale and worn, but distinguished even now,
though less gorgeously, by a beauty that might be imagined bright

enough to glimmer with its own light in a dim cathedral aisle, and had no need to shrink from the severer test of the mid-day sun."[129] When Miriam appears briefly to Kenyon, as she rides in a carriage with "the light of a gas-lamp"[130] flaring upon her face, and he is beckoned to come near, he sees her in richer garb and finally interprets the change as partly owing to a gem worn upon her bosom, "something that glimmered with a clear, red lustre, like the stars in a southern sky. Somehow or other, this colored light seemed an emanation of herself, as if all that was passionate and glowing, in her native disposition, had crystallized upon her breast, and were just now scintillating more brilliantly than ever, in sympathy with some emotion of her heart."[131] During the Carnival season Miriam appears to Kenyon "in one of those brilliant costumes largely kindled up with scarlet, and decorated with gold embroidery,"[132] though her smile shines out of melancholy eyes. There is still a "gleam of that fantastic, fitful gayety"[133] as she realizes how short her time with Donatello is. And when Kenyon meets her during their "sacred hour" in the midst of Carnival time, he is sure "that a pale, tear-stained face" is "hidden behind her mask."[134] So Hawthorne has pictured the always mysterious but changing character of Miriam by interfused colored light, making her resemble the conjuror's image to which he likens her.

Donatello, with his love of "the blessed daylight"[135] and his fear of the dark is himself like "one bright ray" of sunshine that "contrived to shimmer in and frolic around the walls"[136] of Miriam's shadowy chamber as he dances for her. The same ray of sunlight in the suburban villa that glimmers through Miriam's gloomy meditations, responds "pleasantly to Donatello's glance."[137] During the dance, he seems "to radiate jollity out of his whole nimble person."[138] But the appearance of the model at the Fountain of Trevi sets Donatello "all aflame with animal rage";[139] there is "a tiger-like fury gleaming from his wild eyes."[140] Yet it is his love for Miriam (when he sees her wild gestures and is warned to cast her off) that makes "a higher sentiment"[141] brighten upon his face. After the murder, "the glow of rage" is "still lurid on Donatello's face," and flashes out again "from his eyes."[142] But there comes also "the glow of that intelligence which passion had developed in him."[143] Later there settles over him "a dense and dark cloud,"[144] the dismal mood of his bewilderment "with the novelty of sin and grief."[145] Once Kenyon sees "a smile shining on his face"[146] that brings back the Faun, and once he sees Donatello's eyes glare wildly "like a wolf that meets you in the forest,"[147] when Kenyon mentions Miriam's name. But now Donatello, for the most part, lives in shadows; for the boy has now discovered for himself the old truth that "Time flies over us, but leaves its shadow behind."[148] The young master who once made the peasants' hovels glow "like sunshine," who, they said, "never darkened a doorway in his life,"[149] has lost the "pure, white, lustre,"[150] and must throw a cloud over his transparency, restraining his emotions, masking his face. Finally, at the suggestion of Kenyon that peace may come through service to mankind, "his face" brightens "beneath the stars."[151] And when at last he feels the blessing of the bronze pontiff upon his spirit, his eyes shine "with a serene and hopeful expression."[152] At Carnival time, when he makes it clear to Kenyon that his attempt to obtain earthly justice for his crime is not from argument "but only a sense, an impulse, an instinct, I believe, which sometimes leads me right," Kenyon sees "some of the sweet and delightful characteristics of the antique Faun." A playfulness comes "out of his heart," and glimmers "like firelight in his actions, alternating, or even closely intermingled, with profound sympathy and serious thought."[153] Firelight now, not sunlight, marks him a human creature; but the light has returned only because of the experience of penance, penitence, and faith, as he struggled toward heaven with his newly-discovered soul.

Hilda is "a fair young girl, dressed in white,"[154] "without a suspicion or a shadow" upon her "snowy whiteness,"[155] so that the artists appropriately call her Hilda the Dove. With "her light-brown ringlets, her delicately tinged, but healthful cheek," her face growing "beautiful and striking, as some inward thought and feeling" brightens, rises to the surface, and then passes out of sight again, it seems "as if Hilda were only visible by the sunshine of her soul."[156] "White doves and white thoughts"[157] are her companions.

She seems "an inhabitant of picture land, a partly ideal creature."[158] As Miriam says, "Hilda does not dwell in our mortal atmosphere; and . . . it will be as difficult to win her heart as to entice
down a white bird from its sunny freedom in the sky."[159] Kenyon
too sees "the white shining purity of Hilda's nature" as "a thing
apart."[160] After the murder the "white Hilda,"[161] sits sorrowing,
"her mind, so like sunlight in its natural cheerfulness," moving
"from thought to thought,"[162] but finding nothing to dwell upon,
for now she has Miriam's "dark secret."[163] When Hilda discovers
personally the existence of evil in the world, it is for her as for all
such persons, "as if a cloud had suddenly gathered over the morning light; so dark a cloud, that there seems to be no longer any
sunshine behind it or above it."[164] And her awful loneliness is "a
shadow in the sunshine," "a mist between her eyes and the pictures," "a chill dungeon," which keeps her "in its gray twilight."[165]
So she is painted, the picture of innocence suffering from another's
crime, painted with a blood spot on her white robe. Only when the
"dark story"[166] can be poured out in the confessional, after long
groping for God in the darkness and finding nothing but "a dread-
ful solitude,"[167] does Hilda shine again as though "imbued with
sunshine" or by "a glow of happiness"[168] that shines out of her. But
the evil deed that "spread out its dark branches so widely, that
the shadow" fell "on innocence as well as guilt"[169] softens and hu-
manizes Hilda, and when she returns she has "a gleam of delicate
mirthfulness in her eyes."[170] Kenyon, with "neither pole star above
nor light of cottage-windows here below," wants her for guide,
counselor, friend, "with that white wisdom" which clothes her "as
a celestial garment"[171]—wants her to guide him home.

By his few references to Kenyon's personal "coloration" or
"light" Hawthorne keeps him in the position of observer and narrator, who can appreciate and interpret other characters, and
whose need of light can be symbolic. His "light-brown beard,"[172]
and "gray blouse"[173] are once mentioned. But it is the lack of color
and need of light that Hawthorne wishes to emphasize as he refers
to Kenyon's "pale, sunless affection"[174] at Monte Beni where he
yearns for Hilda. For Kenyon it is as though "the idea of this girl"

is "like a taper of virgin wax, burning with a pure and steady flame, and chasing away the evil spirits out of the magic circle of its beams. It had darted its rays afar, and modified the whole sphere in which Kenyon had his being." When her lamp goes out, he at once finds himself "in darkness and astray."[175] It is the "white wisdom"[176] for which he pleads in asking Hilda to marry him.

The model is the totally black character of the work. The stories of this dark and bushy-bearded specter suggest that he has been groping for fifteen centuries in the darkness, longing for the blessed sunshine. He winks and turns uneasily from torches, "like a creature to whom midnight would be more congenial than noonday."[177] And he becomes Miriam's shadow. He is like Memmius who had once a moment's grace when he might have received "the holy light into his soul," but resisted the impulse, and "the light of the consecrated tapers, which represent all truth, bewildered the wretched man with everlasting error."[178] The only time the shadow turns "ashy pale"[179] is at Miriam's suggestion that he pray for rescue. He washes "his brown, bony talons" in the Fountain of Trevi like a madman and peers in "as if all the water of that great drinking-cup of Rome must needs be stained black or sanguine."[180] He is totally vile.

With the radiance of light Hawthorne also illuminates the design of his work, as can be discovered by looking at the lighting for his scenes. In order to simplify enough to make the pattern clear, I am going to suggest some eight or nine kinds of "lighting" that it seems to me Hawthorne uses for appropriate scenes: subterranean light, half-light, white light, golden-age light, moonlight, owl-tower light, pictured-window light, heavenly light, and carnival light.

In a chapter called "Subterranean Reminiscences" Hawthorne lets his characters wander "by torchlight through a sort of dream, in which reminiscences of church-aisles and grimy cellars—and chiefly the latter—seemed to be broken into fragments, and hopelessly intermingled." Passages of "dark-red, crumbly stone" evidence human bodies in niches along either side, discernible in torchlight as "white ashes."[181] It is a "labyrinth of darkness, which broods around the little glimmer"[182] of the tapers, their collected torches illuminating one small spot with "the great darkness spread all around it, like that immenser mystery which envelopes our little life."[183] Miriam vanishes into that dismal darkness, to return at last, "discernible by her own torchlight" from the "labyrinth of gloomy mystery." In the "duskiness" "just on the doubtful limit of obscurity, at the threshold of the small, illuminated chapel,"[184] "the smoky light of their torches, struggling with the massive gloom,"[185] reveals the shadow which had appeared "out of the void darkness of the catacomb."[186] Either Miriam led him, or he her, "into the torchlight, thence into the sunshine."[187] "The mysterious, dusky, death-scented apparition"[188] has appeared out of the great mysterious darkness to be an eternal shadow in Miriam's life: out of the surrounding darkness, the shadow of Evil.

It is the mixed character of Miriam that reveals itself in her studio, which seems "to be the outward type of a poet's haunted imagination." In her "shadowy room" with its closed, shuttered, and deeply curtained windows, except that one "was partly open to a sunless portion of the sky," Miriam has the "partial light . . . with its strongly marked contrast of shadow."[189] The "mysterious dusk"[190] of her studio is that of her soul.

Hilda, by contrast, may be seen "in the broad sunlight that brightened the shrine," where she kept alive the flame of the never-dying lamp, amidst "a flock of white doves, skimming, fluttering, and wheeling about the topmost height of the tower, their silver wings flashing in the pure transparency of the air."[191] This is the atmosphere that corresponds to the white light of Hilda's soul.

Outside the city, in the surburban villa, where a sweet "sunshine" gladdens the "gentle gloom"[192] of the leafy trees, where pines lift dense clumps of branches so high they look "like green islands . . . flinging down a shadow upon the turf," where the "dark flames" of cypress "spread dusk and twilight round about them instead of cheerful radiance," where "white and rose-colored" anemones and violets and daisies bloom, there "is an ideal landscape, a woodland scene that seems to have been projected out of the poet's mind."[193] Here in summer, "in the golden sunset," "the sunny shadows," "the flicker of the sunshine, the sparkle of the fountain's gush," "the green freshness"[194]—here, "green and blue lizards"[195] bask in the sun's warmth, and Donatello, unaware of Eden's fatal spell, the final charm of the malaria, throws himself full length upon the turf, or watches from a treetop "the fountains flashing in the sunlight."[196]

The moonlight ramble brings the company down out of the "faded and gloomy apartment"[197] into the courtyard where they look upward to a "sky full of light," which seems to have "a delicate purple or crimson lustre, or, at least, some richer tinge than the cold, white moonshine of other skies."[198] It gleams upon palace architectural ornaments, upon iron-barred windows prison-like in aspect, upon shabbiness and squalor. A cigar-vendor's lantern flares, a homeless dog barks, and falling water is heard but not seen, as the heavy walk begins. The Fountain of Trevi, "glistening, and dimpling in the moonlight,"[199] is reached, its "snowy jets" gushing up, its spouting streams falling "in glistening drops," its rivulets running over stones "mossy, slimy, and green with sedge." "The water, tumbling, sparkling, and dashing," pours itself into "a great marble-brimmed reservoir," filling it "with a quivering tide," "a snowy semi-circle of momentary foam," and "snow-points from smaller jets."[200] The moonshine "illuminating" all and "filling the basin, as it were, with tremulous and palpable light," flings into the basin three shadows, "all so black and heavy that they sink in the water."[201] As the party moves beneath an archway of the Coliseum, the moonlight fills and floods "the great empty space," glows "upon tier above tier of ruined, grass-grown arches," and makes them "even too distinctly visible."[202] But there is duskiness within the arches and there is "the great black cross in the centre," marking "one of the special blood-spots of the earth."[203] "A red twinkle of light" shows itself in the breadth of shadow, glimmers "through a line of arches," now throws "a broader gleam" as it rises out of some abyss of ruin, now is "muffled by a heap of shrubbery." The red light keeps "ascending to loftier and loftier ranges," till it stands "like a star where the blue sky" rests against the Coliseum's topmost wall. Here, surrounded by scenes of "the Savior's passion and suffering" sit the company "enjoying the moonlight and shadow, the present gayety and the gloomy reminiscences of the scene."[204] The model, like "a Gothic horror" enters the "peaceful moonlight scene,"[205] "the moonshine on his face" as he turns toward the artists; and Miriam shrinks back "into the deep obscurity of an arch" to throw off all self-control in a "brief fit of madness."[206] Reaching the precincts of the Forum, they stand upon the spot where a chasm is said to have opened, a "great dusky gap, impenetrably deep," and Miriam thinks "every person takes a peep into it in moments of gloom and despondency," and promises Hilda it will open for her, for "the chasm" is "merely one of the orifices of that pit of blackness that lies beneath us, everywhere."[207] Reaching the edge of the precipice, they can see "a long, misty wreath, just dense enough to catch a little of the moonshine,"[208] showing the course of the unseen river, and the moon gleaming on the dome of St. Peter's. "Literally dreaming on the edge of a precipice,"[209] Donatello and Miriam remain when the others leave. They see from "a deep, empty niche" "shaded from the moon,"[210] a figure come forth. As in a moonlit dream, the murder that Hilda sees is committed.

Withdrawing to his Owl Tower, the Count of Monte Beni moves in another light. "A gray, moss-grown tower," with "gray and yellow lichens"[211] clustering on its face without, it has, as Donatello says, "a weary staircase, and dismal chambers, and it is very lonesome at the summit." Kenyon tells him that "with its difficult steps, and the dark prison-cells you speak of, your tower resembles the spiritual experience of many a sinful soul, which nevertheless, may struggle upward into the pure air and light of Heaven at last!"[212] The narrow turret stair is "lighted in its progress by loopholes and iron-barred windows," and leads to the prisoner's cell. A little higher "a pair of owls" hop into "the darkest corner"[213] of an equally forlorn room. Up another flight of steps, in Donatello's own owl chamber, a "gray alabaster" skull rests "on a cushion of white marble,"[214] beneath the crucifix. One more flight leads to the summit from which Italy can be seen under "the broad, sunny smile of God"[215]—"smoky-hued tracts of the olive-orchards," "white villas, gray convents," gleaming river, and lakes opening "their blue eyes" to reflect heaven. The view is of "two or three varieties of weather . . . all at the same instant of time," here "quiet sunshine," there "great black patches of ominous shadow from the clouds" with a thunder-storm striding out of them. Behind the tempest brightens forth again "the sunny splendor, which its progress" has "darkened with so terrible a frown."[216] Here Kenyon relies on God's providence as he sees a little wider glimpse of His dealings with mankind, but Donatello sees only "sunshine on one spot, and cloud in another, and no reason for it in either case. The sun on you; the cloud on me! What comfort can I draw from this?" For him the experience is not universal but personal: from the little shrub, "with green and glossy leaves," "the only green thing there,"[217] trying to grow in a crevice of the crumbling mortar, he takes "a worm that would have killed it; an ugly creature"[218] and flings it over the battlements. So he will move from prisoned darkness to dusky knowledge, to penance and penitence with gray skull and cross, to the light of heaven, in the struggle of his own soul with the ugly worm of his individual sin.

The light from the pictures on the church walls contrasts sharply with the light of pictured glass. Frescos, painted by the early artists,

> glowing on the church walls, . . . might be looked upon as symbols of the living spirit that made Catholicism a true religion, and that glorified it as long as it retained a genuine life; they filled the transepts with a radiant throng of saints and angels, and threw around the high altar a faint reflection—as much as mortals could see, or bear—of a Diviner Presence. But now that the colors are so wretchedly bedimmed,—now that blotches of plastered wall dot the frescos all over, like a mean reality thrusting itself through life's brightest illusions,—the next best artist to Cimabue or Giotto or Ghirlandaio or Pinturicchio will be he that shall reverently cover their ruined masterpieces with whitewash![219]

What does not fade or change is "the special excellence of pictured glass," with the interfusing light throwing down the hues of "enduring and fadeless pictures." Kenyon believes that "there is no other such true symbol of the glories of the better world, where a celestial radiance will be inherent in all things and persons, and render each continually transparent to the sight of all."[220] When Donatello suggests the horror that there should be "a soul among them through which the light could not be transfused," Kenyon thinks that "perhaps this is to be the punishment of sin . . . that it shall insulate the sinner from all sweet society by rendering him impermeable to light, and, therefore, unrecognizable in the abode of heavenly simplicity and truth," leaving him in "the dreariness of infinite and eternal solitude."[221] The pictures in the windows are brilliant yet dim with reverence "because God himself is shining through them." Donatello sees Him glow "with Divine wrath." Kenyon says, "It is divine love, not wrath!" Still Donatello insists, "Each must interpret for himself."[222] At this point in Donatello's soul's growth, he can still see only the wrath, but at least he can see some light, and he understands that he must see the light for himself. Outside the cathedral, pictured windows are only "an incomprehensible obscurity, without a gleam of beauty." Kenyon interprets the meaning:

> All this . . . is a most forcible emblem of the different aspect of religious truth and sacred story, as viewed from the warm interior of belief, or from its cold and dreary outside. Christian faith is a grand cathedral, with divinely pictured windows. Standing without, you see no glory, nor can possibly imagine any; standing within, every ray of light reveals a harmony of unspeakable splendors.[223]

Catholicism's "multitude of external forms, in which the spiritual may be clothed and manifested," includes these "painted windows" "through which the celestial sunshine, else disregarded, may make itself gloriously perceptible in visions of beauty and splendor."[224] Hilda's pilgrimages to the churches of Rome are often "for the sake of wondering at their gorgeousness." Many "shine with burnished gold," "glow with pictures," show "a quarry of precious stones." Hawthorne says, "Unless words were gems, that would flame with many-colored light upon the page, and throw thence a tremulous glimmer into the reader's eyes, it were vain to attempt a description of a princely chapel."[225] The grandeur of St. Peter's dazzles out of sight the "shadowy edifice" of the imagination. It is not (as Hilda has indefinitely thought) misty, "dim and gray and huge," over-arched by a dome in the cloudy firmament; but rather the "splendor of the actual interior" glows before her eyes like "a gay piece of cabinet-work" or "a jewel-casket, marvelously magnified."[226] Yet Hilda mourns for the "dim, illimitable interior, which with her eyes shut she had seen from childhood." One afternoon, however, "its interior" beams upon her "with all the effect of a new creation." It seems "a magnificent, comprehensive, majestic symbol of religious faith."[227] The pavement of "many-colored marble" stretches out illimitably. "The dome! Rich, gorgeous, filled with sunshine, cheerfully sublime, and fadeless after centuries, those lofty depths seemed to translate the heavens to mortal comprehension, and help the spirit upward to a yet higher and wider sphere."[228] Still troubled at the thought of her mother's spirit finding her "ensnared by these gaudy superstitions," she strays "towards the hundred golden lights that swarm before the high altar." She sees several persons kneel "to kiss the toe of the brazen St. Peter . . . polished bright with former salutations," and "the glory of the church" is "darkened"[229] before her eyes. She kneels for a moment "under the ever-burning lamp that throws its rays upon the Archangel's face"[230] in the pictured struggle of Virtue against Evil (a picture which shadows herself). Somehow a hope, born out of her trouble, begins to glimmer in her dark despair. Seeing the sunshine "through the western windows," throwing "long shafts of light"—the "great beams of radiance," "made visible in misty glory, by the holy cloud of incense"—she feels as if the worship ascending heavenward acquires "celestial substance in the golden atmosphere"[231] to which it aspires, and she thinks of the Catholic privilege of flinging down the "dark burden at the foot of the cross," to go forth "to sin no more, nor be any longer disquieted; but to live again in the freshness and elasticity of innocence."[232] Feeling such an inestimable advantage to belong to Christianity itself, she pours out her "dark story"[233] to the priest and catches a glimpse of "the heavenly light"—not as a Catholic but as "a daughter of the Puritans"[234] in the World's Cathedral. When Kenyon sees her as he leans against "the marble balustrade that surrounds the hundred golden lights," his face shows "anxious gloom." Moving toward him in "the solemn radiance"[235] she seems "imbued with sunshine" or glowing with the happiness that shines out of her. She is a "bright, yet softened image,"[236] her beauty wrought by inward delight. His gloomy words meet her radiant smile; her heart spills over with happiness "like rich and sunny wine."[237] He says the church needs pictured windows; she finds that inconsistent with "so much richness of color," belonging instead with "a gorgeous dimness." He insists that daylight ought not enter here, as it is "out of keeping with the superabundant splendor."[238]

> It should stream through a brilliant illusion of saints and hier-archies, and old scriptural images, and symbolized dogmas, purple, blue, golden, and a broad flame of scarlet. Then, it would be just such an illumination as the Catholic faith allows to its believers. But, give me—to live and die in—the pure, white light of heaven![239]

The puzzled Hilda insists, "I love the white light too!"[240] Though Kenyon, troubled by Hilda's Catholic propensities, is contrasted gloomily with the light she radiates, together they admire as they leave the cathedral, "the remoteness of the glory behind the altar, and the effect of visionary splendor and magnificence imparted by the long bars of smoky sunshine."[241] Then they arrive at a symbolic interpretation which disregards the question of Catholicism. Dis-cussing the recovery of the golden candlestick of the Jews as they wonder whether it might have traveled to this point of the muddy, yellow Tiber, Hilda believes it shall be found again, and when the "seven lights are kindled and burning in it, the whole world will gain the illumination which it needs." She thinks it would make a wonderful "seven-branched allegory, full of poetry, art, philoso-phy, and religion." And "as each branch is lighted, it shall have a differently colored lustre from the other six; and when all the seven are kindled, their radiance shall combine into the intense white light of truth."[242] Such a conception burns brighter the more Kenyon looks at it. In this scene, Catholicism's forms—however far the forms have become only artificial—have suggested the great Christian truths, and the light of heaven has shined through even a smoky radiance of worship upon Virtue struggling with Evil—to bless with heavenly light.

Hawthorne paints the scene in the Corso in Carnival time with brilliant colors. Kenyon cannot appreciate "the long, blue streamer of Italian sky" above the splendid merriment—"bushels upon bushels of variously colored confetti,"[243] balconies flaunting "gay and gorgeous carpets, bright silks, scarlet cloths with rich golden fringes," "Gobelin tapestry, still lustrous with varied hues," or a ducal carriage with "three golden lackeys, clinging in the rear."[244] Yet he wanders through the street, where handfuls of thrown flour or lime hang "like smoke over a battle-field," or whiten "a black coat or a priestly robe," and make the youth's curly locks "irreverently hoary."[245] Miserably wilted nosegays, defiled from being trampled into the "wicked filth of Rome," are caught up from the mud and thrown again like crumpled, crushed hearts that have been "passed from hand to hand along the muddy street-way of life."[246] The "motley maskers"[247] pass before Kenyon "like a thin dream."[248] Though he sees many a contadina in "finery of scarlet, and decked out with gold or coral beads, a pair of heavy ear-rings, a curiously wrought cameo or mosaic brooch, and a silver comb or long stiletto among her glossy hair,"[249] he cannot find Miriam, whom he had seen as one of two figures "with an impenetrable black mask."[250] His care-stricken mood is inappropriate to the Carnival; not so the sudden arrest of the two black-masked figures. And in the midst of it at last appears the "pale, large-eyed, fragile beauty" of Hilda, looking through "the grotesque and gorgeous show, the chaos of mad jollity," for some object to assure her "that the whole spectacle was not an illusion."[251]

Perhaps the remarkable variety in Hawthorne's use of light is nowhere better illustrated than in *The Marble Faun*. The light which shines through his characters and illuminates his design paints the thought.

Scenes

It has already been hinted that in this work, again, Hawthorne paints the soul with Nature's language. Here he specifically causes his three artists to paint their inner selves in their works and to show their inner souls in their studios. Donatello, though not an artist, belongs to a family that creates "Sunshine," lives in a tower that pictures the movement of his soul, and is related to antique Nature and to the Nature of the suburban villa. The larger views of Rome or Italy speak pictures of civilization. Typically, Hawthorne draws together within each picture specific symbolic details to point his Truth.

Miriam's art is the outward expression of her soul. If one travels with Donatello up the staircase of an old palace to the studio of "Miriam Schaefer, artist in oils,"[252] he will discover in the shadowy room sketch after sketch of woman acting revengefully toward man, though the woman herself suffers, whatever her motive. Miriam says that these are "ugly phantoms that stole out of my mind; not things that I created, but things that haunt me."[253] The spectator will also see "sketches of common life, and the affections that spiritualize it," with the figure of Miriam always "portrayed apart" showing "an expression of deep sadness."[254] Finally, Miriam's self-portrait may be seen, the deep dark eyes, the black abundant hair, the rich sad beauty. And the dark beauty of the character lives in a dusky studio.

Hilda's art works are not original. "Endowed with a deep and sensitive faculty of appreciation," she has "the gift of discerning and worshipping excellence."[255] By this light of sympathy, she comes to a picture's central point, views as it were with the master's own eyes, and attains a perfect comprehension, which her command of hand enables her to copy. She seems to catch "the light which the old master had left upon the original in bestowing his final and most ethereal touch,"[256] and "from the dark, chill corner of a gallery" where "the light" comes "seldom and aslant" brings "the wondrous picture into daylight," and gives "all its magic splendor for the enjoyment of the world."[257] She dwells in an ethereal region, keeping the lamp alight far above the darkness. Her "masterpiece" which presents her own portrait is necessarily copied. She prophesies rather than evidences outwardly the suffering innocence of Beatrice Cenci. Her pictures, like her life, lack, perhaps, "the reality which comes only from a close acquaintance with life," and "with years and experience she might be expected to attain a darker and more forcible touch, which would impart to her designs the relief they needed."[258] Hilda's pure innocence gives her the wonderful insight of an excellent copyist; Hilda's suffering makes her necessarily a less perfect copyist.

Kenyon, the sculptor, lives in a studio where one may see the work *in process*, and where what the artist's "creative power has wrought . . . with a word"[259] takes shape in marble as mechanically skilled men work from the artist's plaster cast to make the outer marble release "the human countenance" which has long existed "within its embrace."[260] Here are both the dead pearl-fisher and the "grand, calm head of Milton," a likeness achieved in part by "long perusal and deep love of the 'Paradise Lost,' the 'Comus,' the 'Lycidas,' and 'L'Allegro.' "[261] Here are sculptured the white hand of Hilda, the "Cleopatra" almost a companion to Miriam, and the unfinished bust of Donatello propounding "the riddle of the soul's growth, taking its first impulse amid remorse and pain, and struggling through the incrustations of the senses."[262] Not a portrayer of his own soul merely, Kenyon rather is the sculptor who gives the three-dimensional image in the undecaying marble, whose work can be seen taking shape.

Donatello's "Sunshine," brought from his cellars by old Tomasco, has "the airy sweetness of youthful hopes, that no realities will ever satisfy." The pale golden liquor provides "more a moral than a physical enjoyment." Since one of its "most ethereal charms" is in its transitory qualities, if you linger "too long upon the draught," it becomes "disenchanted both of its fragrance and its flavor."[263] Never sold for money, impossible to transport, yet its "gentle exhilaration"[264] can be sociably enjoyed in the halls of Monte Beni. "Sunshine" symbolizes or pictures Donatello. And Donatello, the onetime playmate of the creatures of the woods, with his mythical harmony with nature belongs most in the Nature of the suburban villa, where even the birds may recognize him as something akin to themselves or else suppose him to have rooted and grown where they scramble across him as he lies on the turf. Describing the changed Donatello, Hawthorne writes, "Nature, in beast, fowl, and tree, and earth, flood, and sky, is what it was of old; but sin, care, and self-consciousness have set the human portion of the world askew."[265]

The ruins of the Roman world seem to encompass all the past of civilization, and the view of Italy from the summit of the Owl Tower is in effect a view of all human life. Or, to speak of a specific instance, the dead Capuchin, seeming in Miriam's imagination as she looks at the corpse to change into the likeness of the face so terrible in her remembrance, is perhaps a symbol, Hawthorne says, "of the deadly iteration with which she was doomed to behold the image of her crime reflected back upon her in a thousand ways, and converting the great, calm face of Nature, in the whole, and in its innumerable details, into a manifold reminiscence of that one dead visage."[266]

Characters

Each of Hawthorne's four characters is a mixture of Actuality and Meaning; and since Hawthorne centers the tale in Donatello's resemblance to the "Faun" of Praxiteles, the relation of each of the other characters to Donatello as faun will make a good beginning place for study of the characters. Hawthorne pictures the three artists as "simultaneously struck"[267] by the resemblance between Donatello and the "Faun." Miriam finds a "nameless charm" in the idea; Hilda, a perplexity that makes her not "quite like to think about it"; Kenyon makes an interpretation of the need for the Faun: "Nature needed, and still needs, this beautiful creature; standing betwixt man and animal, . . . and interpreting the whole existence of one to the other."[268] These introductory attitudes suggest the characters of the three Actual artists and make Kenyon, the sculptor, the major interpreter of meanings.

Hawthorne has Donatello playfully throw himself into the position of the statue of the Faun at Kenyon's request; then he states the miraculous resemblance. Afterwards he describes not Donatello but the "Faun" so that one can envision its grace and beauty, its charm of geniality and humor, its amiability and sensuality, its easy mirthfulness, "not incapable of being touched by pathos."[269] Then he develops the "character" of the Faun: "no principle of virtue," "true and honest by dint of his simplicity,"[270] capable of being educated through his emotions—"all the genial and happy characteristics of creatures that dwell in woods and fields," "mingled . . . with the kindred qualities in the human soul." He concludes that "the idea may have been no dream, but rather a poet's reminiscence of a period when man's affinity with nature was more strict, and his fellowship with every living thing more intimate and dear."[271] Only then does Hawthorne turn his attention to the character of Donatello in the second chapter entitled "The Faun." In this way he makes the *resemblance* the keynote, by looking first at the statue, then at the character of the young man. In this section Hawthorne says that "it was difficult to make out the character of this young man." He speaks of his being "so full of animal life, . . . so handsome," of his making no impression of incompleteness or of stinted nature; yet he explains that his friends allowed for him as for a child, that he had "an indefinable characteristic" that "set him outside of rules."[272] He suggests the resemblance further by letting Donatello not know his age and thus suggest, to Miriam's humor, his immortality on earth. In the young Italian, then, Hawthorne has a young man who will act in line with his nature and be psychologically true. In the Faun, Hawthorne has an idea which can be philosophically wrought out. Symbolized in the mixed character of Donatello is the Human Soul.

In Miriam, Hawthorne pictures a young woman with a mysterious past, haunted by a "spectral figure" that was her evil fate. "Not of the feeble nature which takes advantage of that obvious and poor resource in earthly difficulties," Hawthorne says, "she flung herself upon the world, and speedily created a new sphere."[273] "She was a beautiful and attractive woman, but based, as it were, upon a cloud, and all surrounded with misty substance; so that the result was to render her sprite-like in her most ordinary manifestations."[274] Caught by the "mysterious fascination" of the ill-omened model, morally estranged by her dark past, Miriam remains shadowy. But Hawthorne suggests, "Yet, let us trust, there may have been no crime in Miriam, but only one of those fatalities which are among the most insoluble riddles propounded to mortal comprehension; the fatal decree by which every crime is made to be the agony of many innocent persons, as well as of the single guilty one."[275] The early glimpse of Miriam as an idea is in Hilda's painting of Beatrice; yet the reader is quite sure she has many resemblances to Kenyon's temptress Cleopatra. Not quite Cleopatra, "fierce, voluptuous, passionate, tender, wicked, terrible, and full of poisonous and rapturous enchantment,"[276] yet the picture Hawthorne gives of Miriam is far from "incompatible with any shadow of darkness or evil."[277] If Hawthorne could keep the character of Miriam mysteriously dark, he could have a mixed character whose Actuality was rich, tantalizing, but not totally evil, yet whose Idea suggested an avenue through which Evil could tempt Donatello in a "Fall of Man" pattern. This means that even as she insists that she is not of Cleopatra's sisterhood, Miriam must arouse Kenyon's suspicion and the reader's.

Hilda as an idea represents the pure white light of Truth; as a young girl, however, she needs the sturdier quality, the deeper insight, that she gains from her great sorrow; and she shows the soul's growth through knowledge of the evil in the world. As Kenyon says of Hilda, "the white shining purity of Hilda's nature is a thing apart; and she is bound, by the undefiled material of which God molded her, to keep that severity which I, as well as you, have recognized."[278] At the level of Idea, this means Hilda's total rejection of Miriam in terms that while they keep Hilda true to that self, sound cruelly harsh:

If I were one of God's angels, with a nature incapable of stain, and garments that never could be spotted, I would keep ever at your side, and try to lead you upward. But I am a poor, lonely girl, whom God has set here in an evil world, and given her only a white robe, and bid her wear it back to Him, as white as when she put it on.[279]

At the same time Hilda suggests, more on the Actual level, that the "powerful magnetism" of Miriam "would be too much" for her. And speaking on both levels at once, she says, "The pure, white atmosphere, in which I try to discern what things are good and true, would be discolored."[280]

Kenyon's position as Actual observer and sculptor and his position as any human being attempting to understand God, Man, and the Universe can be much more easily blended into a single unified character. Since he is recognizably the person to whom the women turn for advice, reasonably a person who might strike up a friendship with Donatello and be invited to his tower, and at the same time a man of great sympathy and understanding, his judgments are frequently not only acceptable but seem to echo just what Hawthorne himself might have said. "The sculptor's sensibility, clear thought, and genius,"[281] make him capable of arriving at an interpretation of Truth at a more realistic, practical level than Hilda can attain as an individual; while his idealistic view of her white wisdom may be accepted as a romantic lover's picture or, at the level of meaning, a love of the intense white light of Truth.

Incidents

If Hawthorne's characters in this work are thought of as representative of "sides" of an idea, it may be that he suggests this in the single sentence quoted above as universalizing his Truth: "Every human life, if it ascends to truth or delves down to reality, must undergo a similar change; but sometimes, perhaps, the instruction comes without the sorrow; and oftener the sorrow teaches no lesson that abides with us."[282] Both Donatello and Kenyon ascend to Truth; Hilda and Miriam delve down to reality. In Kenyon the instruction comes without great and lasting sorrow; in Miriam, one wonders whether the sorrow has taught an abiding lesson.

The over-all structure of *The Marble Faun* has already been suggested, but perhaps one or two things may be said of the development through a series of scenes. An outline of the shift in scenes will indicate generally how Hawthorne moves from place to place to paint his meaning. Again it is noteworthy that in the fifty chapter titles no verb appears, while over half of the titles name characters, art objects, or places, and another twelve name happenings.

The arrangement of the big pictures in this gallery may be seen something like this: three artists observing a boy and a statue; three persons in the catacomb with a fourth, shadowed by a dusky figure, just entering the circle; Miriam in a dusky studio; Hilda tending the lamp in the shrine; Hilda and Beatrice; a faun and nymph in a sylvan dance, with a shadow entering; Kenyon (with Hilda) getting a glimpse of Miriam kneeling to the model; Kenyon showing Miriam "Cleopatra"; the company of artists in a room; the company on a moonlight ramble; Miriam and Donatello alone on the edge of the precipice, with Hilda glimpsing the murder; Kenyon and the murderers with the dead monk; Donatello rejecting Miriam; Hilda rejecting Miriam; Donatello passing by the windows of the Owl Tower as he moves down; Donatello moving up the stairway of the Owl Tower with Kenyon; Donatello and Kenyon, atop the Owl Tower, Kenyon viewing the world beneath cloud and sunshine, Donatello saving the plant from the worm; Donatello rejected by the animals; Kenyon catching the look of crime on Donatello's bust, and Donatello approving; Kenyon talking to Miriam in the marble saloon; Donatello, with Kenyon, on the penitential pilgrimage (stopping at shrines by the wayside, giving to the poor, seeing light through pictured windows, standing to receive the bronze pontiff's benediction); Hilda alone in her tower; Hilda alone in a picture gallery; Hilda confessing in the World's Cathedral; Hilda with Kenyon; Kenyon as the lamp goes out; Kenyon searching for Hilda; Kenyon watching the flight of doves; Kenyon meeting the disguised Donatello and Miriam; Kenyon at the Carnival, glimpsing the masked Miriam and Donatello, as Hilda hits him with a thrown rose-bud; Kenyon and Hilda in the light from the eye of the Pantheon, with the dark figure of Miriam watching and blessing them.

In this work Hawthorne was attempting to picture the growth of the soul, first by the development in Donatello, but also in terms of its development in Hilda, Miriam, and Kenyon. This means a complication of three parallel plots. Hawthorne names his first and last chapters with the same title, "Miriam, Hilda, Kenyon, Donatello," and works out the four developments skilfully. The one particular point in the middle of the work where he, to some extent, both pictures a part of the total story of all four characters and symbolizes the total story is in the chapters "The Owl Tower" and "On the Battlements." In "The Owl Tower" Donatello's struggle is symbolized and Kenyon's final view glimpsed; in the following chapter, Hilda's spirit speaks to Kenyon and Miriam's voice to Donatello. Hawthorne reduced the problems of four plots by making Miriam haunt Donatello's footsteps and by placing Kenyon with Donatello as friend and observer. But it was still necessary to picture Hilda's loneliness and the growth of her soul and to picture Kenyon's search for Hilda until he came to win the "truth" for himself. These sub-plots require a number of chapters between the high point of the bronze pontiff's benediction and the last pictures of Donatello with Miriam, when Donatello's purpose to give himself up to earthly justice completes the picture of his soul's growth.

The ambiguities resultant upon Hawthorne's method of creating two-level characters center in this work in four areas, all meant to remain shadowy. Donatello's connections with the race of fauns are developed as myths in which Hawthorne depends on traditions which at times conflict and thus enforces his idea while allowing the reader to accept or reject the myths. The hints about the furry ears related to an idea he meant merely to have a good time with. The passage in which Donatello calls the animals is in a doubly removed setting where Kenyon seems to hear the sounds of the creatures but sees only the brown lizard. For Miriam's past, too, Hawthorne offers a number of conflicting reports which successfully increase the shadows of ambiguity. And, as seen earlier, he gave a highly imaginative account of where Hilda might have been during her absence, again simply having a good time while he kept the shadows. One of the difficulties, however, that arises in the structural pattern of *The Marble Faun* centers in the mixture of Actuality and Imagination in the characters of Hilda and Miriam. Miriam, a "Beatrice" from the beginning of the story, can be more fully realized than Hilda, who comes to resemble "Beatrice" only after she witnesses the crime. By the point of Hilda's rejection of Miriam, the reader's sympathies are more likely to rest with Miriam, with whose more complete character he has been made better acquainted and forced to sympathize all along. But as far as Hawthorne's idea is concerned, Hilda's rejection is entirely justified. Probably Hawthorne attempted to circumvent this difficulty by the rather long ambiguous passage later in the work in which he lets Hilda wonder whether she has done well to turn from Miriam, who was her friend (but he carefully indicates that he supposes her "misled by her feelings"[283] into these fancies). Undeniably, however, Hawthorne fails to picture Hilda as an Actuality as vividly as would be desirable to blend with as high an idea as she represents, while with Miriam he is almost painfully successful in portraying Actuality. The necessary ambiguity of this incident is too weak and comes too late to be fully satisfactory.

One area which was not meant to remain shadowy for the sake of the tale nevertheless raised a question which was really outside of the story itself—the question of the "fortunate fall." Miriam raises the question, being somewhat taken with the idea; Kenyon feels it is not for mortal man to answer; Hilda totally rejects it even as a thought because "it annuls and obliterates whatever precepts of Heaven are written deepest within us."[284] And Hawthorne himself clearly agrees that Kenyon "rightly"[285] felt this idea to be perilous.

CONCLUSION

In the romances, as in the tales, Hawthorne's artistry in all its phases evidences the Transcendental aesthetic. In mingling Actuality and Imagination, in asserting Truth, in shining the light of Imagination through his pictures, in arranging scenes in correspondence with Nature, and in patterning incidents to show his thought, he is using Transcendental symbolism.

Conclusion

THE INVESTIGATIONS of these chapters have showed that Nathaniel Hawthorne was a Transcendental symbolist. His aesthetic theories were his own individual development of what may be termed the Transcendental aesthetic. A conscious artist, he worked out in beautiful detail the specific theories which he held of the work of the Artist.

It is clear that the development of his theories was coincident with his Transcendental associations. His acquaintance with the Peabody sisters and his marriage to Sophia; his associations with Bronson Alcott, Margaret Fuller, and Emerson; his attentive observations at Brook Farm; his friendship with Thoreau during "The Old Manse" years; his reading of major Transcendentalists—all contributed to the growth and refinement of aesthetic theories which he began to publish in tales and continued to express in prefaces to romances.

The Transcendental aesthetic of Emerson, similar to that of Alcott, Thoreau, and Margaret Fuller, was an extension of his metaphysical beliefs. The Transcendental aesthetic, however, touched other writers not holding Transcendental metaphysical beliefs—notably the Brahmins and Herman Melville as well as Hawthorne. Hawthorne recognized and stated the far-reaching influence of the Emersonian ideas as an influence not only upon others but upon himself.

Emerson saw the Over-Soul reflected through the evil as shadowed in things of earth. This is Hawthorne's high Reality reflected in muddy waters. Emerson saw the Artist as Representative Man, inspired to the pursuit of Beauty and enabled by Nature's language. This is Hawthorne's Artist of the Beautiful. For Emerson, light was the best of painters. For Hawthorne, the light of Imagination created the mirrored picture. Both men insisted that Truth is the highest purpose of the Work of Art and that light would mirror Truth. Emerson realized Man as the central figure in a frame of corresponding Nature and saw the Artist—at the thought level—creating such pictures of Man in a right series and procession. Hawthorne, in his purpose to reveal the truth of the human heart, placed Man in Nature in the same fashion—mingling Actuality and Imagination (at the thought level) and making his procession of scenes in the Neutral Territory reveal his Truth.

Such an understanding of Hawthorne's aesthetic intentions makes a passage-way by which the reader or critic can be led into the interior of Hawthorne's works, a preface to depths of meaning which the richly varied tales and romances have to reveal. Hawthorne's mingling of the Actual and the Imaginative uses specific details in varied ways, for the symbols are fluxional. His assertions of Truth are variously made. The true critic must appreciate Hawthorne's masterful handling of light to infuse his characters with life in intricately and artistically painted scenes. He must note how Hawthorne sees Man against Nature's scenery, how he mixes his characters of Actuality and Imagination, how the procession of scenes paints the truth of the human heart. Such a critic must not only permit Hawthorne the ambiguous shadows necessary to his method of handling character but must appreciate the enrichment of the unified meaning by those very shadows. Such a critic, sensitive to Hawthorne's own attempts to open the way to the understanding of his works, may then allow the Artist's minutely and "mechanically" beautiful butterfly to rest for a moment upon his own finger, and perhaps he may catch one glimpse of an even more beautiful Ideal butterfly disappearing into the celestial atmosphere.

Notes

CHAPTER I

[1] Preface to "Rappaccini's Daughter," *The Complete Works of Nathaniel Hawthorne, with Introductory Notes*, ed. George Parsons Lathrop (12 vols., Riverside Edition; Boston: Houghton, Mifflin and Co., 1883), II, 107. All subsequent references to Hawthorne's *Works* are to this edition. *Doctor Grimshawe's Secret; a Romance, by Nathaniel Hawthorne*, ed. Julian Hawthorne (Boston: J. R. Osgood & Co., 1883) is Vol. XIII of this edition.

[2] Hawthorne's words in a passage deleted from "The Hall of Fantasy" before it appeared in the *Mosses* collection. For a reproduction of the February, 1843, text see *The Pioneer: A Literary Magazine*, ed. James Russell Lowell (New York: Scholars' Facsimiles & Reprints, 1947), pp. 52–53.

[3] For histories of the Transcendental philosophy see Harold Clarke Goddard, *Studies in New England Transcendentalism* ("Columbia University Studies in English," Series II, Vol. II, No. 3; New York: The Columbia University Press, 1908), Henry David Gray, *Emerson: A Statement of New England Transcendentalism as Expressed in the Philosophy of Its Chief Exponent* ("Leland Stanford Junior University Publications," University Series; Stanford, California: Stanford University, 1917), and Octavius B. Frothingham, *Transcendentalism in New England: A History* (New York: G. P. Putnam's Sons, 1876).

[4] Randall Stewart, *Nathaniel Hawthorne: A Biography* (New Haven: Yale University Press, 1948).

[5] *See* Marion L. Kesselring, "Hawthorne's Reading, 1828–1850," *Bulle-*

tin of the New York Public Library, LIII (February, March, April, 1949), 55–71, 121–38, 173–94.

6 Hawthorne said in the preface to the 1851 edition of *Twice-Told Tales* that his purpose was "to open an intercourse with the world," *Works*, I, 17.

7 Caroline W. (Healey) Dall, *Margaret and Her Friends: or Ten Conversations with Margaret Fuller upon the Mythology of the Greeks and Its Expression in Art* (Boston: Roberts Bros., 1895), pp. 17–22.

8 *Love Letters of Nathaniel Hawthorne, 1839–41 and 1841–63* (2 vols.; Chicago: Privately Printed, The Society of the Dofobs, 1907), I, 107.

9 *The American Notebooks by Nathaniel Hawthorne*, ed. Randall Stewart (New Haven: Yale University Press, 1932), p. 78. All references to *American Notebooks* are to this edition; when Mrs. Hawthorne's edition is used (including a few pages not available in MS to Mr. Stewart), citation will be made to *Works*, Vol. IX.

10 *Love Letters*, II, 4ff.

11 Lindsay Swift, *Brook Farm: Its Members, Scholars, and Visitors* (National Studies in American Letters; New York: The Macmillan Co., 1900), pp. 8–9.

12 *Journals of Ralph Waldo Emerson, 1820–1876*, ed. Edward Waldo Emerson and Waldo Emerson Forbes (10 vols.; Boston: Houghton Mifflin Co., 1909–14), IV, 479. (This citation appears under the date June 13, 1838.) Subsequent references to Emerson, *Journals* are to this edition.

13 Rose Hawthorne Lathrop, *Memories of Hawthorne* (Boston: Houghton, Mifflin and Co., 1897), p. 29.

14 *Ibid.*, p. 16.

15 This Transcendental flight is from undated letters from Sophia to Elizabeth Peabody in the spring and summer of 1838 in Julian Hawthorne, *Nathaniel Hawthorne and His Wife: A Biography* (2 vols.; Boston: James R. Osgood and Co., 1884), I, 186. In Lathrop, *Memories*, p. 181, a letter from A. Bronson Alcott to Sophia (September 12, 1836) asks whether she has seen Emerson's *Nature*; if not, he suggests she let him send her a copy. Both Miss Peabody (Elizabeth) and S. A. Peabody, however, appeared in Emerson's *Journal* list of names to receive presentation copies; see citation from unpublished section of a MS *Journal* in Kenneth Walter Cameron's introduction to *Nature (1836) by Ralph Waldo Emerson* (New York: Scholars' Facsimiles & Reprints, 1940), pp. iv-v.

16 *Love Letters*, I, 103 (December 1, 1839).

17 *Ibid.*, p. 207ff.

18 The quotation appears probably some time after the reading, for Hawthorne has forgotten the precise source when he writes (March 23,

1848): "But it is with children as Mr [*sic*] Emerson, or somebody else, says it is with nature—you cannot see them so well when you look at them of set purpose. The best manifestations of them must take you at unawares," *ibid.*, p. 199. Stewart (*ibid.*, p. 325) recognizes this as an extension of Emerson's idea expressed in *Nature, Works*, I, 19:

> "The shows of day, the dewy morning, the rainbow, mountains, orchards in blossom, stars, moonlight, shadows in still water, and the like, if too eagerly hunted, become shows merely, and mock us with their unreality. Go out of the house to see the moon, and 't is mere tinsel; it will not please as when its light shines upon your necessary journey. The beauty that shimmers in the yellow afternoons of October, who ever could clutch it? Go forth to find it, and it is gone; 't is only a mirage as you look from the windows of diligence."

[19] Julian Hawthorne gives an account of Hawthorne's connection with the essays in *Hawthorne Reading: An Essay* (Cleveland, The Rowfant Club, 1902), pp. 120–21:

> "Emerson sent Hawthorne the volumes of his essays as they appeared, with his autograph in each of them; and the first edition of his 'Poems,' a slender volume, but full of the purest poetry, perhaps, ever written. Hawthorne read the essays, but was captivated by them somewhat less than his wife. 'I admired Emerson as a poet of deep beauty and austere tenderness,' said he, 'but sought nothing of him as a philosopher. And in truth the heart of many an ordinary man had, perchance, inscriptions which he could not read.' "

However, since Emerson, *Journals*, V, 519–20 (March 19, 1841) lists Sophia's name rather than Hawthorne's to receive a copy of *Essays, First Series*, this is probably the copy to which Julian has reference. Hawthorne's name is listed to receive the second volume of essays, Emerson, *Journals*, VI, 536–37 (October 15, 1844).

[20] *Ibid.*, pp. 441–42. The entry is dated August 25.

[21] Letters to Elizabeth Hoar, May 7–8, 1842; Charles King Newcomb, May 8; William Emerson, May 8; Margaret Fuller, May 9, in *The Letters of Ralph Waldo Emerson*, ed. Ralph L. Rusk (6 vols.; Morningside Heights: Columbia University Press, 1939), III, 50–53.

[22] *Love Letters*, II, 92 (May 27, 1842).

[23] *American Notebooks*, p. 176. The date is April 8, 1843.

[24] *Letters*, III, 97–99; Emerson in a letter to Hedge (November 21 and 25, 1842) says that last week he had invited a company to hear Alcott and his friends and Hawthorne came.

[25] *Love Letters*, II, 149 (June 10, 1844).

[26] George William Curtis, *Literary and Social Essays* (New York:

Harper & Bros., 1894), p. 25. The convenient location of the portrait of Dante may be questioned.

[27] *American Notebooks*, p. 160. This is dated August 16, Tuesday, 1842, but clearly was written a few days later. See pp. 159–61.

[28] *Ibid.*, p. 145.

[29] *Ibid.*, p. 166.

[30] *Ibid.*, p. 169; see pp. 166–69. Hawthorne purchased the *Musketaquid* for only seven dollars and wished he could acquire Thoreau's skill for so reasonable a rate.

[31] *Ibid.*, p. 175.

[32] Hawthorne writes of Thoreau that "he is a good writer—at least, he has written one good article, a rambling disquisition on Natural History in the last Dial," *ibid.*, p. 167; and says of the other unsigned article, "Then I read Margaret's article on Canova, which is good," *ibid.*, p. 177.

[33] *Ibid.* The article appeared in *The Dial*, III (April, 1843), 417–54. Signed "C. L.," it is attributed to Charles Lane by George Willis Cooke, *An Historical and Biographical Introduction to Accompany THE DIAL as Reprinted in Numbers for The Rowfant Club* (2 vols.; Cleveland: The Rowfant Club, 1902).

[34] "The Hall of Fantasy," *The Pioneer*, pp. 52–53.

[35] *American Notebooks*, p. 177.

[36] *Ibid.*, pp. 166–67. This entry is dated September 1, 1842. Thoreau's article appeared in *The Dial* for July, 1842.

[37] Cf. his comments on the exclusiveness of Transcendentalists, *ibid.*, p. 167; and his symbolic handling of Transcendentalism in "The Celestial Railroad," *Works*, II, 224.

CHAPTER II

[1] These particular names all appear in a single paragraph of "The Over-Soul," *The Complete Works of Ralph Waldo Emerson*, ed. Edward Waldo Emerson (12 vols., Centenary Edition; Boston: Houghton, Mifflin and Co., 1903–1904), II, 268–70. All references to *Works* are to this edition.

[2] *Ibid.*, p. 139.

[3] "Nature," *ibid.*, I, 64.

[4] "Worship," *ibid.*, VI, 213.

[5] "Progress of Culture," *ibid.*, VIII, 221.

[6] "Nature," *ibid.*, I, 24. In "The Transcendentalist," *ibid.*, p. 354, Emerson explains the Transcendentalists' choice of Beauty: "In the eternal trinity of Truth, Goodness, and Beauty, each in its perfection including the three, they prefer to make Beauty the sign and head," and their

reason is cited, *ibid.*, p. 355: "We call the Beautiful the highest, because it appears to us the golden mean, escaping the dowdiness of the good and the heartlessness of the true."

7 "Modern Aspects of Letters," *The Early Lectures of Ralph Waldo Emerson*, ed. Stephen E. Whicher and Robert E. Spiller (Cambridge: Harvard University Press, 1959), I (1833–1836), 382. This volume will be referred to as *Early Lectures* in subsequent citations. Cf. the lecture "Michael Angelo Buonaroti," *ibid.*, p. 110, where Emerson explains that artist's interrelation of the trinity Beauty, Truth, and Goodness: "As in the first place he sought to approach the Beautiful by the study of the True, so he failed not to make the next step of progress and to seek Beauty in its highest form, that of Goodness."

8 "Powers and Laws of Thought," *Works*, XII, 17.

9 "The Bohemian Hymn," *ibid.*, IX, 359.

10 "Nature," *ibid.*, I, 34.

11 "The Poet," *ibid.*, III, 14.

12 "Nature," *ibid.*, I, 26.

13 "Plato; or, The Philosopher," *ibid.*, IV, 62.

14 "Beauty," *ibid.*, VI, 306. From the body of man, to the celestial sphere of man's mind, to the higher sphere of his moral system, "all things ascend," Emerson explains in "Wealth," *ibid.*, pp. 124–25.

15 "History," *ibid.*, II, 12. Related always to the "terrific unity, in which all things are absorbed. . . . Nature is the manifold. The unity absorbs. . . . Nature opens and creates. These two principles reappear and interpenetrate all things, all thought; the one, the many," Emerson says in "Plato; or, The Philosopher," *ibid.*, IV, 51. He found Oneness and Otherness as the base of the constitution of the world; in *ibid.*, p. 48, he set as the problem of thought the separation and reconciliation of these two:

"The mind is urged to ask for one cause of many effects; then for the cause of that; and again the cause, diving still into the profound: self-assured that it shall arrive at an absolue and sufficient one,—a one that shall be all . . . . Urged by an opposite necessity, the mind returns from the one to that which is not one, but other or many, from cause to effect; and affirms the necessary existence of variety, the self-existence of both, as each is involved in the other."

Emerson's emphasis on individuality is of the individuality in relationship to unity. His explanation of his poem "The Sphinx," makes this clear, as quoted from 1859 notebook, in notes on the poem, *ibid.*, IX, 412:

"The perception of identity unites all things and explains one by another. . . . But if the mind live only in particulars, and see only differences (wanting the power to see the whole—all in each), then the world addresses to this mind a question it cannot answer, and each new fact tears it in pieces, and it is vanquished by the distracting variety."

16 "Beauty," *ibid.*, VI, 303.

17 "Shakespeare; or, The Poet," *ibid.*, IV, 216.

18 "Address" (Divinity School), *ibid.*, I, 131. Cf. "Beauty," *ibid.*, VI, 301, and "Nature," *ibid.*, I, 50, for emphasis on seeing the more delicious beauty through the forms.

19 "Compensation," *ibid.*, II, 101.

20 "Intellect," *ibid.*, II, 340.

21 *Ibid.*, III, 4.

22 "Swedenborg; or The Mystic," *ibid.*, IV, 121.

23 "Nature," *ibid.*, I, 27.

24 "The Over-Soul," *ibid.*, II, 270.

25 "Self-Reliance," *ibid.*, p. 45.

26 "Education," *ibid.*, X, 133.

27 *Journals*, II, 520.

28 "New England Reformers," *Works*, III, 282.

29 "Immortality," *ibid.*, VIII, 333. Every man becomes both a partialist and a universalist, a partialist because he is one of Nature's manifold effects; a universalist because he partakes of the Identity.

30 "Michael Angelo," *ibid.*, XII, 219.

31 "Fate," *ibid.*, VI, 8.

32 "Heroism," *ibid.*, II, 249.

33 "Music," *ibid.*, IX, 365.

34 "The Over-Soul," *ibid.*, II, 296. When man opens his heart and mind to the sentiment of virtue, "he learns that his being is without bound; that to the good, to the perfect, he is born, low as he now lies in evil and weakness," Emerson explains in the Divinity School "Address" in *ibid.*, I, 120. "Every thing has two sides, a good and an evil," runs the doctrine of compensation; however, the soul is a deeper fact, "Compensation," *ibid.*, II, 120.

35 "Nature," *ibid.*, I, 45.

36 "The Method of Nature," *ibid.*, p. 202.

37 "Destiny," *ibid.*, IX, 31. In "The Tragic," Emerson sees that "as the salt sea covers more than two thirds of the surface of the globe, so sorrow encroaches in man on felicity," *ibid.*, XII, 405, and in what many would consider un-Emersonian tones he continues:

> "I do not know but the prevalent hue of things to the eye of leisure is melancholy. In the dark hours, our existence seems to be a defensive war, a struggle against the encroaching All, which threatens surely to engulf us soon, and is impatient of our short reprieve."

The good does not make up all the picture, for "evermore in the world is this marvellous balance of beauty and disgust, magnificence and rats," he says in "Considerations by the Way," *ibid.*, VI, 255.

[38] "Spiritual Laws," *ibid.*, II, 155.

[39] "Domestic Life," *ibid.*, VII, 126.

[40] "Let us build altars to the Blessed Unity," Emerson says; "the indwelling necessity plants the rose of beauty on the brow of chaos, and discloses the central intention of Nature to be harmony and joy," "Fate," *ibid.*, VI, 48.

[41] "Nature," *ibid.*, I, 73–74. "Society gains nothing whilst a man, not himself renovated, attempts to renovate things around him," Emerson states in "New England Reformers," *ibid.*, III, 261. In "The Fugitive Slave Law," *ibid.*, XI, 234, he says the devil nestles comfortably into all constitutions; "to interpret Christ it needs Christ in the heart."

[42] "English Literature: Introductory," *Early Lectures*, pp. 224–25.

[43] "The Enchanter," *Works*, IX, 372. Cf. "The Poet," *ibid.*, III, 15ff.

[44] *Ibid.*, p. 30.

[45] *Ibid.*, p. 6.

[46] "Poetry and Imagination," *ibid.*, VIII, 38.

[47] Emerson criticizes Goethe in his "Goethe; or, The Writer," for failure on these very points, *ibid.*, IV, 284.

[48] "The Over-Soul," *ibid.*, II, 289.

[49] "Poetry and Imagination," *ibid.*, VIII, 29.

[50] *Journals*, VII, 500–501. The statement continues, "and, secondly, the way things actually fall out, that is, Fate. Fate and Faith, these two; and it seems as if justice were done, if the Faith is vindicated in the sentiments of the heroes of the tale, and Fate in the course and issue of the events." See "Poetry and Imagination," *Works*, VIII, 31, for the assertion that poetry is faith.

[51] *A Correspondence between John Sterling and Ralph Waldo Emerson*, ed. Edward Waldo Emerson (Boston: Houghton, Mifflin and Co., 1897), pp. 36–37.

[52] "The Transcendentalist," *Works*, I, 338.

[53] "Art," *ibid.*, VII, 40.

[54] "Poetry and Imagination," *ibid.*, VIII, 21.

[55] "Art," *ibid.*, VII, 50.

[56] "Inspiration," *ibid.*, VIII, 271.

[57] From "Fragments on the Poet and the Poetic Gift," *ibid.*, IX, 333.

[58] "Poetry and Imagination," *ibid.*, VIII, 39.

[59] "Experience," *ibid.*, III, 69.

[60] *Ibid.*, IX, 8.

[61] "Poetry and Imagination," *ibid.*, VIII, 31.

[62] "The Poet," *ibid.*, III, 39. "Beauty chased he everywhere," says Emerson of his ideal poet Seyd, in "Beauty," *ibid.*, IX, 275.

63 "Nature," *ibid.*, I, 19. Cf. "Experience," *ibid.*, III, 49.

64 "The Poet," *ibid.*, p. 4.

65 "Poetry and Imagination," *ibid.*, VIII, 42.

66 "Inspiration," *ibid.*, p. 274.

67 *Ibid.*, II, 332.

68 "Goethe; or The Writer," *ibid.*, IV, 281.

69 "Intellect," *ibid.*, II, 336.

70 "The Poet," *ibid.*, III, 13.

71 "Goethe; or, The Writer," *ibid.*, IV, 262.

72 "Nature," *ibid.*, I, 23.

73 *Ibid.*, p. 43.

74 *Ibid.*

75 "Poetry and Imagination," *ibid.*, VIII, 30.

76 "Michael Angelo," *ibid.*, XII, 233. The great painter-sculptor was not taken by mere superficial beauty but saw through it.

77 "The Poet," *ibid.*, III, 20.

78 "Poetry and Imagination," *ibid.*, VIII, 19.

79 "Intellect," *ibid.*, II, 335.

80 See "Shakspear [First Lecture]," *Early Lectures*, pp. 289ff.

81 "The Poet," *Works*, III, 18–19.

82 "Poetry and Imagination," *ibid.*, VIII, 17.

83 *Ibid.*

84 *Ibid.*, p. 27.

85 "The Poet," *ibid.*, III, 34.

86 See W. T. Harris, "Ralph Waldo Emerson," in *Atlantic*, L (August, 1882), 238–52, and cf. his "The Dialectical Unity in Emerson's Prose," *Journal of Speculative Philosophy*, XVIII (April, 1884), 195–202, for evidence of early suggestions in the direction of such an interpretation. Walter Blair and Clarence Faust use Emerson's key to Plato's method in a more extensive analysis and demonstrate Emerson's use of his theory in "Emerson's Literary Method," *Modern Philology*, XLII (November, 1944), 79–95. Vivian C. Hopkins, *Spires of Form: A Study of Emerson's Aesthetic Theory* (Cambridge: Harvard University Press, 1951) emphasizes the spiral in a study of the creative process, the work of art, and the reception by the observer. Sherman Paul, *Emerson's Angle of Vision: Man and Nature in American Experience* (Cambridge: Harvard University Press, 1952) develops Emerson's view of Man and Nature to understand his aesthetics. Ray Benoit, "Emerson on Plato: The Fire's Center," *American Literature*, XXXIV (January, 1963), 487–98, catches a similar vision.

87 "Plato; or, The Philosopher," *Works*, IV, 68.

88 *Ibid.*, p. 56.

89 "Michael Angelo," *ibid.*, XII, 218.

90 "Poetry and Imagination," *ibid.*, VIII, 17.

91 *Journals*, IX, 424–25.

92 See *Works*, X, note on p. 557 for this quotation of a passage from the lecture which was omitted in the essay "The Preacher." Emerson quotes from *Méthode et Entretien d'Atelier* by Thomas Couture.

93 "Europe and European Books," *The Dial*, III (April, 1843), 515.

94 "Perpetual Forces," *Works*, X, 78.

95 "Beauty," *ibid.*, VI, 302–304.

96 *Ibid.*, X, 557.

97 "Nature," *ibid.*, I, 15.

98 *Ibid.*

99 "Poetry and Imagination," *ibid.*, VIII, 45. See also "Nature," *ibid.*, I, 50.

100 *Journals*, VIII, 98–99.

101 Edward Waldo Emerson, in *Works*, VI, note on p. 427, quotes an 1860 *Journal* entry, "Nature is a mere mirror, and shows to each man only his own quality."

102 "Beauty," *Works*, VI, 294.

103 "The Poet," *ibid.*, III, 9–10.

104 "The Man of Letters," *ibid.*, X, 255–56. In "Europe and European Books," *The Dial*, III (April, 1843), 515, he writes, "His fable must be a good story, and its meaning must hold as pure truth."

105 "The Poet," *Works*, III, 11.

106 "Nature," *ibid.*, I, 23–24.

107 *Ibid.*, p. 43.

108 *Ibid.*, p. 44.

109 "Nominalist and Realist," *ibid.*, III, 234.

110 "Poetry and Imagination," *ibid.*, VIII, 17.

111 "Nature," *ibid.*, I, 20–21.

112 *Ibid.*, p. 32.

113 *Ibid.*, p. 9.

114 "Poetry and Imagination," *ibid.*, VIII, 12.

115 "Behavior," *ibid.*, VI, 169.

116 "Poetry and Imagination," *ibid.*, VIII, 13.

117 These remarks are made on Emerson's having looked at the painter S. G. Ward's drawings and prints, *Journals*, V, 33. This portion is highly abridged in the first paragraph in the essay on "Art," *Works*, II, 351.

118 "Nature," *ibid.*, I, 67.

119 "The Poet," *ibid.*, III, 13.

120 "Spiritual Laws," *ibid.*, II, 156.

121 "Goethe; or, The Writer," *ibid.*, IV, 261.

122 "Poetry and Imagination," *ibid.*, VIII, 43.

123 "Shakspear [Second Lecture]," *Early Lectures*, p. 311.

124 "Nature," *Works*, I, 54.

125 *Ibid.*, pp. 51–52.

126 "Art," *ibid.*, II, 356.

127 "Illusions," *ibid.*, VI, 319.

128 "Books," *ibid.*, VII, 216.

129 *Ibid.*

130 "Poetry and Imagination," *ibid.*, VIII, 23.

131 "Fate," *ibid.*, VI, 42.

132 "Nominalist and Realist," *ibid.*, III, 245–46.

133 "Compensation," *ibid.*, II, 102.

134 "Self-Reliance," *ibid.*, p. 50. Cf. "That which I call right or goodness, is the choice of my constitution," in "Spiritual Laws," *ibid.*, p. 140.

135 "Plato; or, The Philosopher," *ibid.*, IV, 51.

136 "The Method of Nature," *ibid.*, I, 204.

137 "The Poet," *ibid.*, III, 20.

138 "Hall of Fantasy," as published in the *Pioneer*, p. 53.

139 The "Orphic Sayings" referred to appeared in I (July, 1840), 85–98 and I (January, 1841), 351–61. Page numbers are cited with each quotation. The paragraph indications are not necessarily Alcott's.

140 *The Dial*, I (July, 1840), 97.

141 *Memoirs of Margaret Fuller Ossoli*, ed. R. W. Emerson, W. H. Channing and J. D. Clarke (2 vols.; Boston: Phillips, Sampson and Co., 1852), II, 15–18.

142 Margaret Fuller Ossoli, *Life Without and Life Within: or, Reviews, Narratives, Essays, and Poems*, ed. Arthur B. Fuller (New York: The Tribune Association, 1859), p. 391.

143 *Ibid.*

144 *Memoirs of Fuller*, I, 342.

145 "A Short Essay on Critics," *The Dial*, I (July, 1840), 7.

146 "Fragmentary Thoughts from Margaret Fuller's Journal," *Life Without and Life Within*, p. 348.

147 *The Writings of Henry David Thoreau* (20 vols., Walden Edition; Boston: Houghton Mifflin Co., 1906), I, 182. Hereafter cited *Writings of Thoreau*.

148 *Journals* (ed. Bradford Torrey and F. H. Allen as 14 vols. of the Walden edition of Thoreau), III, 155f. Hereafter cited as Thoreau, *Journals*.

149 "A Week," *Writings of Thoreau*, I, 350.

150 Thoreau, *Journals*, III, 236.

151 "A Week," *Writings of Thoreau*, I, 79.

152 *Ibid.*, p. 310.

153 "Letter to Harrison Blake," *ibid.*, VI, 173–74.

154 "A Week," *ibid.*, I, 94–95.

155 *Ibid.*, p. 369.

156 *Ibid.*, pp. 399–400.

157 *Ibid.*, p. 106.

158 Thoreau, *Journals*, I, 167.

159 "A Week," *Writings of Thoreau*, I, 353.

160 *Ibid.*, p. 351.

161 Charles Reid Metzger in *Thoreau and Whitman: A Study of Their Esthetics* (Seattle: University of Washington Press, 1961) thinks "possibly the most important thing about Thoreau's aesthetics is its different emphasis." Not so broad as Emerson's, it is more emphatic, exploring especially two facets Thoreau found relevant to his own life, "economy and the primacy of the individual life," p. 38.

162 See Lowell's 1855 lecture, "The Function of the Poet," available in *Major American Poets*, ed. Harry Hayden Clark ("American Literature Series"; New York: American Book Co., 1936), pp. 528–37, for a single rather complete statement of the Transcendental aesthetic. Holmes, in scattered passages through *The Autocrat of the Breakfast Table* (1857), asserts a sympathy with Transcendental theories of art. See especially the remarks of his friend the Poet which introduce Chapter V. In an 1870 lecture, "Mechanism in Thought and Morals," (See for excerpts, *Oliver Wendell Holmes: Representative Selections*, ed. S. I. Hayakawa and Howard Mumford Jones ["American Writers Series"; New York: American Book Co., 1939], pp. 377–99), he expresses a belief in inspiration quite in accord with his explanation of the inspired writing of "The Chambered Nautilus," a poem which itself has Transcendental meanings.

163 The friendship Hawthorne felt for Longfellow extended to appreciation for his poetry. He wrote Longfellow in the last year of his own life: "I take vast satisfaction in your poetry, and take very little in most other men's, except it be the grand old strains that have been sounding all through my life." Quoted in *American Notebooks*, note on page 317.

164 *The Works of Henry Wadsworth Longfellow*, ed. Samuel Longfellow (14 vols., Standard Library Edition; Boston: Houghton, Mifflin and Co., 1886–91), VIII, 291. Subsequent citations to Longfellow *Works* are to this edition.

165 *Ibid.*, p. 141.

166 *Ibid.*, p. 150.

167 "Table-Talk," *Final Memorials of Henry Wadsworth Longfellow*, ed. Samuel Longfellow (Boston: Ticknor and Co., 1887), p. 378.

168 Longfellow, *Works*, VIII, 28.

169 "Michael Angelo: A Fragment," *ibid.*, VI, 144.

170 *Ibid.*, p. 167.

171 Flemming in *Hyperion, ibid.*, VIII, 174–75.

172 *Ibid.*, p. 366.

173 *Ibid.*, p. 173.

174 See Kavanaugh's talk with Mr. Churchill, *ibid.*, pp. 415–16.

175 *Ibid.*, III, 267.

176 See his criticism of Emerson in a letter to Evert Duyckinck, *The Letters of Herman Melville*, ed. Merrell R. Davis and William H. Gilman (New Haven: Yale University Press, 1960), pp. 78–80. Melville reports being agreeably surprised at an Emerson lecture, and says, "I love all men who *dive*," but remarks "I could readily see in Emerson, notwithstanding his merit, a gaping flaw. It was, the insinuation, that had he lived in those days when the world was made, he might have offered some valuable suggestions." See also "Marginalia," in *Essays* by R. W. Emerson; First Series (Boston, 1847), as quoted in *The Portable Melville*, ed. Jay Leyda ("The Viking Portable Library"; New York: The Viking Press, 1952), p. 601.

177 He complains that Emerson's "belly . . . is in his chest, & his brains descend down into his neck," *Letters*, p. 80. Contrarily, Hawthorne is an artist with both heart and mind; see "Hawthorne and His Mosses," where the Truth-seeker is identified with Hawthorne, who is a man of "intricate, profound heart" and "great, deep intellect," *Portable Melville*, pp. 404ff.

178 Where Emerson wrote, "The good, compared to the evil which he sees, is as his own good to his own evil," Melville's marginal comment began, "A Perfectly good being, therefore, would see no evil,—But what did Christ see?—He saw what made him weep," "Marginalia," quoted in *ibid.*, p. 600. And where Emerson extended this correspondence to the Poet's use, saying, "Also, we use defects and deformities to a sacred purpose, so expressing our sense that the evils of the world are such only to the evil eye," Melville asks vehemently, "What does the man mean?" *ibid.*, p. 601. It was the "great power of blackness" in Hawthorne that so fixed and fascinated Melville; see "Hawthorne and His Mosses," *ibid.*, pp. 406–407.

179 *Mardi, The Works of Herman Melville* (12 vols., Standard Edition; London: Constable and Co., Ltd., 1922–23), IV, 54.

180 *Moby-Dick; or, The Whale*, ed. Luther S. Mansfield and Howard P. Vincent (Vol. VI of *Complete Works*, ed. Howard P. Vincent; New York: Hendricks House, 1952) p. 114. All citations to *Moby-Dick* are to this edition.

181 *Ibid.*, p. 520.

182 *Mardi, Works*, IV, 328.

183 *Moby-Dick*, p. 310.

184 *Ibid.*, pp. 161–62.

[185] *Ibid.*, p. 427.

[186] "Hawthorne and His Mosses," *Portable Melville*, p. 400.

[187] *Mardi, Works*, IV, 276–77.

[188] *Ibid.*, p. 326.

[189] *Ibid.*, p. 55.

[190] *Ibid.*, p. 326.

[191] *Ibid.*, p. 329.

[192] *Letters*, p. 70.

[193] *Ibid.*, p. 71.

[194] *The Confidence Man*, ed. Elizabeth S. Foster (New York: Hendricks House, 1954), p. 207. All citations to *The Confidence Man* are to this edition.

[195] *Mardi, Works*, IV, 328.

[196] *The Confidence Man*, pp. 206–207.

[197] *Letters*, p. 146.

[198] *The Confidence Man*, p. 77.

[199] Merlin Bowen, *The Long Encounter: Self and Experience in the Writings of Herman Melville* (Chicago: University of Chicago Press, 1960).

[200] *The Confidence Man*, pp. 270–71.

[201] *Mardi, Works*, IV, 327.

[202] A recent study of Melville's theories is a University of Illinois dissertation by Allen Hayman, "Herman Melville's Theory of Prose Fiction: in Contrast with Contemporary Theories," *Dissertation Abstracts*, XXI (June, 1961), p. 3782.

[203] Goddard, p. 201.

[204] Frothingham, p. 355. Cf. Vernon Louis Parrington, *The Romantic Revolution in America, 1800–1860*, Vol. II of *Main Currents in American Thought: An Interpretation of American Literature from the Beginnings to 1920* (New York: Harcourt, Brace and Co., 1927), pp. 379ff.

[205] This is a portion of a passage on his contemporaries which Hawthorne deleted from "The Hall of Fantasy" before publishing it in the *Mosses* collection. See the *Pioneer*, pp. 52–53.

[206] Hawthorne, *Works*, II, 107.

[207] "The Old Manse," *ibid.*, p. 13.

[208] See *Nature*, Emerson, *Works*, I, 17: "The dawn is my Assyria; the sunset and moonrise my Paphos. . . ."

[209] Cited in Bertha Faust, *Hawthorne's Contemporaneous Reputation: A Study of Literary Opinion in America and England, 1828–1864*. (Ph.D. Dissertation; Philadelphia: Pennsylvania University, 1939), p. 112. The reviewer wrote in *Tait's Edinburgh Magazine*, XXII (January, 1855), 33–41.

210 Hawthorne, *Works*, II, 41–42.

211 *Ibid.*, V, 43. The contrast in environment is between the people Hawthorne meets at the Custom House and such associates as the Brook Farmers, Emerson, Ellery Channing, Thoreau, Hillard, Longfellow, and Alcott. It is noteworthy that Longfellow's name appears in the group, indicating a higher appreciation for the group as a whole.

CHAPTER III

1 "Preface," *The Snow-Image*, Hawthorne, *Works*, III, 385.

2 *Ibid.*, XII, 349.

3 "Preface," *The Snow-Image, ibid.*, III, 388.

4 *Ibid.*

5 James Thomas Fields, *Hawthorne* (Boston: J. R. Osgood and Co., 1876), p. 59.

6 "Preface," *The House of the Seven Gables, Works*, III, 13.

7 *Ibid.*, II, 139.

8 "The Artist of the Beautiful," *ibid.*, p. 525.

9 *Love Letters*, I, 5.

10 *Ibid.*, p. 113.

11 *Ibid.*, p. 122.

12 "The Artist of the Beautiful," *Works*, II, 524.

13 *Passages from the French and Italian Note-Books, ibid.*, X, 545. Italics mine.

14 *American Notebooks*, p. 201.

15 "The Old Apple Dealer," *Works*, II, 503.

16 "The Artist of the Beautiful," *ibid.*, p. 525.

17 "A Virtuoso's Collection," *ibid.*, pp. 558–59.

18 "Rappaccini's Daughter," *ibid.*, p. 139.

19 "The Old Manse," *ibid.*, p. 16. The poet in "The Canterbury Pilgrims" in his "vague reverie, which he called thought," watched the moonlight mingling with the water of a spring; "in its crystal bosom, . . . beholding all heaven reflected there, he found an emblem of a pure and tranquil breast." See *ibid.*, III, 524. This echoes Hawthorne's making of the symbol of the spiritual capacity in the soul; since the lesson could be drawn from any mud puddle and was taught us everywhere, it must be true.

20 *American Notebooks*, p. 170.

21 *French and Italian Note-Books, Works*, X, 282.

22 *Ibid.*, I, 509.

23 *Ibid.*, p. 514.

24 *The Marble Faun, ibid.*, VI, 298.

25 *American Notebooks*, p. 188.

26 *The English Notebooks by Nathaniel Hawthorne*, ed. Randall Stewart (The Modern Language Association of America, General Series XIII; New York: Modern Language Association of America; London: Oxford University Press, 1941), p. 101. Further references to *English Notebooks* are to this edition.

27 Author comment in *Septimius Felton, Works*, XI, 240.

28 *American Notebooks*, p. 106.

29 *Love Letters*, I, 65.

30 "The Birthmark," *Works*, II, 69.

31 *American Notebooks*, p. 197.

32 "Earth's Holocaust," *Works*, II, 449.

33 "Sunday at Home," *ibid.*, I, 34.

34 *Ibid.*, II, 407–408.

35 *Ibid.*, p. 413.

36 *American Notebooks*, p. 97.

37 "Rappaccini's Daughter," *Works*, II, 142.

38 "Egotism; or, The Bosom Serpent," *ibid.*, p. 306.

39 *American Notebooks*, p. 98.

40 *Grandfather's Chair, Works*, IV, 637.

41 Speaking of his involuntary reserve that he supposes gives his writings objectivity, Hawthorne says, "And when people think that I am pouring myself out in a tale or essay, I am merely telling what is common to human nature, not what is peculiar to myself. I sympathise with them— not they with me," *Love Letters*, II, 80.

42 "The Old Manse," *Works*, II, 44.

43 "The Procession of Life," *ibid.*, p. 240. This recalls Emerson's belief that the Poet would confess "his advantage was a knack." See "New England Reformers," Emerson, *Works*, III, 281.

44 *The House of the Seven Gables, Works*, III, 59.

45 *The Marble Faun, ibid.*, VI, 221.

46 "The Great Stone Face," *ibid.*, III, 432–33.

47 *Love Letters*, I, 96.

48 "Drowne's Wooden Image," *Works*, II, 362.

49 *English Notebooks*, pp. 74–75.

50 "Benjamin West," *Works*, XII, 145–46.

51 "The Old Manse," *ibid.*, II, 30–31.

52 "The Artist of the Beautiful," *ibid.*, p. 525.

53 *The House of the Seven Gables, ibid.*, III, 216.

54 "The Snow-Image," *ibid.*, p. 406.

55 *Ibid.*, II, 70–71. For readability, I have omitted the comma that occurs after *itself* in this quotation. This echoes Emerson's idea that

poetry as a talent "is a magnetic tenaciousness of an image, and by the treatment demonstrating that this figment of thought is as palpable and objective to the poet as is the ground on which he stands, or the walls of houses about him," "Poetry and Imagination," Emerson, *Works*, VIII, 27.

56 *American Notebooks*, p. 168.

57 *Works*, IX, 207.

58 *Love Letters*, II, 64.

59 *Ibid.*, pp. 64–65. Cf. Emerson's "Keep the intellect sacred. Revere it. Give all to it," "The Celebration of Intellect," Emerson, *Works*, XII, 130.

60 *French and Italian Note-Books, Works*, X, 394.

61 *Ibid.*, IX, 28.

62 Fields, p. 70.

63 *Ibid.*, p. 79.

64 *Ibid.*, p. 77.

65 *Ibid.*, p. 37.

66 *The Marble Faun, Works*, VI, 313–14.

67 "The Snow-Image," *ibid.*, III, 396.

68 *Ibid.*, p. 436.

69 *English Notebooks*, p. 114.

70 *French and Italian Note-Books, Works*, X, 27.

71 *Ibid.*, p. 398.

72 *Ibid.*, VI, 166.

73 These are the words of the Man of Intelligence to the seeker after Truth in "The Intelligence Office," *ibid.*, II, 379.

74 *English Notebooks*, p. 249.

75 See "The Problem," Emerson, *Works*, IX, 8.

76 *Works*, III, 386.

77 "The Custom House," *ibid.*, V, 50.

78 *Ibid.*, II, 194.

79 *American Notebooks*, p. 18.

80 *Ibid.*, p. 8.

81 *Ibid.*, p. 78.

82 *English Notebooks*, pp. 446–47.

83 *Ibid.*, p. 182.

84 *Works*, V, 438.

85 The painter of "The Prophetic Pictures" names the gift of seeing the inmost soul the artist's proudest—but often melancholy—gift, *ibid.*, I, 202.

86 *Ibid.*, II, 516.

87 *Ibid.*, V, 52.

88 *French and Italian Note-Books, ibid.*, X, 187.

[89] *English Notebooks,* pp. 333–34. Hawthorne develops the brief revelation of the mystery in a similar passage in the *American Notebooks,* pp. 241–42:

> "I have before now experienced, that the best way to get a vivid impression and feeling of a landscape, is to sit down before it and read, or become otherwise absorbed in thought; for then, when your eyes happen to be attracted to the landscape, you seem to catch Nature at unawares, and see her before she has time to change her aspect. The effect lasts but for a single instant, and passes away almost as soon as you are conscious of it; but it is real, for that moment. It is as if you could overhear and understand what the trees are whispering to one another; as if you caught a glimpse of a face unveiled, which veils itself from every wilful glance. The mystery is revealed, and after a breath or two, becomes just as much a mystery as before."

[90] *The Blithedale Romance, Works,* V, 394.

[91] *American Notebooks,* p. 199. This is a quotation of a passage in Emerson's "Nature," which Hawthorne extends to include children and, in a later passage, external objects. Cf. Emerson, *Works,* I, 19: "The beauty that shimmers in the yellow afternoons of October, who ever could clutch it? Go forth to find it, and it is gone; 't is only a mirage as you look from the windows of diligence," and his hint at the greater beauty:

> "But this beauty of Nature which is seen and felt as beauty, is the least part. The shows of day, the dewy morning, the rainbow, mountains, orchards in blossom, stars, moonlight, shadows in still water, and the like, if too eagerly hunted, become shows merely, and mock us with their unreality."

[92] *The Marble Faun, Works,* VI, 371. See also *Works,* X, 88, for a comparison with a view in St. Peter's, when for a moment its magnificence gleams upon the soul; it is like catching suddenly the deepest beauty of a landscape and the sky.

[93] *English Notebooks,* pp. 518–19.

[94] *American Notebooks,* p. 81.

[95] *English Notebooks,* p. 567.

[96] Fields, p. 29.

[97] Preface to "Rappaccini's Daughter," *Works,* II, 107–8.

[98] "Preface," *Twice-Told Tales, ibid.,* I, 16.

[99] Preface to "Rappaccini's Daughter," *ibid.,* II, 107.

[100] *Ibid.,* p. 108.

[101] Fields, p. 59.

[102] "The Custom House," *Works,* V, 53–54.

[103] *Ibid.,* p. 57.

[104] *Ibid.*, p. 43.

[105] *Love Letters*, I, 40.

[106] *Ibid.*, p. 110.

[107] *Ibid.*, pp. 197–98.

[108] *Ibid.*, p. 16.

[109] *Works*, V, 54–56. With Hawthorne's picture in the moonlit room, cf. Emerson in "Beauty," *Works*, VI, 304: "My boots and chair and candlestick are fairies in disguise, meteors and constellations. . . . Chaff and dust begin to sparkle and are clothed about with immortality. And there is a joy in perceiving the representative or symbolic character of a fact, which no bare fact or event can ever give."

[110] "Preface," *The House of the Seven Gables, Works*, III, 14.

[111] Horatio Bridge, *Personal Recollections of Nathaniel Hawthorne* (New York: Harper & Bros., 1893), p. 125.

[112] "Preface," *The House of the Seven Gables, Works*, III, 15.

[113] "Preface," *The Blithedale Romance, ibid.*, V, 321–22.

[114] "Preface," *ibid.*, VI, 15.

[115] "Conclusion," *ibid.*, p. 522.

[116] Fields, p. 72.

[117] "Preface," *Grandfather's Chair, Works*, IV, 429–30.

[118] *Ibid.*, II, 462.

[119] *Ibid.*, III, 396.

[120] *Ibid.*, p. 394.

[121] Preface to "Rappaccini's Daughter," *ibid.*, II, 107.

[122] *Ibid.*, XIII, 109.

[123] *Ibid.*, II, 211.

[124] *French and Italian Note-Books, ibid.*, X, 124.

[125] "The Old Apple Dealer," *ibid.*, II, 495.

[126] "Preface," *The House of the Seven Gables, ibid.*, III, 13.

[127] "Passages from a Relinquished Work," *ibid.*, p. 461.

[128] "The Old Manse," *ibid.*, p. 13.

[129] This is in Hawthorne's 1854 analysis of his *Mosses from an Old Manse*, Fields, p. 59.

[130] *Ibid.*, p. 21.

[131] In "Beauty," Emerson, *Works*, VI, 294.

[132] *The Marble Faun, Works*, VI, 76–78.

[133] *English Notebooks*, p. 556.

[134] Letter to Charles A. Putnam, *The Critic*, N. S. III (January 17, 1885), 30.

[135] "Preface," *The House of the Seven Gables, Works*, III, 14–15.

[136] *Ibid.*, p. 15.

[137] "Alice Doane's Appeal," *ibid.*, XII, 280.

[138] "To a Friend," *Our Old Home, ibid.,* VII, 16. Hawthorne explains that he had intended the things in *Our Old Home* for part of fiction never now to be written and into which he had proposed to put "more of various modes of truth."

[139] "The Artist of the Beautiful," *ibid.,* II.

[140] *Ibid.,* I, 193.

[141] *Ibid.,* V, 64.

[142] Fields, p. 21.

[143] Bridge, p. 112.

[144] *Works,* III, 471.

[145] *Love Letters,* I, 109.

[146] *Works,* III, 13.

[147] *Ibid.,* II, 196.

[148] *Ibid.,* p. 71.

[149] *The House of the Seven Gables, ibid.,* III, 254.

[150] Fields, p. 77.

[151] See "Conclusion" to *The Marble Faun* and cf. Hawthorne's correspondence with John Lothrop Motley, whose criticism Hawthorne found so apt that he says, "If your note had come a few days sooner, I believe I would have printed it in a postscript which I have added to the second edition, because it explains better than I found it possible to do the way in which my romance ought to be taken." And Motley had said:

"I like those shadowy, weird, fantastic, Hawthornesque shapes flitting through the golden gloom, which is the atmosphere of the book. I like the misty way in which the story is indicated rather than revealed; the outlines are quite definite enough from the beginning to the end, to those who have imagination enough to follow you in your airy flights."

Hawthorne answered, "You take the book precisely as I meant it." Letters quoted in Biographical Sketch of Hawthorne, *Works,* XII, 537–38.

[152] *English Notebooks,* p. 454.

[153] *French and Italian Note-Books, Works,* X, 333–34.

[154] *English Notebooks,* p. 550.

[155] *Ibid.,* p. 75.

[156] These are the words of Laurence, the most sensitive listener to the *Grandfather's Chair* stories, *Works,* IV, 498.

[157] *French and Italian Note-Books, ibid.,* X, 425.

[158] *English Notebooks,* p. 607.

[159] *Works,* XII, 288–89.

[160] "The Custom House," *ibid.,* V, 56.

[161] Emerson, *Journals,* VIII, 98–99.

[162] In the "Preface" Hawthorne defines his blending of actual and imagined. His remark on the name Pyncheon was called forth in a letter to Fields (see p. 32) after an *actual* Pyncheon had taken offence.

[163] "Preface," *The Blithedale Romance, Works*, V, 321.

[164] "Preface," *The Marble Faun, ibid.*, VI, 15.

[165] That Hawthorne considered exercising his fancy upon realities which he did not always get to use is most interestingly attested in "Browne's Folly," where only the description of the scene and the assertion of some forgotten intention remain. His notebooks again and again record raw material actualities: mayor's banquets, old folks' hospitals, street scenes, or a castle of Popes for the setting of historical romances. When his imagination suffered the wretched dullness, he wrote Sophia: "The utmost that I can hope to do, will be to portray some of the characteristics of the life which I am now living, and of the people with whom I am brought into contact, for future use." *Love Letters*, I, 81.

[166] *The House of the Seven Gables, Works*, III, 332.

[167] *English Notebooks*, p. 158.

[168] See *English Notebooks*, p. 165, for ponds as mirrors of the beautiful; *American Notebooks*, p. 147, for the river as an open eye in earth's countenance; *Works*, IX, 545, for Lake Leman as "the most radiant eye that the dull earth ever opened to see heaven withal."

[169] *English Notebooks*, p. 96. Cf. quotation from Emerson in note 109 above.

[170] "Lady Eleanore's Mantle," *Works*, I, 314.

[171] For the development of this idea see "The Prophetic Pictures," especially *ibid.*, p. 199.

[172] *Love Letters*, II, 46.

[173] *Works*, XIII, 347.

[174] *English Notebooks*, p. 556.

[175] Fields, p. 29.

[176] *Works*, III, 182.

[177] *Ibid.*, I, 26.

[178] *Ibid.*, p. 49.

[179] *Dr. Grimshawe's Secret, ibid.*, XIII, 351–52.

[180] *French and Italian Note-Books, ibid.*, X, 402.

[181] *American Notebooks*, p. 47.

[182] *French and Italian Note-Books, Works*, X, 246.

[183] *English Notebooks*, p. 614.

[184] *Septimius Felton, Works*, XI, 330.

[185] "Preface," *The House of the Seven Gables, ibid.*, III, 15.

[186] *American Notebooks*, p. 83.

[187] *Ibid.*, p. 249.

[188] "Thomas Green Fessenden," *Works*, XII, 262.

189 *Ibid.*, V, 51–52.

190 Bridge, p. 125.

191 *Works*, XI, 82.

192 *Ibid.*, XII, 519.

193 *Love Letters*, II, 45.

194 *American Notebooks*, p. 30.

195 *Works*, XIII, 347–48.

196 "Preface," *The Marble Faun*: "The author proposed to himself merely to write a fanciful story, evolving a thoughtful moral," *ibid.*, VI, 15.

197 "Preface," *The House of the Seven Gables, ibid.*, III, 15.

198 "The Custom House," *ibid.*, V, 54.

199 In "The Gentle Boy," the expression "a scene occurred" introduces the entrance of Catharine into the pulpit and "an unexpected scene occurred" presents the timid boy to her later; see *ibid.*, I, 99 and 102.

200 Preface to "Rappaccini's Daughter," *ibid.*, II, 107.

201 *The Ancestral Footstep, ibid.*, XI, 491.

202 The first remark is dated May 11, this one May 17, *ibid.*, p. 515.

203 *French and Italian Note-Books, ibid.*, X, 132. Italics mine.

204 Fields, p. 21.

205 *Works*, XI, 293.

206 *Dr. Grimshawe's Secret*, Appendix, *ibid.*, XIII, 348, 352.

207 See "Preface," *The Blithedale Romance, ibid.*, V, 322–23.

208 Harold Blodgett, "Hawthorne as Poetry Critic: Six Unpublished Letters to Lewis Mansfield," *American Literature*, XII (May, 1940), 177–78, 181.

209 "Preface," *The House of the Seven Gables, Works*, III, 15.

210 "Preface," *The Blithedale Romance, ibid.*, V, 321.

211 Blodgett, pp. 177–78.

212 *Works*, III, 13–14.

213 "The Custom House," *ibid.*, V, 57.

214 For a study of Hawthorne's idea of the Artist in which Hawthorne's notebook citations are said to picture a Romantic Artist which the configurations of his works oppose, see Millicent Bell, *Hawthorne's View of the Artist* (Albany: State University of New York, 1962). This critic makes Hawthorne disagree diametrically with himself, particularly by reading "The Artist of the Beautiful" ironically. As she says in her preface, the book really becomes a study of Hawthorne; but since it fails to picture Hawthorne's Artist clearly and completely (despite some fine insights), it moves so far from Hawthorne as to suggest in conclusion that the persistent theme of guilt in Hawthorne's work may be accounted for in that he insisted on being an artist when "every sign from man and Heaven indicated that the choice was a cursed one," p. 204.

CHAPTER IV

[1] Hawthorne, *Works*, I, 79.

[2] *Ibid.*, I, 92.

[3] *Ibid.*, II, 389.

[4] See for example Edward Dawson, *Hawthorne's Knowledge and Use of New England History: A Study of Sources* (A Summary of a Thesis, Vanderbilt University; Nashville, Tennessee: Private Ed., Distributed by the Joint University Libraries, 1939); David S. Lovejoy, "Lovewell's Fight and Hawthorne's 'Roger Malvin's Burial,'" *New England Quarterly*, XXVII (December, 1954), 527–31; and G. Harrison Orians, "The Source of Hawthorne's 'Roger Malvin's Burial,'" *American Literature*, X (November, 1938), 313–18.

[5] *Works*, II, 381.

[6] *Ibid.*, p. 91.

[7] *Ibid.*, p. 109.

[8] *Ibid.*, I, 74.

[9] *Ibid.*, II, 93.

[10] *Ibid.*, III, 498.

[11] *Ibid.*, I, 70.

[12] *Ibid.*, p. 75.

[13] *Ibid.*, p. 78.

[14] *Ibid.*, p. 80.

[15] *Ibid.*, p. 84.

[16] *Ibid.*, II, 62.

[17] *Ibid.*, pp. 63–64.

[18] *Ibid.*, p. 65.

[19] *Ibid.*, p. 69.

[20] *Ibid.*, I, 104.

[21] *Ibid.*, II, 106.

[22] *Ibid.*, p. 123.

[23] *Ibid.*, pp. 122–23.

[24] *Ibid.*, p. 141.

[25] *Ibid.*, pp. 141–42.

[26] *Ibid.*, p. 212.

[27] *Ibid.*, p. 406.

[28] *Ibid.*, III, 485.

[29] *Ibid.*, p. 495.

[30] For an excellent study of Hawthorne's use of light, see Walter Blair, "Color, Light, and Shadow in Hawthorne's Fiction," *New England Quarterly*, XV (March, 1942), 74–94.

[31] *Works*, I, 70.

[32] *Ibid.*, p. 71.

[33] *Ibid.*, p. 72.

[34] *Ibid.*, p. 71.

[35] *Ibid.*, p. 72.

[36] *Ibid.*, p. 73.

[37] *Ibid.*, p. 74.

[38] *Ibid.*, p. 76.

[39] *Ibid.*, p. 79.

[40] *Ibid.*, p. 80.

[41] *Ibid.*, p. 81.

[42] *Ibid.*, p. 82.

[43] *Ibid.*, p. 83.

[44] *Ibid.*, p. 84.

[45] *Ibid.*, p. 89.

[46] *Ibid.*, p. 87.

[47] *Ibid.*, p. 92.

[48] *Ibid.*, p. 93.

[49] *Ibid.*, p. 94.

[50] *Ibid.*, p. 112.

[51] *Ibid.*, p. 108.

[52] *Ibid.*, p. 113.

[53] *Ibid.*, p. 99.

[54] *Ibid.*, p. 92.

[55] *Ibid.*, p. 52.

[56] *Ibid.*, p. 53.

57 *Ibid.*, p. 54.
58 *Ibid.*, p. 55.
59 *Ibid.*, p. 59.
60 *Ibid.*, p. 62.
61 *Ibid.*, p. 63.
62 *Ibid.*, p. 65.
63 *Ibid.*, p. 66.
64 *Ibid.*, p. 67.
65 *Ibid.*, II, 112.
66 *Ibid.*, p. 132.
67 *Ibid.*, p. 146.
68 *Ibid.*, p. 111.
69 *Ibid.*, p. 119.
70 *Ibid.*, p. 113.
71 *Ibid.*, p. 119.
72 *Ibid.*, p. 120.
73 *Ibid.*, p. 121.
74 *Ibid.*, p. 128.
75 *Ibid.*, p. 130.
76 *Ibid.*, p. 123.
77 *Ibid.*, p. 122.
78 *Ibid.*, p. 139.
79 *Ibid.*, p. 142.
80 *Ibid.*, p. 106.
81 *Ibid.*, p. 91.
82 *Ibid.*, p. 98.
83 *Ibid.*, p. 99.
84 *Ibid.*, p. 100.
85 *Ibid.*, p. 102.
86 *Ibid.*, p. 103.
87 *Ibid.*, pp. 103–104.
88 *Ibid.*, p. 104.
89 *Ibid.*, p. 105.
90 *Ibid.*, p. 106.
91 *Ibid.*, p. 220.
92 *Ibid.*, p. 221.
93 *Ibid.*, p. 222.
94 *Ibid.*, p. 234.
95 *Ibid.*, III, 478.

96 *Ibid.*, p. 479.
97 *Ibid.*
98 *Ibid.*, p. 480.
99 *Ibid.*, p. 483.
100 *Ibid.*, p. 484.
101 *Ibid.*
102 *Ibid.*, p. 485.
103 *Ibid.*, p. 489.
104 *Ibid.*, p. 493.
105 *Ibid.*, p. 495.
106 *Ibid.*, p. 496.
107 *Ibid.*, II, 382.
108 *Ibid.*, p. 403.
109 *Ibid.*, p. 406.
110 *Ibid.*, I, 70.
111 *Ibid.*, III, 493.
112 *Ibid.*, p. 497.
113 *Ibid.*, p. 498.
114 *Ibid.*, II, 111.
115 *Ibid.*, p. 110.
116 *Ibid.*, p. 100.
117 *Ibid.*, I, 73.
118 *Ibid.*, p. 97.
119 *Ibid.*, p. 110.
120 *Ibid.*, p. 104.
121 *Ibid.*, II, 225.
122 *Ibid.*, p. 216.
123 *Ibid.*, p. 234.
124 *Ibid.*, p. 222.
125 *Ibid.*, p. 217.
126 *Ibid.*, p. 229.
127 *Ibid.*, III, 486.
128 *Ibid.*
129 *Ibid.*, p. 487.
130 *Ibid.*, II, 396.
131 *Ibid.*, p. 142.
132 *Ibid.*, p. 119.
133 *Ibid.*, p. 139.

134 Austin Warren, ed. *Nathaniel Hawthorne, Representative Selections, with Introduction, Bibliography, and Notes* ("American Writers Series"; New York: American Book Co., 1934), p. 367.

135 *Works*, II, 108.
136 *Ibid.*, I, 54.
137 *Ibid.*, pp. 59–60.
138 *Ibid.*, pp. 60–61.
139 *Ibid.*, III, 494.
140 *Ibid.*, p. 498.
141 *Ibid.*, I, 89.
142 *Ibid.*, p. 122.

143 *Ibid.*, II, 214.
144 *Ibid.*, p. 217.
145 *Ibid.*, p. 215.
146 *Ibid.*
147 *Ibid.*, p. 221.
148 *Ibid.*, p. 229.
149 *Ibid.*, p. 142.

CHAPTER V

1 *Ibid.*, V, 51.
2 *Ibid.*, p. 52.
3 *Ibid.*
4 The gradual transition from the present to the remote past in "The Custom House" artistically emphasizes the remoteness of the happenings in the story.
5 *Ibid.*, p. 68.
6 See *ibid.* and Fields, p. 21.
7 *Works*, V, 307.
8 For criticism of *The Scarlet Letter* which emphasizes the characters' truth to their own natures, see Gordon Roper's introduction in his edition of *The Scarlet Letter and Selected Prose Works by Nathaniel Hawthorne* (New York: Hendricks House, Farrar, Straus, 1949) and cf. Walter Blair, "Discussion Guide to *The Scarlet Letter. . . ,*" *The United States in Literature*, ed. Walter Blair *et al.* ("America Reads," ed. Robert C. Pooley; Chicago: Scott, Foresman and Co., 1963), p. 315.
9 *Ibid.*, p. 174.
10 *Ibid.*, p. 176.
11 *Ibid.*, pp. 177–78.
12 *Ibid.*, p. 180.
13 *Ibid.*, p. 230.
14 *Ibid.*, p. 304.
15 *Ibid.*, p. 77.
16 *Ibid.*, pp. 107–108.
17 *Ibid.*, p. 112.
18 *Ibid.*, p. 201.
19 *Ibid.*, p. 310.
20 *Ibid.*, p. 207.
21 *Ibid.*, p. 113.
22 *Ibid.*, p. 200.
23 *Ibid.*, p. 221.

24 *Ibid.*, p. 303.
25 *Ibid.*, p. 306.
26 *Ibid.*, p. 312.
27 *Ibid.*, p. 175.
28 *Ibid.*, p. 232.
29 *Ibid.*, p. 241.
30 *Ibid.*, p. 297.
31 *Ibid.*, p. 74.
32 *Ibid.*, p. 95.
33 *Ibid.*, p. 107.
34 *Ibid.*, p. 109.
35 *Ibid.*, p. 243.
36 *Ibid.*, p. 253.
37 *Ibid.*, p. 309.
38 *Ibid.*, p. 311.

39 *Ibid.*, pp. 79–80.
40 *Ibid.*, p. 82.
41 *Ibid.*, p. 139.
42 *Ibid.*, p. 156.
43 *Ibid.*, p. 158.
44 *Ibid.*, pp. 204–205.
45 *Ibid.*, p. 303.
46 *Ibid.*, p. 115.
47 *Ibid.*, p. 114.
48 *Ibid.*, pp. 126–27.
49 *Ibid.*, p. 272.
50 *Ibid.*, p. 221.
51 *Ibid.*, p. 73.
52 *Ibid.*, p. 75.
53 *Ibid.*, p. 87.
54 *Ibid.*, p. 91.
55 *Ibid.*, p. 131.
56 *Ibid.*, p. 179.
57 *Ibid.*, p. 182.
58 *Ibid.*, pp. 183–84.
59 *Ibid.*, pp. 186–87.
60 *Ibid.*, p. 189.
61 *Ibid.*, p. 220.
62 *Ibid.*, p. 221.
63 *Ibid.*, p. 228.
64 *Ibid.*, p. 243.
65 *Ibid.*, p. 244.
66 *Ibid.*, p. 250.
67 *Ibid.*, p. 255.
68 *Ibid.*, p. 288.
69 *Ibid.*, p. 295. Italics mine.
70 *Ibid.*, p. 301.
71 *Ibid.*, p. 312.
72 *Ibid.*, p. 71.
73 *Ibid.*, p. 104.
74 *Ibid.*, p. 120.
75 *Ibid.*, p. 211.
76 *Ibid.*, p. 220.
77 *Ibid.*, p. 234.
78 *Ibid.*, p. 246.
79 *Ibid.*, p. 265.
80 *Ibid.*, p. 259.
81 *Ibid.*, p. 102.
82 *Ibid.*, p. 213.
83 *Ibid.*, p. 248.
84 *Ibid.*, p. 172.
85 *Ibid.*, VI, 107.
86 *Ibid.*, p. 458.
87 *Ibid.*, p. 463.
88 *Ibid.*, p. 189.
89 *Ibid.*, p. 15.
90 *Ibid.*, p. 523.
91 *Ibid.*, p. 15.
92 *Ibid.*, p. 20.
93 *Ibid.*, p. 272.
94 *Ibid.*, p. 511.
95 *Ibid.*, p. 124.
96 *Ibid.*, p. 273.
97 *Ibid.*, p. 323.
98 *Ibid.*, p. 147.
99 *Ibid.*, p. 126.
100 *Ibid.*, p. 510.
101 *Ibid.*, p. 517.
102 *Ibid.*, p. 19.
103 *Ibid.*, p. 302.
104 *Ibid.*, p. 309.
105 *Ibid.*, p. 488.
106 *Ibid.*, p. 349.
107 *Ibid.*, p. 28.
108 *Ibid.*, p. 36.
109 *Ibid.*, p. 44.
110 *Ibid.*, p. 49.
111 *Ibid.*, p. 52.
112 *Ibid.*, p. 66.
113 *Ibid.*, p. 65.
114 *Ibid.*, p. 66.
115 *Ibid.*, p. 67.
116 *Ibid.*, p. 95.
117 *Ibid.*, p. 103.
118 *Ibid.*, p. 102.
119 *Ibid.*, p. 119.
120 *Ibid.*, p. 157.
121 *Ibid.*, p. 188.
122 *Ibid.*, p. 197.

123 *Ibid.*, p. 207.
124 *Ibid.*, p. 210.
125 *Ibid.*, p. 322.
126 *Ibid.*, p. 324.
127 *Ibid.*, p. 330.
128 *Ibid.*, p. 350.
129 *Ibid.*, p. 364.
130 *Ibid.*, p. 450.
131 *Ibid.*, p. 451.
132 *Ibid.*, p. 482.
133 *Ibid.*, p. 490.
134 *Ibid.*, p. 506.
135 *Ibid.*, p. 40.
136 *Ibid.*, p. 64.
137 *Ibid.*, p. 95.
138 *Ibid.*, p. 107.
139 *Ibid.*, p. 177.
140 *Ibid.*, p. 176.
141 *Ibid.*, p. 187.
142 *Ibid.*, p. 203.
143 *Ibid.*, p. 204.
144 *Ibid.*, p. 234.
145 *Ibid.*, p. 235.
146 *Ibid.*, p. 252.
147 *Ibid.*, p. 265.
148 *Ibid.*, p. 253.
149 *Ibid.*, p. 274.
150 *Ibid.*, p. 289.
151 *Ibid.*, p. 309.
152 *Ibid.*, p. 361.
153 *Ibid.*, pp. 490–91.
154 *Ibid.*, p. 69.
155 *Ibid.*, p. 72.
156 *Ibid.*, p. 81.
157 *Ibid.*, p. 136.
158 *Ibid.*, p. 81.
159 *Ibid.*, p. 147.
160 *Ibid.*, p. 331.
161 *Ibid.*, p. 238.
162 *Ibid.*, p. 240.
163 *Ibid.*, p. 245.
164 *Ibid.*, pp. 375–76.

165 *Ibid.*, p. 377.
166 *Ibid.*, p. 406.
167 *Ibid.*, p. 409.
168 *Ibid.*, p. 414.
169 *Ibid.*, p. 485.
170 *Ibid.*, p. 510.
171 *Ibid.*, p. 520.
172 *Ibid.*, p. 142.
173 *Ibid.*, p. 141.
174 *Ibid.*, p. 318.
175 *Ibid.*, p. 465.
176 *Ibid.*, p. 520.
177 *Ibid.*, p. 45.
178 *Ibid.*, p. 48.
179 *Ibid.*, p. 118.
180 *Ibid.*, p. 176.
181 *Ibid.*, p. 39.
182 *Ibid.*, p. 41.
183 *Ibid.*, p. 42.
184 *Ibid.*, p. 44.
185 *Ibid.*, p. 45.
186 *Ibid.*, p. 46.
187 *Ibid.*, p. 47.
188 *Ibid.*, p. 52.
189 *Ibid.*, p. 57.
190 *Ibid.*, p. 58.
191 *Ibid.*, p. 69.
192 *Ibid.*, p. 90.
193 *Ibid.*, p. 91.
194 *Ibid.*, p. 93.
195 *Ibid.*, p. 94.
196 *Ibid.*, p. 95.
197 *Ibid.*, p .158.
198 *Ibid.*, p. 170.
199 *Ibid.*, p. 172.
200 *Ibid.*, p. 173.
201 *Ibid.*, p. 175.
202 *Ibid.*, p. 182.
203 *Ibid.*, p. 183.
204 *Ibid.*, p. 184.
205 *Ibid.*, p. 185.
206 *Ibid.*, p. 186.

207 *Ibid.*, p. 191.
208 *Ibid.*, p. 198.
209 *Ibid.*, p. 199.
210 *Ibid.*, p. 202.
211 *Ibid.*, p. 291.
212 *Ibid.*, p. 292.
213 *Ibid.*, pp. 293–94.
214 *Ibid.*, p. 295.
215 *Ibid.*, p. 296.
216 *Ibid.*, p. 297.
217 *Ibid.*, p. 298.
218 *Ibid.*, p. 299.
219 *Ibid.*, p. 348.
220 *Ibid.*, p. 349.
221 *Ibid.*, p. 350.
222 *Ibid.*, p. 351.
223 *Ibid.*, pp. 351–52.
224 *Ibid.*, p. 392.
225 *Ibid.*, p. 393.
226 *Ibid.*, p. 397.
227 *Ibid.*, p. 398.
228 *Ibid.*, p. 399.
229 *Ibid.*, p. 400.
230 *Ibid.*, p. 401.
231 *Ibid.*, p. 403.
232 *Ibid.*, p. 404.
233 *Ibid.*, p. 406.
234 *Ibid.*, p. 412.
235 *Ibid.*, p. 413.
236 *Ibid.*, p. 414.
237 *Ibid.*, p. 415.
238 *Ibid.*, pp. 416–17.
239 *Ibid.*, p. 417.
240 *Ibid.*
241 *Ibid.*, p. 419.
242 *Ibid.*, p. 422.
243 *Ibid.*, p. 495.
244 *Ibid.*, p. 496.
245 *Ibid.*, p. 497.
246 *Ibid.*, p. 498.

247 *Ibid.*, p. 499.
248 *Ibid.*, p. 500.
249 *Ibid.*, p. 502.
250 *Ibid.*, p. 501.
251 *Ibid.*, p. 512.
252 *Ibid.*, p. 55.
253 *Ibid.*, p. 62.
254 *Ibid.*, p. 63.
255 *Ibid.*, p. 74.
256 *Ibid.*, p. 76.
257 *Ibid.*, p. 78.
258 *Ibid.*, p. 72.
259 *Ibid.*, p. 140.
260 *Ibid.*, p. 141.
261 *Ibid.*, p. 143.
262 *Ibid.*, p. 434.
263 *Ibid.*, p. 258.
264 *Ibid.*, p. 260.
265 *Ibid.*, p. 277.
266 *Ibid.*, p. 222.
267 *Ibid.*, p. 21.
268 *Ibid.*, p. 27.
269 *Ibid.*, p. 23.
270 *Ibid.*, p. 24.
271 *Ibid.*, p. 25.
272 *Ibid.*, p. 28.
273 *Ibid.*, p. 488.
274 *Ibid.*, p. 39.
275 *Ibid.*, p. 115.
276 *Ibid.*, p. 153.
277 *Ibid.*, p. 154.
278 *Ibid.*, p. 331.
279 *Ibid.*, p. 243.
280 *Ibid.*
281 *Ibid.*, p. 488.
282 *Ibid.*, p. 439.
283 *Ibid.*, p. 488.
284 *Ibid.*, p. 520.
285 *Ibid.*, p. 492.

Bibliography

PRIMARY SOURCES

The Dial. 1840–1844.

Emerson, Ralph Waldo. *The Complete Works of Ralph Waldo Emerson.* Edited by Edward Waldo Emerson. 12 vols. Centenary Edition. Boston: Houghton, Mifflin and Co., 1903–1904.

———. *A Correspondence between John Sterling and Ralph Waldo Emerson.* Edited by Edward Waldo Emerson. Boston: Houghton, Mifflin and Co., 1897.

———. *The Early Lectures of Ralph Waldo Emerson.* Edited by Stephen E. Whicher and Robert E. Spiller. Cambridge: Harvard University Press, 1959.

———. *Journals of Ralph Waldo Emerson, 1820–1876.* Edited by Edward Waldo Emerson and Waldo Emerson Forbes. 10 vols. Boston: Houghton Mifflin Co., 1909–14.

———. *The Letters of Ralph Waldo Emerson.* Edited by Ralph L. Rusk. 6 vols. Morningside Heights: Columbia University Press, 1939.

Hawthorne, Nathaniel. *The American Notebooks by Nathaniel Hawthorne.* Edited by Randall Stewart. New Haven: Yale University Press, 1932.

———. *The Complete Works of Nathaniel Hawthorne, with Introductory Notes.* Edited by George Parsons Lathrop. 12 vols. Riverside Edition. Boston: Houghton, Mifflin and Co., 1883.

————. *Doctor Grimshawe's Secret; a Romance, by Nathaniel Haw-thorne.* Edited by Julian Hawthorne. Riverside Edition, *The Complete Works of Nathaniel Hawthorne,* Vol. XIII. Boston: J. R. Osgood & Co., 1883.

————. *The English Notebooks by Nathaniel Hawthorne.* Edited by Randall Stewart. The Modern Language Association of America, General Series XIII. New York: Modern Language Association of America; London: Oxford University Press, 1941.

————. *Love Letters of Nathaniel Hawthorne, 1839–41 and 1841–63.* 2 vols. Chicago: Privately printed, The Society of the Dofobs, 1907.

Holmes, Oliver Wendell. *Oliver Wendell Holmes: Representative Selections.* Edited by S. I. Hayakawa and Howard Mumford Jones. "American Writers Series." New York: American Book Co., 1939.

Longfellow, Henry Wadsworth. *Final Memorials of Henry Wads-worth Longfellow.* Edited by Samuel Longfellow. Boston: Tick-nor and Co., 1887.

————. *The Works of Henry Wadsworth Longfellow.* Edited by Samuel Longfellow. 14 vols. Standard Library Edition. Boston: Houghton, Mifflin and Co., 1886–91.

Melville, Herman. *The Confidence Man.* Edited by Elizabeth S. Foster. New York: Hendricks House, 1954.

————. *The Letters of Herman Melville.* Edited by Merrell R. Davis and William H. Gilman. New Haven: Yale University Press, 1960.

————. *Moby Dick; or, The Whale.* Edited by Luther S. Mansfield and Howard P. Vincent. Vol. VI of *Complete Works.* Edited by Howard P. Vincent. New York: Hendricks House, 1952.

————. *The Portable Melville.* Edited by Jay Leyda. "The Viking Portable Library." New York: The Viking Press, 1952.

————. *The Works of Herman Melville.* 12 vols. Standard Edition. London: Constable and Co. Ltd., 1922–23.

Ossoli, Margaret Fuller. *Life Without and Life Within; or, Re-views, Narratives, Essays, and Poems.* Edited by Arthur B. Fuller. New York: The Tribune Association, 1859.

The Pioneer: A Literary Magazine. Edited by James Russell Lowell. New York: Scholars' Facsimiles & Reprints, 1947.

Thoreau, Henry David. *The Writings of Henry David Thoreau.* 20 vols. Walden Edition. Boston: Houghton Mifflin Co., 1906.

SECONDARY SOURCES

Bell, Millicent. *Hawthorne's View of the Artist.* Albany: State University of New York, 1962.

Benoit, Ray. "Emerson on Plato: The Fire's Center," *American Literature*, XXXIV (January, 1963), 487–98.

Blair, Walter. "Color, Light, and Shadow in Hawthorne's Fiction," *New England Quarterly*, XV (March, 1942), 74–94.

Blair, Walter and Faust, Clarence. "Emerson's Literary Method," *Modern Philology*, XLII (November, 1944), 79–95.

Blair, Walter, *et al. The United States in Literature.* "America Reads." Edited by Robert C. Pooley. Chicago: Scott, Foresman and Co., 1963.

Blodgett, Harold. "Hawthorne as Poetry Critic: Six Unpublished Letters to Lewis Mansfield," *American Literature*, XII (May, 1940), 173–84.

Bowen, Merlin. *The Long Encounter: Self and Experience in the Writings of Herman Melville.* Chicago: University of Chicago Press, 1960.

Bridge, Horatio. *Personal Recollections of Nathaniel Hawthorne.* New York: Harper & Bros., 1893.

Brooks, Van Wyck. *The Flowering of New England: 1815–1865.* The Modern Library of the World's Best Books. New York: The Modern Library, 1936.

Cameron, Kenneth Walter. *Emerson the Essayist.* 2 vols. Raleigh, N. C.: The Thistle Press, 1945.

———. (ed.) *Nature (1836) by Ralph Waldo Emerson.* New York: Scholars' Facsimiles & Reprints, 1940.

Carpenter, Frederic Ives. *Emerson Handbook.* "Handbooks of American Literature." New York: Hendricks House, 1953.

Chandler, Elizabeth Lathrop. *A Study of the Sources of the Tales and Romances Written by Nathaniel Hawthorne before 1853.* "Smith College Studies in Modern Languages," Vol. VII, No. 4. Northampton, Mass.: Smith College, 1926.

Clark, Harry Hayden. (ed.) *Major American Poets.* "American Literature Series." New York: American Book Co., 1936.

Cooke, George Willis. *An Historical and Biographical Introduction to Accompany THE DIAL as Reprinted in Numbers for The Rowfant Club.* 2 vols. Cleveland: The Rowfant Club, 1902.

Curtis, George William. *Literary and Social Essays.* New York: Harper & Bros., 1894.

Dall, Caroline W. (Healey). *Margaret and Her Friends; or Ten Conversations with Margaret Fuller upon the Mythology of the Greeks and Its Expression in Art.* Boston: Roberts Bros., 1895.

Dawson, Edward. *Hawthorne's Knowledge and Use of New England History: A Study of Sources.* A Summary of a Thesis, Vanderbilt University. Nashville, Tennessee: Private Edition, Distributed by The Joint University Libraries, 1939.

Emerson, Ralph Waldo, Channing, W. H. and Clarke, J. F. *Memoirs of Margaret Fuller Ossoli.* 2 vols. Boston: Phillips, Sampson and Co., 1852.

Faust, Bertha. *Hawthorne's Contemporaneous Reputation: A Study of Literary Opinion in America and England, 1828–1864.* Ph.D. Dissertation. Philadelphia: Pennsylvania University, 1939.

Fields, James Thomas. *Hawthorne.* Boston: J. R. Osgood and Co., 1876.

Foster, Charles H. "Hawthorne's Literary Theory," *Publications of the Modern Language Association,* LVII (March, 1942), 241–54.

Frothingham, Octavius Brooks. *Transcendentalism in New England: A History.* New York: G. P. Putnam's Sons, 1876.

Goddard, Harold Clarke. *Studies in New England Transcendentalism.* "Columbia University Studies in English," Series II, Vol. II, No. 3. New York: The Columbia University Press, 1908.

Gray, Henry David. *Emerson: A Statement of New England Transcendentalism as Expressed in the Philosophy of Its Chief Exponent.* "Leland Stanford Junior University Publications," University Series. Stanford, California: Stanford University, 1917.

Harris, W. T. "The Dialectical Unity in Emerson's Prose," *Journal of Speculative Philosophy,* XVIII (April, 1884), 195–202.

———. "Ralph Waldo Emerson," *Atlantic,* L (August, 1882), 238–52.

Hawthorne, Julian. *Hawthorne Reading: An Essay.* Cleveland: The Rowfant Club, 1902.

———. *Nathaniel Hawthorne and His Wife: A Biography.* 2 vols. Boston: James R. Osgood and Co., 1884.

Hayman, Allen. "Herman Melville's Theory of Prose Fiction: in Contrast with Contemporary Theories," *Dissertation Abstracts,* XXI (June, 1961), 3782.

Hopkins, Vivian C. *Spires of Form: A Study of Emerson's Aesthetic Theory.* Cambridge: Harvard University Press, 1951.

Kesselring, Marion L. "Hawthorne's Reading, 1828–1850," *Bulletin of the New York Public Library,* LIII (February, March, April, 1949), 55–71, 121–38, 173–94.

Lathrop, Rose Hawthorne. *Memories of Hawthorne.* Boston: Houghton Mifflin and Co., 1897.

Lovejoy, David S. "Lovewell's Fight and Hawthorne's 'Roger Malvin's Burial,'" *New England Quarterly,* XXVII (December, 1954), 527–31.

Matthiessen, Francis Otto. *American Renaissance: Art and Expression in the Age of Emerson and Whitman.* London and New York: Oxford University Press, 1941.

Metzger, Charles Reid. *Emerson and Greenough: Transcendental Pioneers of an American Esthetic.* Berkeley: University of California Press, 1954.

———. *Thoreau and Whitman: A Study of Their Esthetics.* Seattle: University of Washington Press, 1961.

O'Connor, Evangeline Maria (Johnson). *An Analytical Index to the Works of Nathaniel Hawthorne.* Boston: Houghton, Mifflin and Co., 1882.

Orians, G. Harrison. "The Source of Hawthorne's 'Roger Malvin's Burial,'" *American Literature,* X (November, 1938), 313–18.

Parrington, Vernon Louis. *The Romantic Revolution in America, 1800–1860.* Vol. II, *Main Currents in American Thought: An Interpretation of American Literature from the Beginnings to 1920.* New York: Harcourt, Brace and Co., 1927.

Paul, Sherman. *Emerson's Angle of Vision: Man and Nature in American Experience.* Cambridge: Harvard University Press, 1952.

Roper, Gordon. (ed.) *The Scarlet Letter and Selected Prose Works by Nathaniel Hawthorne.* New York: Hendricks House, Farrar, Straus, 1949.

Stewart, Randall. *Nathaniel Hawthorne: A Biography.* New Haven: Yale University Press, 1948.

Stovall, Floyd. (ed.) *Eight American Authors: A Review of Research and Criticism.* Modern Language Association of America, Revolving Fund Series, No. 19. New York: The Modern Language Association of America, 1956.

Swift, Lindsay. *Brook Farm: Its Members, Scholars, and Visitors.* National Studies in American Letters. New York: The Macmillan Co., 1900.

Warren, Austin. (ed.) *Nathaniel Hawthorne: Representative Selections, with Introduction, Bibliography, and Notes.* "American Writers Series." New York: American Book Co., 1934.

Index